# Looters, Photographers, and Thieves

## The Fairleigh Dickinson University Press Series in Italian Studies

General Editor: Dr. Anthony Tamburri, Dean, John D. Calandra Italian American Institute (Queens College-CUNY)

The Fairleigh Dickinson University Press Series in Italian Studies is devoted to the publication of scholarly works on Italian literature, film, history, biography, art, and culture, as well as on intercultural connections, such as Italian-American Studies.

Recent Publications in Italian Studies

Verdicchio, Pasquale, *Looters, Photographers, and Thieves: Aspects of Italian Photographic Culture in the Nineteenth and Twentieth Centuries* (2011)

Parati, Graziella, and Anthony Julian Tamburri (eds.), *The Cultures of Italian Migration* (2011)

Trubiano, Marisa S., *Ennio Flaiano and His Italy: Postcards from a Changing World* (2010)

Halliday, Iain, *Huck Finn in Italian, Pinocchio in English: Theory and Praxis of Literary Translation* (2009)

Serram Ilaria, *The Imagined Immigrant: The Images of Italian Emigration to the United States between 1890 and 1924* (2009)

Lucamante, Stefania (ed.), *Italy and the Bourgeoisie: The Re-Thinking of a Class* (2009)

Van Order, Thomas, *Listening to Fellini: Music and Meaning in Black and White* (2008)

Billiani, Francesca, and Gigliola Sulis, *The Italian Gothic and Fantastic: Encounters and Rewritings of Narrative Traditions* (2008)

Orton, Marie, and Graziella Parati (eds.), *Multicultural Literature in Contemporary Italy* (2007)

Scambray, Ken, *Queen Calafia's Paradise: California and the Italian-American Novel* (2007)

Polezzi, Loredana, and Charlotte Ross (eds.), *In Corpore: Bodies in Post-Unification Italy* (2007)

Parati, Graziella, and Marie Orton (eds.), *Multicultural Literature in Contemporary Italy* (2007)

Francese, Joseph, *Socially Symbolic Acts: The Historicizing Fictions of Umberto Eco, Vincenzo Consolo, and Antonio Tabucchi* (2006)

Kozma, Jan (trans.), Grazia Deledda, *Marianna Sirca* (2006)

On the Web at http://www.fdu.edu/fdupress

# Looters, Photographers, and Thieves

## Aspects of Italian Photographic Culture in the Nineteenth and Twentieth Centuries

Pasquale Verdicchio

Fairleigh Dickinson

FAIRLEIGH DICKINSON UNIVERSITY PRESS
*Madison · Teaneck*

Published by Fairleigh Dickinson University Press
Co-published with The Rowman & Littlefield Publishing Group, Inc.
4501 Forbes Boulevard, Suite 200, Lanham, Maryland 20706
www.rowmanlittlefield.com

Estover Road, Plymouth PL6 7PY, United Kingdom



British Library Cataloguing in Publication Information Available

**Library of Congress Cataloging-in-Publication Data**

Verdicchio, Pasquale, 1954–
Looters, photographers, and thieves : aspects of Italian photographic culture in the nineteenth and twentieth centuries / Pasquale Verdicchio.
p. cm. — (The Fairleigh Dickinson University Press series in Italian studies)
Includes bibliographical references and index.
ISBN 978-1-61147-018-5 (cloth : alk. paper) — ISBN 978-1-61147-019-2 (ebook)
1. Photography—Social aspects—Italy—History—19th century. 2. Photography—Social aspects—Italy—History—20th century. I. Title.
TR183.V47 2011
770.945'09034—dc23 2011013475

∞™ The paper used in this publication meets the minimum requirements of American National Standard for Information Sciences—Permanence of Paper for Printed Library Materials, ANSI/NISO Z39.48-1992.

Printed in the United States of America

# Contents

# Acknowledgments

This book is the result of a slowly evolving and changing sense of seeing. There are many people to thank for having helped me through the process, family and friends, and many who have never known me but whose work in art, photography, literature and cinema has been my training ground. More concretely, I would like to thank Liesbeth van den Bosch for her support over the years, for having made available the time and space in which to concentrate my efforts toward the writing and completion of these pages; with her I have shared many of the experiences that have formed this vision. I also thank my children, Mara and Giuliano. Their seeing the world through new eyes taught me to open my own. Infinite gratitude goes to my parents, Elda and Mario, for always supporting my endeavors. Many thanks to my colleague, Stephanie Jed, whose support and mentorship over the years has been invaluable, and to all those I have neglected to mention but who, nevertheless, have a place on my visual horizon.

Very early stages of some of the work contained in this book has appeared or will appear in essays published in the following: "Verismo, narrator, and reality: Giovanni Verga," in *Selecta: Journal of Pacific Northwest Council on Foreign Languages*. Vol. 12, 1991, 74-78; "Tina Modotti: Life Through the Ground-Glass," in *Dear Vocio* exhibition catalogue. University of California, San Diego, 1997. 8-19; "Imaging America: The Photography of Lewis Hine and Jacob Riis," in *Public Space, Private Lives: Race, Gender, Class and Citizenship in New York, 1890-1929*. European Contributions to American Studies, No. 53. Amsterdam: VU University Press, 2004. 333-340; "Authoring Images: Photography as Literary Art" in

*Enlightening Encounters between Photography and Italian Literature.* Giorgia Alaù and Nancy Pedri editors; "Baron von Gloeden's Sicilian Arcadia" in *Descant*, Sicily issue, 154 (vol. 42, No. 3, Fall 2011). Michelle Alfano and Venera Fazio, eds. I thank the editors and publishers of these publications for their support.

Finally, I wish to express my gratitude to the UCSD Academic Senate for the Research Grants that made this project possible, and the Office of the Dean of the Arts and Humanities Division, in the person of Prof. Seth Lerer, for support toward the publication of the manuscript.

# Introduction

Questions of national, racial, ethnic and cultural identity have over the last few decades settled at the center of cultural criticism in North America and elsewhere. These questions go hand in hand with critiques of national narratives in that they have had a defining influence in the formation, maintenance or critique of the concept of nation since its first manifestations in the late 1700s. The elements that go into creating parameters of national behavior, culture and character have been the dominion of forces both external and internal to the nation states to which they have been applied.

The medium of photography, invented after the emergence of the modern nation-state, found fertile ground within that discourse and was fundamental in the creation of nationalist images and imaginaries. Photography became an instrument of primary importance in the delineation of national characteristics and the definition of anthropological categories that might facilitate the establishment of national and international hierarchies. Photography at the service of imperialism and colonialism further upheld pseudo-scientific anthropological constructs that, to a great extent, still exert their influence in international relations today. This sort of documentation became a widespread practice that pitted body types and physiognomies in a war of survival in which the ability to create and sustain systems of classification empowered by military might and violence ensured supremacy.

The efficacy of photography in establishing hierarchical types and maintaining the definition of what was represented as being "other," or not quite legitimately empowered, is slightly different from that of its later cousin, cinematography. The photograph's lack of an apparent narrative structure works to its advantage as an insidious tool of *speculative narration*, in the way that it purports to mirror the world and offer an expansion of its meaning by its speculated images. Photography's stillness and silence holds its subjects within a realm of unreality against which they can apparently do little. The struggle for the possibility of a word or action that might liberate them from being imaged also subtracts from them the opportunity for objection. In other words, it deprives them of agency. By this I do not mean to claim innocence for cinematography, so I will simply say that film works in a no-less intensive manner. Cinema's narrativity puts into prominence national images or codes that tap into a "spectatorial familiarity" that manipulates audiences to self-identify with a narrative context and stories.[1]

Although it is widely recognized that the discourse on visual culture has mostly been formed under the influence of linguistics and semiotics, the progress toward defining an independently active theoretical vocabulary for the visual has been slow. The reluctance to name Walter Benjamin as a direct influence by a number of contemporary visual culture writers is notable, but his presence is nevertheless evident. And, while I do not intend to offer either a Marxist, post-structuralist or semiotic reading of photography herein, this work is in its substance informed by Benjamin's fundamental work on the visual. It is disingenuous to suggest that Benjamin's theories of the visual are outdated or of service only within a strictly Marxist critical discourse. To so dismiss even his most often quoted essay, "The Work of Art in the Age of Mechanical Reproduction," would be to purposefully undermine the evolution of visual cultural criticism and its contemporary value.[2]

Benjamin's analysis of the visual may be locked within a generally Marxist frame of reference, but it can hardly be said to be useful only within that context. After all, the medium of photography itself is slippery enough to resist complete manipulation by any ideological constraints. Even in its highly capitalistic manifestation as advertising, photographic images are ambiguous, or polyvalent enough to often contradict the very message they seem to convey. The essay "The Work of Art" continues to be a fundamental resource for its proposal of both photography and film's function as conditioners of image production and reproduction. Benjamin traces therein the development of reproduction technologies (typography, engraving, and eventually photography) for their impact on human culture and the value system of Western art. Benjamin's analysis and discourse bestows upon photography a potential that, in his words, "is useful for the formulation of revolutionary demands in the 'politics of art.'"[3]

One of Benjamin's most significant observations in this essay is in relation to how photography's mechanical functions bestow upon it the ability to "keep pace with speech."[4] By closely linking the revolutionary demands in the politics of art and photography's approximation of speech Benjamin appears to be reaching for a formulation by which photography could be representative of a new language that is in its unfolding potentially revolutionary. If we consider how, in certain situations where there has been an attempt to curtail the spread of information, whether from war areas through the use of "embedded" journalists," or from the oppressive situation in Tibet by the Chinese, the role of photographic images relayed via new technologies has been fundamentally important as a counter-hegemonic alternative. Further, what might at first appear to be limitations of the medium could be read to be potentially useful and radical representational traits. First and foremost, and not only applicable to photography, "even the best reproduction of a work of art is lacking in one element: its presence in time and space, its unique existence at the place where it happens to be."[5] What could at first glance appear to be a strong de-contextualizing or de-historicizing tool may, conversely, function to bestow upon photography the privilege of functioning as a classless medium of democratic representation. This function may become more apparent when associated with issues of ownership and representational authority with regards to photographic production, re/production and dissemination. In this case, rather than a subject's loss of impact and diminishment of a subject's historical testimony through reproduction, photography connotes a removed mode by which to emphasize the import of events and those involved in them through the reduction of their glamorously unique value as entertainment.[6]

Given this, there is still, however, a distinction that must be made between historical testimony and another type of historicity. While Benjamin uses the term "aura" to describe a product's historicity, we must question how historicity is maintained if we consider that the mission of the anthropological photograph is to set visually descriptive categories into historical cement via photography. I would therefore like to propose that, within an extended set of parameters, a photograph could be considered a process of historical imprinting that contains a certain amount of culturally resistant density.

While there are plenty of explicit examples of the use of photography to support anthropological determinism, there are many less explicit expressions that counter the uses of the photographic image in the service of national programming. To this end, the present work will explore the functionally more active and successful instigation of a certain type of visual rhetoric directly related to the creation and definition of national identity.

The path of this book will be delineated by the work of photographers such as the Alinari brothers, Tina Modotti, Baron von Gloeden, Lewis

Hine, Herbert Riis, Giovanni Verga, and to a lesser extent other photographers whose work has gone into defining the terms and diverse aspects of national imaginary. While masked by other rhetorical impositions, costumes and traditional dress, representations of classical modes and poses, socially aware documentation, the works of the photographers herein all have had a pertinent impact on varying terms of national identity. Whether they create a revolutionary image or a sedate image that offers its subjects up to the whims of colonially minded forces is a matter of ideological purpose and pursuit on the part of the photographers. What we are left with today are the photographs, and through these we must do our best to read and interpret the images they cast through the knowledge we may have gathered via our own cultural conditioning and responses to the visual.

Much has been written about national cinemas and national literatures. Might we then not ask if there could be such a thing as national photography? Pier Paolo Pasolini's notion of film as a progressive accumulation of images that creates an ever-expanding sequential language resistant to definition until the last image is produced might be of help here. As such, images would qualify for a nationalist label only when created and produced within a restrictive context such as Fascism, an ideology that functions by assertion, delineation, definition, circumscription and imposition of meaning. Yet, photography has frequently been instrumentalized to such ends, and plenty of examples of what might be termed national photographic projects can be quoted. Under close scrutiny such projects might not readily be recognized as primarily or singularly nationalist, but more as anthropologically or sociologically normative ones that came to serve nationalist or imperialist interests.

Indeed, Edward Curtis' catalogue of the "vanishing race" of American Indians, or even the photographic documentation of prisoners in the Nazi camps of the Third Reich, could be read in this retrospective sense. Photographic compendia such as the *Family of Man* exhibition, organized by Edward Steichen in 1955 for New York Museum of Modern Art, proposed a figural global family that asked its audience to imagine the erasure of national borders through an illustration of universals.[7] A wonderful idea, were it not that the universals pictured of a post-World War II world were the results of strife and conflict which the exhibit rendered invisible. Considering the apparent spaces of communication and diffusion created by photography, we might consider it a "democratic" medium accessible to most everyone and, as such, one that might negate nationalisms.

While the body of critical work on national cinemas and literatures has grown by leaps and bounds, a similar body of work on photography is all but absent. Therefore, one of the questions that I intend to at least partially address throughout the pages of this book regards the viability of proposing a concept of national photography. As a progression of still images film has been bestowed the qualification of national among others, so why should it not be applicable to its basic unit, the photograph. An investigation of the genre/medium distinctions between film and photography might in fact lead to an understanding of how photography could work toward the dissolution of nationalist categories. Through such a perspective we might discern, even in initiatives such as the famous "Family of Man" exhibit, criticized as a romanticized view of humanity, a more radical sense of the photographic image.

The photographers discussed in this book have either direct or indirect ties to Italy, yet I have chosen to focus on their activity because of that country's unique position within the West. This small piece of land jutting out into the Mediterranean, short on natural resources, with a continuously struggling economy, and as a country that has lost a proportionally large percentage of its population through emigration, continues to this day to show a multitude of facets that support its first world status while parts of it remain relegated to the realm of underdevelopment. Photography in the Italian context has been instructive and instrumental for a wide variety of ideologically based cultural investigations. It has served in defining a normative figure of *italianità* (Italianness), and it has served to document and preserve the subaltern cultures that would in turn deny that essentialized character. The work done by the cultural anthropologist Ernesto De Martino in the southern regions of the peninsula in the 1950s is a prime example of the latter.

Today, as a leader in the fashion industry, Italy produces an endless stream of photographs that supposedly define a quintessentially Italian style. However, the international army of male and female supermodels and their photographers produce images that are more representative of the globalizing tendencies that burn through our local sensitivities than of localized realities. Photography today, in the context of fashion, advertising and commercialism, has commodified the body and neutralized it into a generalized figure dressed in the skin of a supposedly more progressed culture.

The Italian South has been under the scrutiny of the photographic lens of foreigners and locals to a disproportionate amount vis-à-vis other regions. The book *Lo sguardo da sud* (1999) analyzes the underlying choices that guide this phenomenon through a series of "conversations" with Southern photographers.[8] Goffredo Fofi's introductory notes conjure up examples that support a representation of the south that is mostly cinematographic; among those included to testify to the role of photography in the south is theatre and film director Mario Martone. This begs an important question regarding the Italian South in relation to the overall nation. Do other representational terms exist outside of the set of images that neorealist cinema outlined; images that go beyond the ethnographic catalogue that has become the stereotype?

The photographers of *Lo sguardo da sud* tend to agree on some issues that directly address photography's place in Southern Italy, terms that are generally applicable to the larger Italian situation. Past and present photographic conditions in the South have as their precursors an ethnographic/anthropological tradition that has always directly engaged the social sphere. Even landscape photography reflects an approach that wants to communicate a social reality or expresses the need to find, in the absence of human subjects, recourse toward new approaches in recording a particular reality.

Although ambiguously Southern, because of his location in the North of the South, Mario Giacomelli is a photographer whose work has consistently blurred the margins between the landscape and those who inhabit it. His collapsing of perspective and flattening of dimensionality manifest presence as a stain in the land just as a patch of grass might be. And yet, as localized as his photographs are, and as much as they decrease the distance between man and landscape, the influence of "familiar" signs of Italian culture remain evident in the shape of the land as well as the artifacts of humanity. On the other hand, the abandonment of the environment to itself, the subject of photographers such as Mimmo Jodice and Luigi Ghirri, becomes a way to search for previously unseen cultural clues of inhabitation. Jodice, Naples' most renowned contemporary photographer, states, "at the end of the seventies my relationship to the city changed. My uneasiness became internalized and became a silent protest. My photographs showed an empty and rarefied city and the people, who were once central to my photography, disappeared."[9]

The overall opinion of the photographers included in *Lo sguardo* is that there is no definable "southern" photographic tradition. Photography as an instrument has it various manifestations through which it also evolves from something at the use of anthropological documentation and classification, to an element of sociological registration and activism to an artistic tool. The Sicilian photographer Letizia Battaglia, whose photographs recording the infestation of the social, political and cultural spheres by the Mafia in Sicily, makes a case for a more generalized South: "I am interested in the Souths of the world."[10]

If anyone were to look for an Italian North or an Italian South in photography, it would certainly be found in images that reflect well-known stereotypes. Photographic knowledge, what the image makes visible and seems to make available, is what passively imbricates viewers into the construction of recognizable types, which they themselves may very well be. It is important then that, while photography may be used to define difference as well as similarity, the figurative aspects of the medium go toward defining national characteristics that are based on a reductive visual vocabulary. I would venture to say that, what is at stake in photography, from the family snapshot to Presidential portraits, is the very question of nationalism. As it is used to erect a national image, photography simultaneously delimits its range.

While cinema can certainly be considered a carrier of a constructed semiology of national strategies, photography's manifestation of singular events, image by image, appears to contradict the cumulative effect required by an ideological system. Film may indeed be a progression of photographic images, but photography is more than a mere fraction of a sequence. Photography's independence, its ability to sustain a narrative through single images, undermines temporality and, as such, communicates not only the capture and documentation of a moment but also the limits of its historicity. Further, it emphatically makes known the presence of the mechanisms and modes of narrative production that are inherent in the encoding of any image.

The following chapters will explore how photography might function to establish a national catalogue through the practice of what could be called a "national photography," while also identifying photographers whose work is expressedly set against such a category. Chapter 1 will lay the ground for other chapters through a brief consideration of the body as a created image, manipulated, observed and reproduced three dimensionally. As an additional expression of the "mirroring" that such recreations might suggest, the chapter continues with a brief analysis of the portrait as a basic statement of individual and/or national. Portraits, and by extension self-portraits, are a culturally active practice to formally situate familiar and accepted norms already at work within a society. This is true even if a photographer acts against accepted norms and, if sometimes it is not possible to enact alternative modes of portraiture within the conventional landscapes, a "place" for them must be created or sought out.

The baron Wilhelm von Gloeden found this place in Taormina, Sicily, while Mexico and its people enabled the work of Italian expatriate Tina Modotti. Giovanni Verga's native place was Sicily, a region at the margins of the then new Italian nation. Others, like Hine and Riis, worked at the margins of their own society within potential, unrealized and the as yet un-legitimized social spaces of immigrant communities. All in all, these photographers moved between the spaces of the legitimization of bodies for national, political and cultural reasons, and the artificilization of bodies (how they are made to fit) within those same categories.

Following a basic analysis of self-portraits by the above photographers, I will to consider those same photographers' relationships to their usual subjects in an attempt to understand the functions, reasons, sense and significance of self-imaging. While they could be said to be an exploration of what might constitute national/extra national/expatriated bodies, the self-portrait sometimes shows correspondences with the photographers' portraits of others. Von Gloeden's exoticized Sicilian boys represent a transitory state that corresponds to the baron's need for a youthful, mystical, mythical culture made static and everlasting by the camera. Von Gloeden's homosexual paradise is, after all, as imaginary as his posed classical compositions. He is the lonely inhabitant of a fiction. Modotti, who did not appear to have intervened or interfered with her subjects by accessorizing or extreme posing or placement, did however in some cases manipulate photos in the dark room to emphasize their social message.

Given the fact that contemporary Italian culture is based on a standardized verbal language whose spread has trailed behind visual sensibilities in permeating the peninsula, Chapter 2 will include a consideration of how the visual, and in particular photography and photographic images, has come to be represented in Italian literature. Beginning with Tommaso Campanella's *City of the Sun* as an early revolutionary example of visual pedagogy, I will then turn to contemporary Italian authors whose engagement of the photographic image is particularly strong, evocative and incisive. The works of novelists Italo Calvino, Leonardo Sciascia and Gianni Celati, all of whom have at some time taken photography as their subject, are indicative of an Italian fascination with figural representations. This penchant for the visual is well represented through the length and breadth of Italian cultural history, so much so that it could very easily be said that Italian culture is much more visual than literary. It is through the work of these authors, who provide a ground upon which a theory of figurative manifestation might be possible somewhere in the move from image to word, or vice versa, that I formulate and address a notion of photography as a literary art. Such an approach, for its approximation of genres and descriptive strategies that propose alternative modes of narrative possibilities, situates this study within the parameters of what we know today as cultural studies.

Chapter 3, "Looters, Photographers, and Thieves: Stolen States of the Image/nation," will delve into a reading of the role of the famous Alinari Archives, by far the most extensive private photographic archive of major national importance. The Alinari activities were in large part responsible for the elaboration and maintenance of a national image that is centered on Tuscany and Florence. I propose to review their images through the expression *fare una bella figura* (to cut a beautiful image), which I take to be a major conditioning factor in Italian self-imaging. The *bella figura* was and is useful in the context of national discourse both in potentializing nationhood in the late 1800s and in today's Italian self-image, especially at a time in history when a prominent political figure such as Silvio Berlusconi is also Italy's major media mogul.

Chapter 4, "Giovanni Verga: Photography and Verismo," will pursue a reading of the photographic images produced by the father of *Verismo,* Italian realism, Giovanni Verga. While it may be possible to trace a correspondence between Verga's literary production and his photographic output, here I will address specific details of his photography that speak to the deconstruction of the idea of *bella figura* explored in Chapter 2. Verga limited his photography to the areas most immediate his everyday life. His subjects were his family and the peasants that peopled the landscape in which he grew up, as well as the stories of his *Verismo* period. While I will discuss Verga's own self-portraits in the opening chapter, it is his photographs of the peasants I am most interested in addressing here. Not only were these peasants the same subjects of his writing, but they were also the individuals who would make up the emigrant masses who would eventually embark for the Americas. The potentiality as emigrants embodied by his subjects is a compelling trait that, while not necessarily discernible in the photographs, nevertheless offers terms of comparison from which the following chapter takes form.

Chapter 5, "Imaging America: The Photography of Lewis Hine and Jacob Riis," turns to the images produced by the American photographers Lewis Hine and Herbert Riis. They are the most recognized documenters of the immigrant influx into the United States of America around the end of the nineteenth and beginning of the twentieth centuries. Their imagery has become a useful catalogue of historical types for those who have sought to represent the diversity of the American ethnic landscape as it developed during that particular wave of immigration. Today, we can extend the readings applicable to the work of Hine and Riis beyond their status as factual documents and question the status that those photographs imparted on their subjects. While their work might not have been strictly driven by ideology, Hine and Riis cannot be detached from the structures of knowledge and power of their time. The ensuing results of their photographic production are of extreme importance to the image we have of ourselves today as residents of North America.

Hine and Riis' catalogue of humanity served the purpose of nation building by erasing the origins of the subjects and accordingly replaced them with one, unifying, American identity. Nevertheless, their photographs also marked these bodies irrevocably as different in the American imaginary, the effects of which persist to this day. It is this marking that I then follow, in an attempt to trace a line of correspondence between the figural representations emphasized by Hine and Riis and those of Verga.

The final chapters will address the work of two very dissimilar photographers: Tina Modotti and Baron von Gloeden. Chapter 6, "Imaginative Contradictions: von Gloeden's Disruptive Bodies of Representation," approaches the Baron von Gloeden's photographs of young Sicilian boys within the parameters of a fascination for the Mediterranean that borders on colonial documentation. The baron, apparently a persecuted homosexual, found in Sicily the possibility to lead a freer and more creatively expressive life. In Taormina he begins a long series of photographic representations of the young men mostly in and around the city. The young men are photographed almost always in the nude, wearing fictionalized trappings of a past and classical period that provides the backdrop for photographs that become popular among the Grand Tour travelers to the island. Today, the baron's photographs are highly sought-after collector's items, yet, even as we have advanced in our critical enquiry to take into account various forms of colonialism, the question as to whether von Gloeden's freedom of expression impedes his subjects' own freedom has yet to be addressed.

Italy and Sicily are in a particularly interesting position as both Mediterranean and European regions. As liminal territories they lend themselves to particularly fruitful analyses of hybrid cultural manifestations representative of emerging extra-national situations or extensions of otherwise seemingly unitary situations such as the EU and NATO. Perhaps even more interesting than this is the fact that there seems to be a reluctance to address issues such as these both within a European context and within the purview of cultural studies. The reasons for the exclusions are not clear, but the consideration that colonialism may be present within the home boundaries of the colonizers is certainly disruptive of some deeply rooted colonial and post-colonial critiques. This is more than evident in how von Gloeden's works are read today, and how some critics go as far as to redefine his subjects' identities as non-European.

After a brief historical-biographical account of Tina Modotti's life, her photographic and political work, Chapter 7, "Tina Modotti: Life Through the Ground-glass," will consider her work in light of the fact that she herself was an immigrant to the US and then Mexico. It is important to note that Mexico provided Modotti with an environment in which her activism and her art flourished and drew closer to some of the ideals that contrasted the Fascist culture that had taken hold in her Italian homeland. Her short-lived photographic career had a lasting influence on Mexican photography, through the work of Manuel Alvarez Bravo among others, and created a subset of photographic practice that carries a particularly "feminine" approach. As I will demonstrate, Modotti's series *The Women of Tehuantepec* is paramount in her production as a declaration of the power of women culturally, socially and politically.

Modotti and von Gloeden found themselves able to express their identities outside of their own national context; an expatriate Italian and an expatriate German, the two photographers found abroad the possibility to express their true selves. Yet, differently from Modotti, von Gloeden did not seem to identify socially or culturally with his subjects; all the while, they served to enable his own self-expression. Ironically, it was through the denial of those subjects' identities and the superimposition of his own classical system of signification, that von Gloeden attempted to reconstitute his own image through what I call "ethnic cross-dressing."

The final chapter, "Autobiographical Postscript as a Way of Conclusion: Belabored Bodies, Believable Fictions, Belated Images," is a brief reading of an out of focus photograph that sparked my initial interest in photographic images as "documents" and provided the stimulus for this book. Within the photograph rest the terms discussed through each chapter and, as a concluding image that has not quite found its focus, it stands as a depository of manifestations and possibilities that each figure individually, and the group as a whole, represent. As a denial of *bella figura* by social class and photographic aesthetics, this concluding chapter and photograph suggest that each figure cuts a social space that is inextricably tied to that of every other element in its community.

Recent works on the photographic image have taken on the problem of the specificity of representation as it relates to one group, race, ethnic group or gender. Publications and studies such as *The Black Female Body: A Photographic History*, by Deborah Willis and Carla Williams, *Ground Level*, by James Nachtwey, and *I viaggi nel Sud di Ernesto De Martino* (Ernesto De Martino's Voyages in Southern Italy), by Clara Gallini and Francesco Faeta, have found in the isolation of images by thematic terms an eloquent ground for specific visual formations. It is my hope that this present volume might represent a modest contribution to this most fascinating discourse and the constantly evolving realm of figurative possibilities.

The less than linear and chronological nature of this book is meant to serve as a locus of collection and accumulation. The arguments and images of each chapter thread through and with each other to propose another way of approaching disparate subjects, formats and establish photographers as seers rather than gazers. Some items form a circular and repetitive continuity within the greater range of the argument and, inevitably, as with the endless array of images that pass before us, their consideration may not always find a conclusive end or theoretical resolution. Just like all the images that we receive, produce and ponder, certain issues may be left there to orbit in our unconscious for contemplation and future reference.

Hopefully, this structure will function toward creating a communicative network between the chapters as it exists in my own direct personal experiences with photographs as a collector and as a sometime photographer, and as with all of us a frequent subject of photographs. To a certain extent, these categories all dictate the choice of photographers and photographs considered herein and provide the interpretative and critical space by which I have engaged the material. Finally, I hope that rather than simple conclusions, I might have been able to point out gaps where more questions will be generated for an extension of the network. My attempt has been to work beyond solidified terms of reference, in both photography and literature, toward more fluid and open spaces. Given the fact that much of the photography considered within the pages of this book is in dialogue with, or the product of, national or colonial programmatic agendas, it is only fair to ask what potential spaces for intervention upon them might remain if it is not done outside of established categories.

## NOTES

1. Rachel Gabara, "A Poetics of Refusal: Neorealism from Italy to Africa," in *Italian Neo-Realism in a Global Context*, edited by Laura Ruberto and Christi Wilson (Detroit: Wayne State University Press: 2007), 191.
2. Walter Benjamin, "The Work of Art in the Age of Mechanical Reproduction," in *Illuminations: Essays and Reflections* (New York: Schocken Books, 1987), 217–51.
3. Ibid., 218.
4. Ibid., 219.
5. Ibid., 220.
6. Ibid., 221.
7. Edward Steichen, *The Family of Man* (New York: Museum of Modern Art, 1955).
8. Goffredo Fofi, "Introduzione," in *Lo sguardo da sud*, edited by Alessandra Mauro (Napoli: l'ancora, 1999).
9. Alessandra Mauro, *Lo sguardo da sud: conversazioni su sud e fotografia* (Napoli: l'ancora, 1999), 22.
10. Ibid., 79.

# 1

# The Raw and the Cooked-Up

## *Opening Thoughts on Bodies*

To a body[1]

The curls of a man; the brow that they hide,
A living soul inside; the tender skin;
And the folds of his suit at his lap,
All things that I saw as a child.
P. P. Pasolini

### WORKING BODIES OF THE IMAGINARY

Pier Paolo Pasolini's poem "To a body" (*A un cuarp*) represents a memory of the poet's infatuation with a (male) body that he has observed. The details and traits reported are physical and sensual, both real and imagined. They enliven what might initially appear to be a simple description of the author's sexual desire. More significant, however, is the fact that the poem is written in a language that is marginal within the hegemonic territory of "Italian" linguistic culture. Friulano was a marginal language that, previous to Pasolini's own engagement of it, did not exist in written form.[2] The hidden aspect of this linguistic and cultural expression that awaits liberation and unveiling makes its use of it directly sensual, makes its expression distinctly and uniquely physiological. This poem and its language are "the folds of [a] suit" that await unfolding, undoing and exposure. The poem "A un cuarp" tends to function like the snapshot of an emerging culture for its ability to capture the expressions of a body during a transitive and therefore limited moment of expression.

As a snapshot of a body's informative capabilities, what it alludes to, and what it entices, this poem elicits reading and interpretation. It invites one to go beyond the mere surface of the thing itself to the hidden story behind it, to the real or fictional narrative it simulates.[3] The body itself informs or gives shape to the response of the reader/viewer who, upon reading it, transitions into a literary and poetic interpretative space. Rather than the words describing or injecting a notion of what the image might be and give it shape, it is the body itself that informs our perception of it. As such, these verses, like any other medium that might allow for this sort of function, are a good place to begin to work toward a consideration of photography as an intimately physiological process. This undermines any description of such a medium as a one-way, unidirectional illustrative technology and moves toward a consideration that recognizes the interactivity of perception.

The terms by which photography functions influence the perception of the bodies depicted or captured to the extent that the bodies' own informative effects on the medium are often overlooked. In other words, to literally accept the objective sense of the photographs without considering how the technology might have to adjust in order to represent a body. Such a shift of perspective requires a consideration of the technological parameters by which the subjects of photography are pictured. No matter what prescriptive formulas might be offered, what "automatic" settings we might engage on a camera, each subject requires an adjustment in focus, light, composition and more, in order to technologically render the "best" image possible. This simple reality that guides photography is one of an array of possible ways in which subjects/bodies inform the technology and establish a relationship of interdependence with it.

Slouching toward the two-hundred-year mark of the invention of photography, the incredible leaps in its evolution through technological innovation are mostly lost to the greater part of the population who partakes of it nowadays. The generations who know photography only as a digital medium, those who have never inserted a roll of film into a camera, let alone know what film is, can only have a limited sensitivity to the photographic camera as a truly interactive instrument by which each photographer chooses lens, film type and speed, shutter speed and lens aperture. Until recently, and even with some of the point and shoot film cameras, a process of decision-making was required that played a role in the quality and effect of the resulting images.

Undeniably, even the most automatic of digital cameras requires the photographer to at least push the on/off button. Beyond that, the work entailed in recording images has become more and more distanced from what we might have once called an active agent. Indeed, agency could now be said to have become almost a secondary appendage whose function has been reduced to turning on the camera, point and shoot. So programmed has this become that the non-action of the digital/automatic photographer has, with point and shoot, come to name a whole sector of camera types that defines the passive role of those who use it.

At this point I would suggest that the interactions I have described above, in the brief reading of Pasolini's poem and my considerations of how a subject might reciprocally inform a technology, the main function of which is considered to be that of disseminating information, must bring into the discourse an aspect of human (inter)action in making photographs that can only be called *labor*.[4] Very little has been said about this aspect of photography. Vilém Flusser's addresses it tangentially in his *Toward a Philosophy of Photography*, but limits it to the workings of the "apparatus." While Flusser's engagement of the mechanical labor of the camera is important, I propose that the human element must at some point or other come into the picture, so of to speak, as a fundamental point of reference for the labor involved in *making* and not *taking* images. Translating Flusser's observations regarding the camera to a human circumstance turns the terms of reference to my purpose:

> The Latinate term *apparatus* stems from the verb *apparare*, which is *to prepare*. Latin also contains the verb *praeparare*, however; the difference is one of prefixes: *ad* and *prae*. The most available translation for *apparare* in English would be to *make ready*.[5]

The close relationship between the apparatus and the preparatory procedures required by a photographer before an image can be recorded implies the identification of a human component to bring the labor process to fruition. If it is true that we can know culture through its *apparati*, as Flusser and others have suggested, including the eighteenth-century philosopher Giambattista Vico, then the function of cameras as something ready to be put to a particular use takes on very important meaning. Walter Benjamin's meditations on the production, characteristics and function of image-making in the classic "The Work of Art in the Age of Mechanical Reproduction" continue to be helpful in understanding our relationship to image-making machines, and their evolution over the last 150 or so years. The initial transition from large-format cameras to smaller 120 and 35 mm models facilitated certain types of photography and helped popularize the medium. Today the transition to point-and-shoot and digital has slowly reduced the labor involved in recording images and altered the time frame between exposures.

Flusser generates an interesting and convincing argument regarding the function of cameras. He teases out a definition of the photographic apparatus as involved in the production and information of objects as labor, the end result of which "is called a work."[6] Flusser's, however, is not a wholly firm definition, since the relationship between the camera and the human body is similar to, while also different from, that of other instruments or tools to their users. While some contemporary camera manufacturers have developed "face-recognition" programs and "eye-guided" focusing processes, it remains open for discussion as to whether the camera is an extension of the eye or whether the eye is guided by the camera in its looking.[7] While Flusser turns his discussion toward the photographer to ask whether we might define "such things as *photo-proletarians* and *photo-capitalists*,"[8] I would like to extend Flusser's argument in a different direction. I will here shift my focus slightly to the laboring bodies of photography that are not behind the camera and direct Flusser's argument elsewhere. While "the photographer does not work in the industrial sense of the word," and that, as much as they are part of the apparatus of image-making, photographers "are not meant to change the world, but to change the meaning of the world," I would also contend that photography changes that meaning through the engagement of laboring bodies as subjects and the technicians who aid in the preparation, processing, printing and replication of images.[9]

It is for certain that the relationship of the maker of images with the photographic apparatus has altered the "intellectual" work involved in making cultural signs. This, Flusser suggests, requires a renewed approach in the analysis of culture that, rather than using work as a category of distinction, would involve how subjects themselves might be *informed* by the process.[10] I am therefore interested in bringing to the fore the invisible or missing cog involved in the process of making information. Even in its differentiated form, photography has established since its inception a societal relationship with the human body that partially replicated that of other technologies. Regardless of who was/is behind the camera at the moment of exposure, the subjects being recorded, those *informing* the technology's task, and those who then process(ed) and print(ed) or digitalize the images, thereby *informing* the materials on which the images manifest, were/are those who according to Flusser "work(ed) in function of" the technology. What is even more fascinating in this case is that photo-laborers, not being involved in the initial framing and alignment of the photograph, but rather having a role as models, subjects or laboratory workers, are involved in the production of what is absent or invisible, something that, as the sign of a cultural intentionality within a national scope, has no function or being except as information.

At this point, it may be useful to consider how our perception of bodies has been changed by technology. Although it aids in the picturing or representation of bodies we might also think about how they themselves potentially inform the technology. The title of this chapter carries a not-so-veiled allusion to structural anthropologist Claude Lévi-Strauss' *The Raw and the Cooked*[11] while also suggesting that I am not writing as a structural anthropologist. Lévi-Strauss' notations of "raw" and "cooked" are interesting in that while they fall within a scheme of analysis of cuisine, their terms of reference are indicative of two functional aspects of culture. The "raw" can be taken to refer to any basic cultural practice and the "cooked" to what society might do with it in order to render it palatable, as it were, within hegemonic culture. As such, in relation to photography, we might ask if its social "facts" (its presumed ability to represent "reality" and therefore correctly and truthfully represent ethnicity, race, gender, sexuality and all expressions and manifestations of difference and diversity) are a function of the requirements of a social order or an actual expression of the subjects photographed.

Interestingly enough, today's photographic terminology includes "raw" as a designation of a particular type of digital file. A "raw" file is one that is the least sampled in terms of pixel encoding and therefore includes the maximum amount of pixular information possibly recordable within the limits of any one particular camera's capabilities. It is this "raw" data, which one may choose as an option on most cameras today, which will eventually be "cooked" to fit the specific use that a photograph might be put to. This ability to denote the amount and type of information recorded by digital cameras is an extension and a "making visible" of the choices involved in photography from its very beginnings. The difference that a "raw" file supposedly preserves is a set of encoded facts that in other formats (jpeg or pic for example) are constantly degraded and less true to their first version each time they are opened for viewing and thereby resampled.

All this requires a recasting of *to inform* from a passive process, implying the simple transfer of something already gathered, to a more dynamic and active process of transformation. Meaning is made even by a subject's mere presence, or by a laboratory worker's handling (manipulation) of the basic chemical materials and processes to make apparent an image exposed by someone else seeking to establish meaning.

Before returning to the laboring bodies behind the production of images however, I would like to take a brief detour to consider the possibility of image production without an imaging apparatus. "Image" today has taken an added significance to mean life choices, style choices, and possibly political or ideological adherence. The accoutrements of fashion, body-work, tattooing, piercing, cutting and branding, and all their associated accessories, go to create a particular personal image that is not the result of mechanical production but rather the outcome of self-manipulation. Humans have always been curious of the body that defines them in contrast to other animals and have acted upon that body in ways to further distinguish them. Hairless and upright, of diverse pigmentation, some humans have always felt the need to poke, prod and handle the body in an attempt to find out more about it. Some of the most precise pre-digital attempts at understanding the "raw" aspect of humanness can be seen, among other places, in Renaissance master Leonardo Da Vinci's anatomical drawings. Today, we marvel at their accuracy and artistry, as these satisfy our anthropological scientific curiosity and sense of narcissistic aesthetics.

We also know of the "alchemical" works of the Prince Raimondo de Sangro di Sansevero from the 1700s, still on display in what once was his private chapel in the heart of Naples, that reference for us the blasphemous blending of black arts, religion and science.[12] And, some of the most intriguing representations of the human body and its functions are to be found in the anatomical waxes that became the primary sources and references for the study of medicine and anatomical features pertinent to art. There are the magnificent anatomical waxes by Clemente Susini at the University of Cagliari, prepared between 1803 and 1805, and the anatomical waxes collection of Florence's La Specola (1775), as well as the Museum of Anatomical Waxes by Luigi Cattaneo in Bologna.

The Specola collection was the subject of an especially interesting publication by the German publisher Taschen in 1999 because it inserted the waxes within a contemporary context. It is not accidental that Taschen's publication list clearly outlines a specific interest in the functions, uses and representations of the body in the formation of cultural trends. The waxes would appear to uphold an abstract notion of femininity, propose the body in all its details as a pathway to knowledge, and clearly and emphatically represent reproductive processes as being exclusively associated with the female body. Ludmilla Jordanova's study of images of gender in science and medicine finds figures such as those of La Specola collection to function within a cultural framework that reinforces three eighteenth-century principles about the body. "Disequilibrated social relations have frequently been signaled by a language of gendered anatomy and pathology. There are, of course, powerful polarities at work here, the mark of centuries of dichotomous thought: active/passive, muscles/nerves, action/experience, male/female, public/private and domestic, subject/object, self/other, seeing/seen, reason/passion and desire."[13] These social categories and philosophical trends are clearly evident in the Specola collection and its centerpiece, the "Medical Venus" (Figure 1.1). The intricate wax models that begin to be fashioned during the Enlightenment as study aids and as expressions of the period's ideals are breath taking and startling. As Annette Burfoot notes regarding the Specola waxes, "Nearly everyone walking into the first room of models recoils at the hyper-realism . . . a sense of edging towards the abyss and the horrific is heightened" (Figure 1.2).[14]

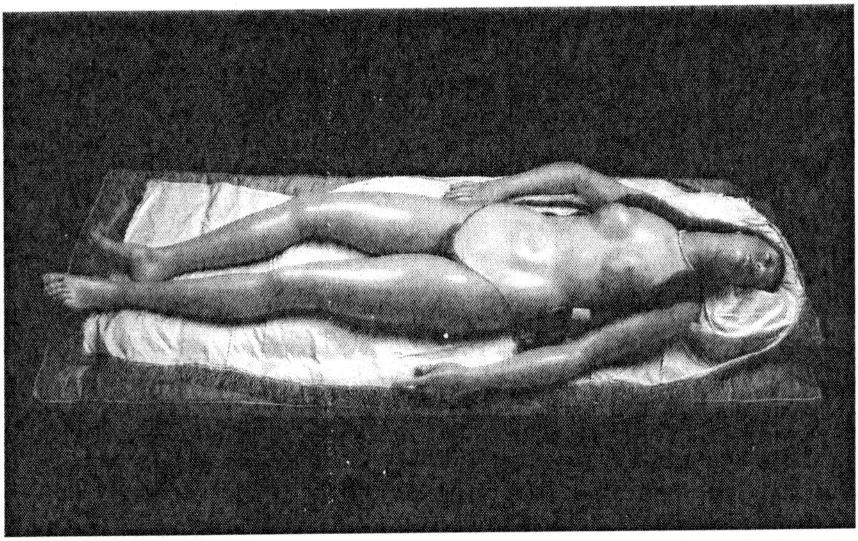

Figure 1.1. *Venere chiusa.* La Specola. Credit: Saulo Bambi, Museo di Storia Naturale, Firenze, Italia

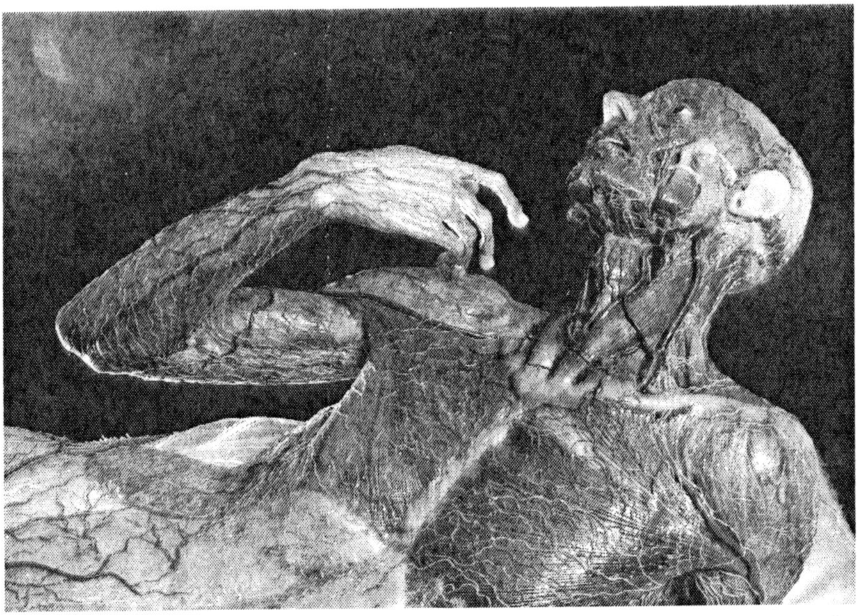

Figure. 1.2. *Wax model showing the superficial lymph vessels.* Museo della Specola, Florence, Clemente Susini 1775–1791. Villani Achille 1950–1960 Fratelli Alinari Museum Collections, Villani Archive, Florence. Credit: Alinari Archives, Florence.

Burfoot suggests that these waxes have provided inspiration to Italian masters of horror cinema such as Dario Argento, which nevertheless does not deny, but rather supports, the notion that part of the fascination for the waxes and Leonardo's earlier drawings is due to their fulfilling a function of discovery of the self.[15] Before the emergence of any external or mechanical "apparatus" that would enable the faithful rendering of the human body, in a nice twist on Christian Genesis, it was the eye in concert with the hands that created these bodies. And, while they might not, in the strictest sense of the word, be images, they appear as images in culture for the power they lend human beings to imagine themselves mirrored inside and out. The re-imaginings of the human body that these drawings and waxes represent tie in very cleanly with French philosopher Michel Foucault's observations regarding the relationship between power and the production of knowledge.[16]

Certainly the knowledge produced by the objects discussed above is supportive of a power structure that intended the dissemination of a certain ideology regarding the body, gender, reproduction and societal roles. The production of the waxes was by no means a disinterested or neutral undertaking, and it is so evidenced by their institutional affiliations and places of preservation. Similarly, making the (not-so-distant) leap to the emergence of the photographic medium, we can see that there too, while expressing moments of apparent democratization, the new medium reflects ideological interests in the knowledge it makes available and the means by which that knowledge is produced.

Cut to a more contemporary fascination with the body that appears to have gone full circle to the more tactile and "hyper-realistic" days of the wax figures. Along with a full complement of television programs such as *Bones*, *C.S.I.*, *Cold Case Files*, *N.C.S.I.*, *Forensic Investigator*, there are medical shows that have mixed the romantic intrigue of soaps such as *General Hospital* with anatomical and physiological intrigue to arrive at shows such as *House* and *Grey's Anatomy*. Today there is no shortage of images to help fulfill our desire to view the human body (preferably someone else's) in a whole variety of positions, dimensions and expressions of multi-layered reality that render still the process of decay. The difference that distinguishes these forms from the anatomical waxes is their function as *entertainment*. They pretend to have a function as sources of knowledge, even as they appear to offer neutral knowledge. And, under the guise of entertainment, they tend to be thought of as unencumbered by a dominant power structure for the apparent "choice" they provide us viewers regarding what and when we watch.

The overly saturated visual horizon concerned with the surfaces of the body, including pornography's ever closer, more and more invasive and probing exploration of every possible variation with orifices of the body, had at some point to give way to new ways experiencing human physicality. Television ventured in to this realm of internal voyeurism with medical and forensic shows and has now entered a phase that seeks to go beyond those into a more divergent realm that includes programming, both fictional and journalistic, on serial killers, the criminal mind, etc.

Cleverly tapping into this deepened interest in the human body that seems to have developed from an insatiable need for a tactility that is real, a number of entertainment firms have set out, and successfully put forth, to show us to ourselves in the most intimate details all under the guise of educational entrepreneurship. As robotics becomes more and more a reality than science fiction, and the traffic of organs is part of a lucrative underground market, the projection of *Blade Runner*'s (1982) replicants and more recent *Terminators* (1984–2009) and *Surrogates* (2009) further play a mimetic game with our apparent troubling inability to recognize our human selves.

## THE RAW AND THE COOKED-UP: BELABORED BODIES AND THE DISPLAY OF HUMANNESS

It has been said that "the photographic portrait cannot and does not want to be the story of those pictured, and it would seem that each individual story can no longer be enclosed within a portrait."[17] Such a statement would seem to recognize the limitations of photography, its unattainable claim to reality. And as this realization has now become apparent to most everyone, there appears to be a need to have to identify some other form of representation to take its place. Given its immateriality and distance from the subjects it records, photography can only be a remote mode of historical documentation. Through photography we are left to deal with living beings reproduced as images that have agency in their own function as cultural expressions. But what if we were to take philosopher Giordano Bruno's hint that "the bodies tell the story" and attempt a mode of reproduction that would enable us to represent human bodies with human bodies themselves? Is it possible for unmediated, material, physically present bodies in all their flesh and blood to *be* their own history?

Recently, a traveling exhibition has made the news for its uniqueness and the stir it has caused on a number of levels including as an attraction and as, for some, a repulsive and disturbing display. The exhibition has traveled to a number of cities around the world, among them Barcelona,

Fort Lauderdale, Buenos Aires, Pittsburgh, San Diego, Las Vegas and New York, but one can simply visit the website www.bodiestheexhibition.com and step into the world of our own materiality exposed:

> BODIES . . . The Exhibition
>
> Celebrate the wonder of the human form in the World Premier of BODIES ... The Exhibition—a phenomenal look at the phenomena we call the human body.
>
> With educational relevance for all ages, this exhibition of real human specimens immerses visitors in the complexities of the human body, telling us the amazing story of ourselves with reverence and understanding.

The Bodies exhibition is not alone in making these claims for education, discovery and research. Others that I was able to find on the web are "Body Worlds," "Body Exploration," "The Universe Within" and "Bodies Revealed," all of which have their associated websites declaring their mission, outlining their procedures for obtaining bodies and selling their T-shirts, catalogues and coffee mugs:

> www.natureandscience.org/bodyworlds/default.asp,www.ourbodytheuniversewithin.com/news.htm
> www.bodiestheexhibition.com/video/bodies-video-broadband-1.mov

The above-quoted narrative opens the initial web portal of the BODIES exhibition. It is followed by links through which one may get to know the exhibition better before visiting and also order tickets and merchandise. The cities listed give an idea of the global appeal of such an exhibition, and the marketing potential that it represents. Tickets can be purchased for the Prague, Lisbon, Pittsburgh, San Diego, Durham, Las Vegas, New York, and Washington stops and more are added as it travels and as word-of-mouth begins to make more people curious.

The official website extends its welcome with "Welcome to BODIES: The Exhibition. A Phenomenal Look at the Phenomenon We Call the Human Body," which is accompanied by an image that will surely be appreciated by most of this world's population that counts soccer (football) as its sport: a skinless body doing a reverse bicycle kick. *GOOOOOOAAAAAAL! Que golazo, de este hombre de la esquadra umana!*

Aside from the poses in which these "beings" are positioned playing soccer, tennis and other sports, in other words ways in which they are brought up to the contemporary expectations of a health-conscious and sports-aware public, there is nothing new about these bodies. We have seen digital simulations of this sort in movies, and we have of course the anatomical waxes discussed above. So, what's so interesting or special about these most recent traveling exhibitions and their promises? Nothing, aside from the fact that these bodies are "real human bodies that have been preserved so they do not decay," otherwise their claim to reality seems remarkably close to that of photography. While there is no projection, reflection or mirroring of the image via mechanical methods in any way, I would propose that the preparation of bodies is very similar to modern technology's production of virtual landscapes.

The success of such a process depends on our own well-stimulated powers of accessing an internal image bank that has accumulated standardized visual referents. It depends on the work of our imagination, whose play is constricted by culturally predefined parameters determined by advertising, television, film, computer games, etc. This contemporary manner of presenting "real bodies," preserved and dissected, is a manner of virtualizing the body that finds correspondence in the production of self-portraits. The externalization of the human body creates a sense of recognition similar to the self-portrait that carries with it a similar sense of incredulity and intimacy. Public reactions to these exhibits testify to this as much as they contrast the "hyper-realism" and sense of the "horrific" that confronts visitors to the Specola Collection waxes.

Since first visiting the *Bodies, the Exhibition* website the popularity of these shows has increased and their impact has been felt in a number of ways. The first page of the website now contains a new insert, a disclaimer and a "NYC Refund Policy" that I had not previously noticed with regards to the origin of the bodies used in the exhibition. Obviously some attention has been brought to this and other displays that use human bodies for display:

> In keeping with the May 23, 2008 Assurance of Discontinuance executed by Premier Exhibitions, Inc. (the "Company") and The Attorney General for the State of New York, the Company agreed to disclose the following regarding BODIES. . . The Exhibition, at South Street Seaport:
>
> (A) "This exhibit displays human remains of Chinese citizens or residents which were originally received by the Chinese Bureau of Police. The Chinese Bureau of Police may receive bodies from Chinese prisons. Premier cannot independently verify that the human remains you are viewing are not those of persons who were incarcerated in Chinese prisons."
>
> (B) "This exhibit displays full body cadavers as well as human body parts, organs, fetuses and embryos that come from cadavers of Chinese citizens

or residents. With respect to the human parts, organs, fetuses and embryos you are viewing, Premier relies solely on the representations of its Chinese partners and cannot independently verify that they do not belong to persons executed while incarcerated in Chinese prisons."

If you would have elected not to attend the Exhibition had you seen these disclosures, and would like your entrance fee to be refunded, please submit a signed statement that includes the following information:

(A) Name and Address;
(B) Proof of having attended the New York Exhibition before May 30th, 2008;
(C) The date before May 30, 2008 on which you attended the New York Exhibition;
(D) A declaration that had you known, read, or understood the above-referenced disclosures, you would not have attended BODIES. . . The Exhibition, at South Street Seaport.

To:

Premier Exhibitions, Inc.
P.O. Box 19035
Atlanta GA 31126

For detailed information regarding the New York General's inquiry and settlement, click here. (PDF)

(http://www.prxi.com/nycrefunds/)

As a disclaimer, this is almost an aside, an intrusion on the apparent intention of the site and exhibit to educate and invite visitors to share in the marvelous display. Potential visitors are asked to consider the process by which these bodies have been produced as a wonderfully innovative procedure at the service of contemporary knowledge:

To help you see what a body really looks like on the inside, this Exhibition uses real human bodies that have been preserved so they do not decay.

A human specimen is first preserved according to standard mortuary science. The specimen is then dissected to show whatever it is that someone wants to display. Once dissected, the specimen is immersed in acetone, which eliminates all body water. The specimen is then placed in a large bath of silicone, or polymer, and sealed in a vacuum chamber. Under vacuum, acetone leaves the body in the form of gas and the polymer replaces it, entering each cell and body tissue. A catalyst is then applied to the specimen, hardening it and completing the process.

> This method of preservation creates a specimen that will not decay. This offers thousands of unique teaching possibilities for educators at all levels, including medical professionals, archeologists and other scientists.
> (www.bodiestheexhibition.com/bodies.html)

It is rather interesting the way in which the process is so deliberately recounted as a matter-of-fact set of the instructions that interestingly recalls those found in old photography manuals for the development and fixing of images. But, again, that might not be a coincidence at all, for here too we are directly involved in re-creating bodies out of bodies. The organizers of these "body" exhibits and those who imagined the possibility of putting real bodies to such use and displaying them before ever-increasing lines of spectators, have created a new category of posthumous labor that forms part of what I will call *belabored bodies,* relatable to and including the living and breathing laboring bodies used in the quest for *imagistic* reality that is photography.

Strangely enough, the attempt to give us, the viewing (and paying) public, a full sense of reality through the use of "real" bodies in contrast to the earlier waxes, drawings, photographs and virtual reconstructions in the end confronts us with "plasticized" or fictionalized bodies. What the process of plasticization does, explained in detail in some of the websites cited above, is to artificialize the bodies. As we step closer to what we are told are "real" bodies, we encounter plastic bodies and are again denied the direct experience of flesh and blood. Again, while this is presented as groundbreaking, the process seems to repeat at least rhetorically if not actually some of the steps of the wax molding and of photography. A subject is chosen, it is prepared, posed, processed and fixed in a certain manner so as to re-present a particular activity or highlight a part of the body deemed worthy of viewing.

Reading further into the website, the organizers have nicely provided a "History of Anatomy" that is useful for both what it tells and what it elides. There is a naming of the milestones in the study of anatomy, an enumeration of the tools and instruments developed throughout that history in order to facilitate its study. Yet, there is no mention of the anatomical waxes that continue to be regarded as fundamental reference points in the evolution of medicine. In place of that we find an almost anxious inclusion of the 1832 British Anatomy Act:

> As the interest in anatomy grows, England passes the Anatomy Act to offer an adequate and legitimate supply of bodies and prevent body snatching, grave robbing, and murdering as means of providing anatomists with cadavers.
>
> (www.bodiestheexhibition.com/bodies.html)

Undeniably, these exhibitions are at some level educational. Schools regularly organize tours to visit and be wowed by the sight of "real" bodies that have been plasticized and dissected. The comments left by visitors, which are also reported on the website, testify that many people take away not only the sense wonder and awe from their experiences, but also lessons regarding the fragile state of the human body:

> "I think the respect and dignity given to these bodies is wonderful"
> "More amazing than any art gallery."
> "I never thought I would get a chance to touch an actual heart!"
> "I am calling my daughter right now to convince her to stop smoking."
> "Everyone should visit this exhibit to see the damage caused by poor lifestyle choices."
> "You have revealed a hidden side of us that we all need to see and learn about."
> "What a great tribute to the human body. From cranium to big toe—I am blown away."
> (Visitor comments: www.bodiestheexhibition.com/bodies.html)

Despite all this, questions remains regarding the origin of the bodies, the disclaimers and the display itself. This is however also not a question that is uniquely related to these exhibitions; it must be asked whether we are at the *Bodies* exhibition or admiring Salgado's famine photographs, images of the Holocaust from WWII or reportage of the Rwandan genocide. As viewers we are caught in a dilemma: we are fascinated by these images of violence beyond their informational function. We are entertained, we are engaged by and asked to ponder the images; we are stopped in our tracks and asked to consider whether the images before us edify the bodies represented or the violence done to them.

I have chosen to insert this brief discussion of anatomical waxes and their modern day emulations within a general discussion of photography because, as a medium, the latter cannot be considered if not within the historical construct of subject/object relations. Photography's representations of what we assume to be real, and the eventual use of those images within contexts that are social, cultural and political require a contemplation on the fascination we hold for our bodies, and on some of the modalities by which we have attempted over time to explore them.

Possibly arising out of an inability to view ourselves as anything aside from what we believe we embody, and as an attempt to discover what a body might suffer, our fascination is most likely with the extent to which bodies are handled, mishandled, manipulated, mutilated, disfigured and demeaned. Photography is a medium in which all of these manipulations can be carried out while maintaining an ambiguous sense of uncertainty as to whether the images might be "real" or not.

At this point it might be useful perhaps to attempt to set out a definition of the term "real," for which I would like to propose that something is rendered "real" when it involves a process of human labor. What this labor might constitute and what form it might take is what I will explore in the following pages. I would like to begin by proposing that most of the labor involved in photography is of a vestigial or phantomatic nature and that, although involved in the photographic process, it is not necessarily the labor involved in taking the photograph (shooting the image) nor does the labor necessarily appear bodily in the final product. The labor I intend to point out is that of the workers who produce the images by handling the materials and giving form, or *informing*, the absent.

Within this group I include those who "model" for photographers, for the reason that in various and different imaging situations they produce images by the presence of their bodies. At times, the photographer herself performs an apparent slight-of-hand that disappears the photographer to have her reappear on the other side of the lens in what we know as a self-portrait. While the issue of self-portraits will be more specifically dealt with in chapters dedicated to certain photographers, here I would like to put forth the question of the function of self-portraits within the activity of image-making. What could the significance of the photographer's transition out from behind the lens and into the focal plane of the photographic apparatus be?

Self-portraits collapse the photographer, subject and processor of the image, into one agent. The terms of the production entail a by-proxy action that is implicated in the views and points-of-view that we might seek to leave of ourselves and our self-image. These variations on the photographing subject, including the shift from the person behind the lens to one who might step in front of his or her own lens, could be thought of as *surrogate imagists.*

Self-portraiture is ultimately connected to the images/representations discussed above because it further expresses a notion of the meaning of human embodiment. There is an underlying understanding of the self-portrait as a mirror of the self, in other words a doubling or reflection of/on the body which would appear to recognize the result of this mirror image as one that suppresses "all difference, denying any distinction between . . . self and . . . others," rather than emphasize individuality, subjectivity, and uniqueness.[18]

## SELF-PORTRAIT FILE

I would like to begin with a couple of considerations. The first is about the discursive space in which self-portraits are produced or in which they might be made possible or impossible. The second consideration has to do with the possible range of mechanisms behind the production of the self-portrait as an attempt to represent the photographer's activities as a "public" intellectual.[19]

Usually, the self-portrait is subsumed as a category of the portrait in art history categories. While this may be fully justified in relation to framing, composition and other morphological categories used to catalogue visual art, the *self* in the portrait requires a more detailed interpretation when used to explore other expressive potentialities. It is quite often the case that artists (among whom I include photographers) might appear to be reluctant to put forth a self-portrait, which is more likely the result of a deeper concern with the meaning of the form within the larger context of the artist's body of work rather than an expression of shyness or modesty.

The individual photographers I explore in this book have all produced, in one way or another, self-portraits. Since we tend to think of self-portraits as an image containing the singular image of the artist, I would like to propose here that it might be possible to include within the form a series of compositional variants that often include others in the frame as well as the expression of the self in other ways beyond its physical presence. The self-portrait is the domain of those who are behind the lens, and the portrait is within the dominion of those who might commission a photographer to enrich a familial gallery of sorts. These portraits are quite different from the more "scientific" portraits of those that are taken to represent anthropological categories. Regardless, the self-portrait may, in the end, constitute an anthropological category all its own.

The Futurist painter Umberto Boccioni's most obvious and obsessive preoccupations were with the effects of repetition, circularity and speed. He explored these effects through a series of well-known paintings that have become symbolic of Futurist ideology. As might be expected, Boccioni was also very intrigued with the possibilities that photography offered. There is a photograph of the artist in which he registers his photographic self-image as a multiple or repetition of himself. The photograph, dated circa 1905, represents five, possibly six, Boccioni. Four Boccioni are shown in various progressions of side profiles from left to right moving in a circle. One has his back to the viewer, and we might imagine an obscured frontal view behind the latter.

The oft-emulated photograph is entitled *Io Noi* (I We) in an obvious attempt to transform, through the crowding of a space with similar yet different images of the same subject, a personal act of self-representation into an act of objectification of that same subject. Boccioni achieved this through the occultation of the *io*, the first person Boccioni, arguably doubly absent by both the compositional rhetoric of the image and the obscuration of its frontal and presumably "true" frontal representation. By emphasizing the representational limits of the medium, *Io noi* exposes the unchallenged claims of the portrait or self-portrait formats. Paradoxically, in so doing, Boccioni expands the horizons of the medium, the parameters and possibilities of which were still at that time determined by a traditional painterly aesthetics and concept of art. Boccioni is among an active group of artists who make it their task to challenge that tradition and begin to define for photography its own particular vocabulary.

*Io Noi* not only questions photography's ability to wholly represent reality as it demonstrates the medium's technical agility, it also reproposes and updates a common visual trope from Medieval and Renaissance frescoes, in which any number of narrative moments are presented within a single frame. Stories and histories, narrative and linear time are collapsed into frames that undermine their logic and sustainability outside of convention and propose *believable fictions* through an imagistic relativity, logically recognizable as fictions but representationally believable.[20] Taken within this set of parameters, I would propose that the self-portraits by the artists presented in this study represent an attempt to invent new "characters" who would define for themselves a place in history rather than reflect historical or cultural literary referents/conventions. The photographers in this study take on the self-portrait not as historical subjects for their own self-interest but to emphasize their proximity as types to existing situations through the creation of their particular *believable fictions*.

Further, the discursive spaces in which the self-portraits are produced are in part fictional and in part a reflection of existing socio-political situations. They must either be tied up in the normative currents of the period or in an attempt to create alternative spaces within a culture. The photographs produced by Tina Modotti and Giovanni Verga are also illustrative of this latter point. Both Modotti and Verga's self-portraits function as proposals for the creation of visual spaces into which the marginal, the unusual, what might be considered outside a social or demographic norm, might find expression. This having been said, how to distinguish their photos of peasants, workers, women and other classes from those of other photographers who might use them to illustrate those populations' abnormality remains a large, though not wholly unapproachable, and fundamental question. The discursive context in which the images are produced, namely one of migrating bodies within, through and across national and nationalistic contexts, might provide a good place to begin that investigation. While I will approach those questions more thoroughly in the chapters dedicated to each photographer, it will suffice here to mention that Modotti and Verga, along with some of my other examples, worked at the margins of nationalist impositions and in favor of subalternity and cultural diversity.

The photographers I am about to discuss do not construct their self-portraits within distracting conventions, in other words within the conventional frameworks of bourgeois portraiture. All of the photographers I will concern myself with here do indeed make themselves the direct and unquestionable focus of their own lens. Yet, what I mean to foreground here is that the term "self-portrait," while laden with significance in our culture and in particular for the presupposition that the subject of the photograph is the primary term of reference, is only *apparently* true in their case. For this particular group of photographers, the self-portrait is an indirect referent for other layers of meaning and signifiers that flow in and out of their whole body of work.

We might want to contemplate the notion that self-portraits (all portraits?) can only be fictions. While, as we shall see with the Baron von Gloeden and his habit of dressing himself in various costumes just as he did his subjects to fictionalize his appearance, his attempt was to lose himself within a population he had previously idealized and fictionalized, the process is somewhat different for other photographers such as Verga and the Alinari Brothers. The latter engaged in what we today might call "straight" photography, without excessive or apparent intervention on the part of the photographer. Nevertheless, if we consider that the Alinari were consciously participating in the cataloguing of Florentine, Tuscan and Italian culture (the order is important for how Italian culture was consciously constructed through the tropes of Florentine Renaissance and its influence on other spheres, regional and national), as an expression of national character, then theirs is no less a fiction than von Gloeden's classicized Sicilian youth.

That these fictions constitute believable constructs goes to the effectiveness of photography as a medium engaged in the creation of believable fictions as apparent reality and to our human penchant for believing what we see. Giovanni Verga, the Italian author and principal representative of *Verismo*, a particularly Italian form of literary Realism, and himself a photographer, while engaging straight photography in recording the peasants of his region much as he did with words, also produced a number of self-portraits. Self-portraits almost require their viewers/readers to read them in relation to a photographer's photos of others. Giovanni Verga would appear to pose the following question through his photographs: *If I, Giovanni Verga, value the un-mediated representation of the Sicilian peasantry both in words and images why would I require any less, or any different, of the images of myself and my family?*

I would suggest that this is the sort of rhetoric that we might look for in photographic images, a rhetoric of representation that tends toward the making of believable fictions as ideological foci; possibly insightful moments that would lead us to understand the processes and causes that guide us from seeing ourselves to believing the images that we see.

## THE ALINARI LABORATORIES

The process of producing what one takes to be, or sees as, the image of one's self and one's social and political environment also defines a social and ideological relationship that could be said to be a self-portrait. Each photographer's position(ing) vis-à-vis the bodies he or she employs in the making of images is a revelatory gaze cast upon his or her own body.

The Alinari Photographic Laboratories were a veritable industry whose involvement in the production and cataloguing of an Italian national image I will outline in a chapter to follow. Here I would like to begin to address a particularly interesting aspect of their infrastructure that remains mostly unconsidered: the working spaces and the labor force that made of the Alinari an incredibly influential cultural phenomenon.

The industrialized aspect of their art could be considered to represent an important example upon which other future readings of photographic labor might be viewed. For example, the identity of their workers, the conditions under which they labored has gone mostly uncommented. While many images of the "Stabilimenti," picturing photographers and laboratory personnel at work in clean and spacious facilities, are preserved in the Alinari Archives, little if anything is known of the individuals who worked in those same spaces (Figure 1.3).

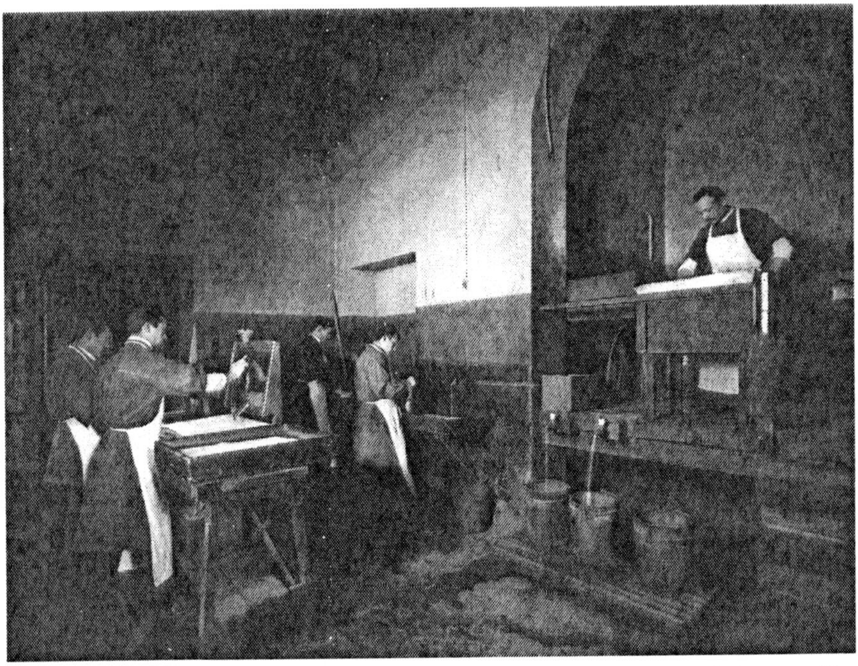

Figure. 1.3. ***View of the laboratory of the Fratelli Alinari company of Florence.*** **The photographers shown in the image are making contact prints. Fratelli Alinari, 1899. Credit: Alinari Archives, Florence.**

In light of these images, it is obvious that the Alinari enterprise could not have functioned if not for a skilled work force. Not only did this personnel have to follow directions in learning the new technology but I would guess that it also participated in the development of that technology to adequately enable a greater sophistication as required by the Alinari's demanding new uses of it.

I would therefore suggest that the Alinari not only engaged photography as a medium through which to isolate, record and accumulate images in keeping with a particular view of the nascent nation, but that they also created (manipulated?) a work force in which those images themselves were instilled as they took part in their creation. The apparently innocent and straightforward task of recording images with a camera became, in the hands of the Alinari and others like them, a mode of cultural pedagogy that passed through the fingertips and eyes of their laborers to the eyes of the nation. It was in this way, by engaging laboring bodies toward the construction of a virtual nation of images, that the Alinari helped take some of the first steps in the creation of a national imaginary. Even before those that they sought to represent had begun to think of themselves as "Italian," Alinari photographs generated a fascination with what the embodiment of a national image might be.

## GIOVANNI VERGA AND THE LABOR OF EMIGRATION

More or less a contemporary of the Alinari, the Sicilian writer Giovanni Verga worked on his own, with no apparent assistants, in exploring the limits of the new technology that was photography. While his brand of Realism, *Verismo*, emphasized the recording of "things as they are" and a removal of the influence of the author's hand, he often made it clear that his photographs were not to be regarded as studies for his writings.

Verga worked in and around his home, and in the fields where he also professed to find the stories of the peasants whose lives he recounted. His photographs include family and self-portraits, as well as individual and group portraits of the peasants who worked the countryside. Verga's are photographs of an unstable reality and his subjects are an absence, both in terms of their participation in Italian society, their marginal economic status, and their future presence (negated by emigration) in the places where they are being photographed. Theirs are the *belabored bodies* whose future absence constitutes as much a laboring body counted upon in order to allow nationalism to function, as their presence was exploited to benefit others.

The bodies that Verga takes care to record and situate in that landscape are paradoxically the bodies that the national program considers superfluous. It is an interesting twist of events then that makes of Verga's photographs a record not of the injustices of social inequality but of exportable labor, of a commodified humanity that is shifted, and shifts, to where it might be considered useful in order to survive. His photos are those of what we might consider to be potential emigrants, their labor *is* emigration, and their exploitation is their being deemed superfluous in their homeland.

## RIIS AND HINE'S IMAGES OF FUTURE LABOR

Interestingly enough, Giovanni Verga's photographs find their complement in another context of nation-building. Lewis Hine and Herbert Riis were photographers working in the United States at the turn of the nineteenth century and who turned their cameras on the teeming masses of immigrants that were reaching the American shores. Theirs represents a compendium of laboring bodies made available for the growing North American nation.

By recording and cataloguing the immigrant masses as they transitioned into American society, Riis and Hine exploited those immigrant bodies toward the creation of a *body of work* of no direct use to those pictured. Their photographs paid little attention to what those bodies signified outside of potential labor. It is of course recognized and appreciated that these photographers also used their documentation to political and social ends in that they argued for improved conditions in the hovels and ghettoes populated by these new immigrants, as well as in the industrial environments in which their bodies were to be engaged.

However, as I shall discuss in the chapter dedicated to Lewis and Hine, it must also be made clear and remembered that the immigrants photographed and catalogued by these two esteemed photographers were viewed and valued as little more than malleable material for the national machinery. Little attention was paid to their cultural and social origin outside of what negative influence it might import and, aside from their labor potential, their contribution was deemed to be rather minimal until many decades after their arrival.

## VON GLOEDEN'S INNOVATIVE LABOR PRACTICES

Perhaps unexpectedly, the Baron von Gloeden was among the first in photography to put into practice a series of innovative labor practices that protected his models and assistants beyond the remuneration they might receive at the time the photographs were taken. Von Gloeden's photographs were very popular with travelers and have maintained their popularity to this day among collectors. He printed and sold many copies of his photographs and the postcards that were made from them.

Known mostly for his classically stylized photographs of young, scantily clad Sicilian youths, von Gloeden used some of the same young men that were his models as laboratory and field assistants. While for his use of young boys in somewhat suggestive poses and contexts we might certainly view his photography as exploitative, his concern for them extended beyond his own needs and desires. We in fact know the names and biographies of many of his models, as well as what became of them within the life of the town of Taormina and beyond. And we also know that his concern for their well-being extended to setting up a system of remunerative royalties for his models.

Von Gloeden then appeared to understand modeling as a labor practice that needed to be recognized for its contribution to the production and eventual sale of images. The system he set up ensured his models and assistants also of future credit for the work produced, royalties on future sales and, in a certain manner, an historical presence in his archives and in the eventual history of photography and culture that would surround the baron's images.

## TINA MODDOTI, THE APPRENTICE'S ASSISTANT

A similar, though somewhat altered relationship between photographer and assistant is that of the activist, photographer, cultural laborer and model Tina Modotti. Her case is particularly interesting because she formed across social classes. Beginning as an immigrant who, among other things, worked in San Francisco's garment industry, Modotti made her way into the art world first by acting in small productions of the Italian American theatre, then as a collaborator/assistant to her husband Robò, and eventually as an assistant and model to the famed photographer Edward Weston.

While all these activities could be categorized as secondary in their social impact and activism, it is in Modotti's own work as a photographer, organizer, activist and writer that she manages to express her laboring body. Hers was always an applied labor that would be better described as apprenticeship, as an intentioned indenturement. The peasants Modotti photographs are not curiosities pictured in quaint landscapes for the enjoyment of those with *sophisticated* tastes. I believe that Modotti regards her subjects much as she thought of herself in the role of subject, in other words as an acquiescing individual lending his or her image in order to gather from its usage a greater insight into the function and use of images and those that they supposedly represented. This directly served her activism and revealed the mechanisms of male/female, dominant/subaltern, boss/worker, subject/object and other binary relationships that required dismantling.

It would seem, much by how the photographic process requires labor and the mode in which it engages laboring bodies that, from the moment man and technology meet, through to the eventual viewing of a photograph, photography could be considered a bodily or physiological act. As we shall see later, writers such as Italo Calvino in his short story "A Photographer's Adventure" (1993) have taken on the issue of photography as a physiological stimulus or response and have addressed its circumstances, ambiguities and problematics through that lens.

Yet, even as the workers behind the camera, in front of the lens, and in the labs of the industry participate in an apparently direct manner in the production of images they, just as industrial workers in other fields, suffer the distance of physiological, psychological, and existential alienation in their production of someone else's vision.

It could be said that the photographic process of labor is blinding in its assumptions regarding the value of certain images over others. This relationship that arises out of the considerations of the photographers cited with their sources has clear physiological and socio-economic effects that suggest even a stronger sense of isolation. This practice of photography, one that enables another's vision, is a process that instills blindness rather than providing enlightening images.

The chapters that follow will then expand on some of the issues and reflections included in this first chapter. I have wanted to present a few thoughts on bodies as a way of entering into the discourse on photographic images and a selected variation on them as a way to begin to approach how meaning is made around bodies. It is always fascinating to me how something that defines our every relationship with the world and around which our egos are so tightly wrapped can only be defined in terms of what lies outside of it. Even more fascinating is the fact that the observations we make are through an organ set into a part of the body neither of which can truly be seen directly. We are held to stake all of our definitions regarding our appearance on *believable fictions* constructed at all levels of society. Some images are produced in the attempt to present and support a national image of sorts, while others are used as a tool toward redefining certain customs and attitudes and propose yet other images, such as self-portraits that represent attempts at defining one's self in terms of received images or more attractive appearances.

As a process that imbues bodies with information, as a technological mode of information by which photographed bodies are inscribed within a particular set of beliefs, an ideology or other such normative aspirations, photography is, as I have described the *informing* process above, an active technology. And yet, information or inscription, or the mode of inscription is what is at stake in this study and as the literary aspect that I think is highly active within photographic images. Even as one of the processing steps in photographic printing is referred to as "fixing" (of the chemical reaction on paper), inscription is not a steadfast "fixing" of the correlation image/subject but refers, rather, to something similar in sense to what Walter Benjamin observed of Chinese painting: "nothing is more fleeting than the appearance of a resemblance, . . . that which [the paintings fix is] never has more that the fixity of clouds."[21]

The emphasis I have brought to my readings of images is not far from Benjamin's own view of the impermanence of the fixity of images and his understanding of inscription in photography as the place where "photography intervenes as the literarization of all the conditions of life, and without which all photographic construction must remain arrested in the approximate."[22]

As such, the ability to read photographs, not only for what they show on the surface but as literary expressions, open to a variety of expansive uses, requires a new literacy that is not tethered to any one particular set of referents but retains "the fixity of clouds." Citing the photographer Mohogol Nagy, Benjamin suggests that "it is not the person ignorant of writing but the one ignorant of photography who will be the illiterate in the future."[23] We have seen over the decades how visual illiteracy and the assumed literalness, rather than literariness, of photography has been manipulated to sway public opinion in many different contexts, cultures and national situation. Today, our presumed sophistication and media-savvy in challenged through the use of simple images and no supporting evidence outside of the say-so of "authorities" through advertising in swaying our consumption choices and the use of visual aids to instigate fear and lead us into conflict.

## NOTES

1. Unless otherwise noted, all translations from the Italian are mine.

> A un cuarp
> I ris umans; li sejs qe n'anima,
> drenti, a platin viva; la piel tinara;
> e li plejs da l'abit tal grin,
> duties robis q'i jodevi di frut.

2. Friulano had been a spoken tongue up to that point. Pasolini's dedication to the language of his mother's region was closely tied to his activism in highlighting the cultural diversity and marginality of regions such as the Friuli. It was this

same attitude that tied him to the populations of the "borgate" of Rome depicted in novels such as *Ragazzi di vita*; to Naples and its culture, recounted in essays such as "Gennariello"; to the post-colonial and emerging "Third" world depicted in films such as *Appunti per un Orestiade Africana* and books such as *Il padre selvaggio*.

3. My use of the verb *to inform* throughout the body of this book should be understood in all its possible meaning variations. It is important to consider its use not only vis-à-vis the notion of carrying "information" from one place to another, the transfer of knowledge, but also, and most importantly in this case, as the representation and manifestation of the essential characteristics of something, of those traits that allow one to become familiar with a subject and, in an active sense, as those elements that give structure and form to something.

4. Vilém Flusser, *Toward a Philosophy of Photography* (Göttingen: European Photography, 1983), 15.

5. Vilém Flusser's small but expansive *Toward a Philosophy of Photography* is among a very small number of works on the medium that begins to shed some light on this, even if in a direction that might be tangential to mine.

The Latinate term "apparatus" stems from the verb "apparare," which is "to prepare." Latin also contains the verb "praeparare," however; the difference is one of prefixes: "ad" and "prae." The most available translation for "apparare" in English would be "to make ready." In this sense, an apparatus would be an object which makes itself ready for something, while a "preparation" would be an object which patiently waits for something. The camera makes itself ready to take pictures, tries to ambush them, is on the lurk for them. This lying in wait for something, this predatory character of the apparatus, must be understood in our attempt to define "apparatus" etymologically. (15)

6. Ibid., 16.

7. Ibid., 17.

8. Ibid.

9. Ibid.

10. Ibid., 18.

11. Claude Lévi-Strauss, *The Raw and the Cooked* (New York: Harper & Row, 1969).

12. Prince Raimondo de Sangro di Sansevero's private chapel has long been a favorite attraction for visitors to the city of Naples. The small chapel includes some very fine examples of Sansevero's alchemy, two bodies illustrating the human nervous system and the circulatory system, a famous marble sculpture of the "Veiled Christ" and other wonders.

13. Ludmilla Jordanova, *Sexual Visions: Images of Gender in Science and Medicine Between the Eighteenth and Twentieth Centuries* (New York: Harvester Wheatsheaf, 1989), 59.

14. Annette Burfoot, "Surprising Origins: Florentine Eighteenth-Century Wax Anatomical Models as Inspiration for Italian Horror," *Kinoeye*, no. 9 (2002): 3.

15. The Italian director Dario Argento began his career as a journalist and screenwriter. Among his most famous collaborations in writing is with Sergio Leone for the film *Once Upon a Time in the West*. He is internationally recognized as a master of the horror/thriller film genre. One of his best-known films is *Suspiria*

(1977). Argento continues to write, produce and direct films in the genre and is widely recognized as a master with a worldwide cult following.

16. See note 2, chapter 3.

17. Goffredo Fofi, "Introduction," *Humana: La presenza dell'uomo in fotografie,* edited by Moreno Gentili (Udine: Art& - Parole e figure, 1996), 23.

18. Jean-François Chevrier, "The Image of the Other," in *Staging the self: Self-portrait Photography 1840s–1980s,* edited by James Lingwood (Plymouth: Plymouth Arts Centre, 1986), 10.

19. The designation of "public" intellectual could be taken to be an extension of Antonio Gramsci's category of organic intellectual. Differently from an organic intellectual, who acts out of and on behalf of a particular constituency, retaining some formal ties with that constituency, the public intellectual tends to be an outsider to all constituencies while challenging all power structures. An exemplary public intellectual would be Pier Paolo Pasolini in the Italian context. The scholar Edward Said, who wrote extensively on the subject (*Representations of the Intellectual: The 1993 Reith Lectures*), is himself considered to have been a public intellectual.

20. The term *believable fictions* is borrowed from Gianni Celati as a way of defining fictions that appear to be wholly familiar to us and that seem to communicate a knowledge already inherently carried. Later in this study *believable fictions* will be reintegrated into a context more properly related to Gianni Celati's fiction. See Celati, in Sironi, 178.

21. Walter Benjamin, "Painting and Graphics," in *The Work of Art in the Age of its Technological Reproducibility and Other Writing on Media,* edited by Michael W. Jennings, Brigid Doherty, and Thomas Y. Levin (Cambridge: Belknap Press, 2008), 214–15. An invaluable collection of Benjamin's writings on media, this book serves to amplify many of the topics and issues addressed in the philosopher's best known essay on the topic, "The Work of Art in the Age of Mechanical Reproduction."

22. Ibid., 294.

23. Ibid.

# 2

# Photography as Literary Art

The art in photography is literary art before it is anything else:
its triumphs and monuments are historical, anecdotal, reportorial,
observational before they are purely pictorial . . .
The photograph has to tell a story if it is to work as art.

—Clement Greenberg[1]

## TOMMASO CAMPANELLA' *CITY OF THE SUN*

I walk around Naples, the place of my birth and developmental years, the city that has fixed a particular cultural image within my imaginary. As I saunter, every aspect and detail of the city and its streets speaks to me. The statue of the Nile and its tributaries in the small piazza known as *'o cuorp' 'e Napule* (the body of Naples);[2] the small shrine to Diego Maradona, who led the Naples soccer team to national titles in the 1980s; the smells of cooking that wind their way along the narrow streets and alleys at certain times of the day; and the juxtaposition of old and new, ancient and contemporary that continually emerges within this urban space. The walls manifest a running commentary on the social and political situation of the city. The walls are part of this population's expressive culture. The graffiti is layered and never ending. An old favorite of mine: BERLUSCA E' LA MUCCA PAZZA! (Berlusconi is the mad cow); declarations of love: LAURA, TI AMO! (Laura, I love you); public notices: IL GOVERNO E' FALLITO! (The government has gone out of business!) (Figure 2.1).

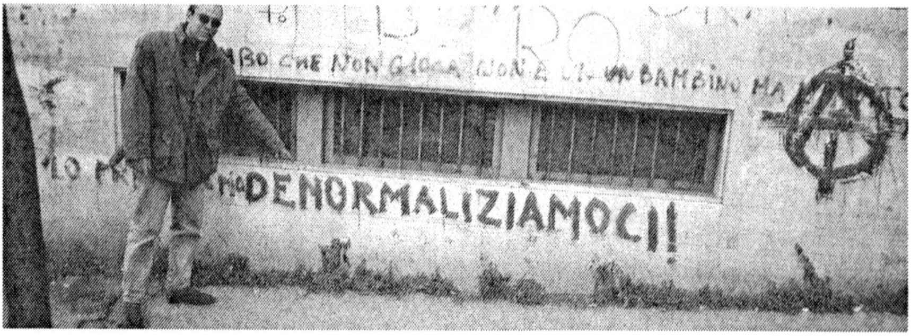


**Figure. 2.1.** ***Denormaliziamoci!*** **Credit: P. Verdicchio.**

Much of what I learned about reading the world, and much of what I take with me as a guidebook, came from the streets of Naples in an educational process that still continues. *Chist'e' 'o paese d'o sole, chist'e' 'o paese d'o mare* (This is the city of sun, this is the city of the sea) as the Neapolitan song goes, and this city of sun continues to educate its population through itself, its streets and walls and sidewalks and churches, and the ever-growing array of images and their combinations. This is a street culture, a communal throbbing, a living and pulsating culture. Nothing is private, except what one carries within. All surfaces, attitudes and behaviors are constantly noticed, read and interpreted. All are absorbed into the expanding and fluid cultural mass. The medium is in fact the "mass(age)" and, as a medium might, the cultural massage channels communication and information through the mass of its constituents.

It is while contemplating the importance of images, appearances and dis-appearances, that I find myself thinking back to Lucy Lippard's quotation of Greenberg, the epigram that opens this chapter. As a declaration that is meant to undermine the status of photography as an art, it falls victim to itself since those are the very aspects that (for Lippard and me) give it value, namely its less than literal and more literary qualities.[3]

Greenberg's give and take attempt to knock photography down a couple of notches establishes it as a vehicle by which "history, anecdote, report, and observation" are an indication of its literariness and, by what he seems to say, what mark its weakness. That "the photograph has to tell a story if it is to work as art" is a roundabout way of declaring that it falls short of being art. But, this is part and parcel of an age-old dispute surrounding photography since its inception. The questions as to whether photography is art, or whether it represents reality, have been debated extensively and answered in the negative and affirmative in an infinite range of modes and discourses. Since I do not intend to take either side of the debate as my point of departure, but rather deal with various aspects of photography that may in fact crisscross disparate fields of interest, I will not engage those same questions here. Photography is not an either or proposition; it is both literary and pictorial, and not one before the other but both simultaneously. The cultural value of images depends on both sides of the argument being available and operable at the same time. Whether as advertising or journalism, as documentation or illustration, a cave painting or the latest in digital technology, images will always project on our psyches evidence of presence and correspondence to a material world of perception. Naples is the city I picture when I think about the function and the power of images. When I think of Naples, its culture and social structure, its pedagogical role in the life of those who inhabit it as a literary visual environment, I do so in learned images of cultural conditioning and value that remind me of Tommaso Campanella's *La città del sole* (*The City of the Sun*).[4]

## SHINING IMAGES FROM THE *CITY OF THE SUN*

A major force in Southern Italian popular resistance, the Dominican monk Tommaso Campanella's self-appointed task was to rid the world of "three evils: tyranny, sophisms, and hypocrisy." His struggle to rid Calabria and the South of foreign domination led to his participation in the anti-Spanish insurgence of 1599, as a result of which he was imprisoned. The Spaniards in the city of Naples extorted a confession from him through continuous torture. Although he was sentenced to death, it was commuted to perpetual imprisonment as a result of the monk's feigned insanity. During his years in prison, until his release in 1629, Campanella penned a number of works, among them *The City of the Sun* (1602). While many utopian works were written during that historical period, *The City* goes further in its proposal of a program of cultural pedagogy clearly aligned with the visual and architectural as apparati of cultural encoding, learning and knowledge.

*The City*'s enveloping layers of seven spiraling walls wrap and wind around its central architecture as they constitute the city's link to the universe, stars and natural world:

> On the interior wall of the first circuit all the mathematical figures are conspicuously painted—figures more in number than Archimedes or Euclid discovered, marked symmetrically, and with the explanation of them neatly written and contained each in a little verse. There are definitions and propositions, etc. On the exterior convex wall is first an immense drawing of the whole earth, given at one view. Following upon this, there are tablets setting forth for every separate country the customs both public and private, the laws, the origins and the power of the inhabitants; and the alphabets the different people use can be seen above that of the City of the Sun.

On the inside of the second circuit, that is to say of the second ring of buildings, paintings of all kinds of precious and common stones, of minerals and metals, are seen; and a little piece of the metal itself is also there with an apposite explanation in two small verses for each metal or stone. On the outside are marked all the seas, rivers, lakes, and streams which are on the face of the earth; as are also the wines and the oils and the different liquids, with the sources from which the last are extracted, their qualities and strength. There are also vessels built into the wall above the arches, and these are full of liquids from one to three hundred years old, which cure all diseases. Hail and snow, storms and thunder, and whatever else takes place in the air, are represented with suitable figures and little verses. The inhabitants even have the art of representing in stone all the phenomena of the air, such as the wind, rain, thunder, the rainbow, etc.

On the interior of the third circuit all the different families of trees and herbs are depicted, and there is a live specimen of each plant in earthenware vessels placed upon the outer partition of the arches. With the specimens there are explanations as to where they were first found, what are their powers and natures, and resemblances to celestial things and to metals, to parts of the human body and to things in the sea, and also as to their uses in medicine, etc. On the exterior wall are all the races of fish found in rivers, lakes, and seas, and their habits and values, and ways of breeding, training, and living, the purposes for which they exist in the world, and their uses to man. Further, their resemblances to celestial and terrestrial things, produced both by nature and art, are so given that I was astonished when I saw a fish which was like a bishop, one like a chain, another like a garment, a fourth like a nail, a fifth like a star, and others like images of those things existing among us, the relation in each case being completely manifest. There are sea-urchins to be seen, and the purple shell-fish and mussels; and whatever the watery world possesses worthy of being known is there fully shown in marvelous characters of painting and drawing.

On the fourth interior wall all the different kinds of birds are painted, with their natures, sizes, customs, colors, manner of living, etc.; and the inhabitants of this city possess the only real phoenix. On the exterior are shown all the races of creeping animals, serpents, dragons, and worms; the insects, the flies, gnats, beetles, etc., in their different states, strength, venoms, and uses, and a great deal more than you or I can think of.

On the fifth interior they have all the larger animals of the earth, as many in number as would astonish you. We indeed know not the thousandth part of them, for on the exterior wall also a great many of immense size are also portrayed. To be sure, of horses alone, how great a number of breeds there is and how beautiful are the forms there cleverly displayed!

On the sixth interior are painted all the mechanical arts, with the several instruments for each and their manner of use among different nations. Along-

> side, the dignity of such is placed, and their several inventors are named. But on the exterior all the inventors in science, in warfare, and in law are represented. There I saw Moses, Osiris, Jupiter, Mercury, Lycurgus, Pompilius, Pythagoras, Zamolxis, Solon, Charondas, Phoroneus, with very many others. They even have Mahomet, whom nevertheless they hate as a false and sordid legislator. In the most dignified position I saw a representation of Jesus Christ and of the twelve Apostles, whom they consider very worthy and hold to be great. Of the representations of men, I perceived Caesar, Alexander, Pyrrhus, and Hannibal in the highest place; and other very renowned heroes in peace and war, especially Roman heroes, were painted in lower positions, under the galleries. And when I asked with astonishment whence they had obtained our history, they told me that among them there was a knowledge of all languages, and that by perseverance they continually send explorers and ambassadors over the whole earth, who learn thoroughly the customs, forces, rule and histories of the nations, bad and good alike. These they apply all to their own republic, and with this they are well pleased.[5]

The function of the walls is declaredly pedagogical. Education begins at the age of three and continues for the rest of one's life. The city is itself a repository and an instrument of knowledge. Living in the City of the Sun means being exposed to all of nature's bounty incessantly and thereby gaining the knowledge necessary for a holistic existence. Man is thusly defined to be an integral component of the earth and the universe. The interesting aspect of this type of educational model is that it is highly dependent on the visual as a first mode of acquisition and interpretation. The inventory of plants, animals, rivers, oceans and every other natural object is integrated into knowledge first through its representation, and then its practical role or use is eventually defined in a way that can be said to represent its niche.

Campanella's inventory distinguishes itself from other specialized and interested inventories, such as those that emerged with imperial or colonial enterprises, by not being designed to construct a hierarchy of value and exchange. The walls of the City of the Sun compose a dialogue that functions to inform and conform human discourse within a meta-historical discourse. Through that humanness it is integrated into the natural world as just one more interactive component that is the precursor of some contemporary redefinitions of the terms of "humanism." Campanella thus proposes and engages images within an insurrectional and revolutionary pedagogy. *The City*'s design, rather than delineate power relations, becomes an instructive model of cultural literacy for its populace.

The images of *The City* are quite literal, tautological for the way in which some are arranged side-by-side with the objects they represent, such as an actual container of olive oil being displayed beside an image of olives. This sort of democratized accessibility and the significatory universe it devises does however bring up questions regarding the role of history. Campanella's revolutionary concept would appear to rest in a notion of history in which the images of/in the city, in their complex, establish a system of continuous interdependence among all things; something that in turn defies hierarchy and reduces the terms by which relationships might be interpreted and integrated. If Campanella's images are tautological in how they encourage identification, they are so in a way that photographs cannot be by their lack of presence in time and space. Therefore, while the images of *The City* may be literal, those represented in photography are literary, including any poetic implications that the term might suggest.

## ITALO CALVINO AND THE SELF-CONSCIOUSNESS OF THE IMAGE MAKER

My choice to begin with Campanella as a way to consider the import of imagery is not due to a consideration of chronological primacy. Italian musings on the world referred as images date well before Campanella's construction of a visual/visionary city. It is in *The City* however that we first find a sense of pictorial pedagogy that does not emphasize objects or their representations as carriers of simulacral meaning but, rather, sees in them the interlacing layers of their existence. It is most evident that Italian contemporary culture and society has been shaped by a visual proclivity that today is known as "Italian style." Verismo and Neorealism, Renaissance and Baroque, contemporary fashion and classical design, all seem to emerge out of a socio-politically conscious desire to state and restate a position or an event visually as a way to ensure its survival through an acknowledgement of a socially and culturally relevant network of meanings. While the rhetoric of both post-World War II Neorealism and Giovanni Verga's Verismo of the late 1800s emphasize an objective reporting of reality, as if there were no difference between the events and their being recounted, it is quite obvious that any telling of events always participates in a restatement and elaboration of them.

Giovanni Verga's self-stated exercise of merely repeating what he claims to have heard from the mouths of everyday people, while bordering on dispassionate reporting, re-states the lives of Sicilian peasants within a language and form of expression that is alien to them. In addition, Verga's stories could be determined to be elaborations of the facts of the lives of those he represents by an external observer who never appears to be socially related to the characters he or she narrates. However, the act of observation and narration undeniably unveil the threads of interconnectedness.

Italo Calvino's tales of the World War II period establish a relationship to the concept of reality, and the effectiveness and inadequacies of language in relation to our feeble attempts at fixing meaning in the world, that is decidedly ambiguous from the start. The identification and function of a visual component in writing is explicitly addressed by Calvino in the essay "Visibilità" (Visibility), from the *Lezioni Americane: Sei proposte per il prossimo millennio* (*Six Memos for the Next Millennium*), (2003).[6] Still in preparation at the time of his death, the lectures were to have been delivered during the 1985–1986 Harvard academic year as the Charles Eliot Nelson Lectures in Poetry, and are representative of "six values, qualities or specificities of literature that are particularly dear to me, and which I will try to situate within the perspective of the new millennium."[7]

Calvino's thoughts on the origins, workings and effects of images begins with a consideration of none other than Dante, who attempts a definition of "imagination" in six verses of "Purgatory XVII" (13–18):

> O imagination, you that distract us
> at times from outward things unknowing
> while a thousand horns sound around us-
>
> Who moves you if it not the senses to do so?
> A light formed in Heaven
> on its own, or projected down by will.[8]

It is at that point in his travels that Dante's pilgrim begins to experience a differentiation in the images he sees: some he sees with his eyes, others he experiences directly as mental images. We are to understand the former as supposedly objective images of reality that one registers in viewing the world, and the second as ones projected or received directly onto/by one's mind, without any external referent. Calvino points out that, for Dante the writer, Dante the pilgrim experiences everything in the latter form, which would seem to imply not only the lack of any dependable objective reality, but also that the visual part of the imagination is either "precedes or accompanies verbal imagination."[9]

The primacy that Calvino (and literary history beginning with Dante and moving through to contemporary writers like Gianni Celati, and possibly to Italian culture in general) claims for visuality or visibility is apparent in all of his works beginning with *The Path to the Nest of Spiders* (1946) and its future preface at the hands of the author. The following passage from "Visibilità" sheds some light on Calvino's extended relationship with the visual, and the function he assigns to it as an innovative cultural element:

> Returning to the literary problem, let's ask ourselves how the imaginary of an era is formed in which literature does no longer look to an authority or a

> tradition as its origin or end, but stakes everything on novelty, originality, and invention. I think that in such a situation the problem of the primacy of the visual image or verbal expression (which is after all a little like the question of the chicken or the egg) leans most likely toward the visual image.[10]

The revelatory discovery of the visual image as the primary mover in the generation of words is that the function of the image is brilliantly and inexorably literary. The only limitation to the process of literary composition possible through images is what we place upon in by our desire to know all of their potential associations. Calvino's meditation on the function of the image in his writing recognizes that when an "image has become abundantly clear in my mind, I begin to develop it into a story, or rather, the images themselves begin to develop their own implicit potential, the stories they carry within themselves."[11]

This method that Calvino describes at the end of his life as fundamental to his writing is similar to the one he suggests at the beginning of his career. Not much seems to have changed in the author's reliance on the world not for the confirmation of some objective reality but for the enhancement of a subjective relationship through which to extend an embrace to a collective and interdependent universe. The *Memo* on "Visibilità" recalls Calvino's preface to *The Path to the Nest of Spiders*: "I set out from that urchin character, from an element of direct observation of reality."[12]

Hailed as the first "neorealist" novel, Calvino's *The Path of the Nest of Spiders* is a fantasy-laden reminiscence of the days of partisan warfare, seen through the eyes of an imaginative nine-year-old boy. The result is far from the nitty-gritty realism we might imagine of such subject matter, especially when qualified by the term "neorealist." However, and especially because it carries the "neorealist" label, Calvino thought it important to return to it in successive editions with an explicative introduction.

The first edition of *The Path* is dated 1947, while the preface, which is additionally interesting for the light it sheds on Calvino's writing style, makes its first appearance in the 1963 edition. The writer takes great pains to outline the historical moment that the country traversed during those years and the opportunities that were revealed with the end of the Fascist era. Cesare Pavese, Elio Vittorini, and Ignazio Silone are among those he mentions as writers who participated in recasting a new culture. All of them were directly involved in championing what can only be called a renaissance of Italian culture that included all forms of art and culture in the years that followed World War II.

The identifying characteristic of the new culture, and the apparent aim of Calvino's first novel, was to construct a collective response to history past and propose directions for an historical future. To this end, Calvino stresses throughout the preface that he was not after something that expressed "his" point of view but a more general vision representative of all who had gone through the experience of Fascism, the war, the resistance and the eventual "liberation." He therefore declares *The Path* to be a book that was "born anonymously," an aspect of the novel that the writer seems to consider its most valuable and lasting by stating that "this is what especially touches us today; the anonymous voice of that time, stronger than our still-uncertain individual reflections."[13]

The collectivity idealized by Calvino and others during that period does however create a contrast with the very form of the work and preface. During the course of the preface, Calvino uses a technique that will recur in his other works: reiteration and starting over. The preface shows what appear to be at least six new or false starts which rhetorically support the attempt "to get it right," and a practical illustration of the historical moment and cultural activity of his generation. While stressing that "*neorealism* was not a school," Calvino continues to stress the collective aspect of his exercise.[14] He proposes that the dominant trait of neorealism might be "a contamination or constraint suffered by literature for extra-literary reasons, . . . a collection of voices, largely marginal, a multiple discovery of the various Italies, even—or particularly—the Italies previously unknown to literature."[15] We know as fact that the "collective voice" of the Resistance was indeed multi-faceted in its regional origins and political affiliations. We have testimony of this in many works, fictional and not, dealing with that period. Among the best known of them is Roberto Rossellini's film, *Rome, Open City* (1946), in which the Nazi commander Bergman unsuccessfully tries to use the Resistance's internal differences to generate division among the ranks.[16]

The Italies to which Calvino refers are those that were part of a national imaginary that had a rather restricted notion of itself, mostly fed by the speculative information of photographic representations such as those of the Florentine Alinari brothers and an idealized national literature represented by Dante Alighieri. Yet, Calvino also differentiates between the "realism" of his national project of the post-World War II period and that of Giovanni Verga, whose Verismo works concentrated on the Sicilian peasantry. By making this distinction, Calvino seems to propose a difference between regional realism and national realism that shifts from verist detail to imaginative anonymity. This should not be read as an attempt to diminish Verga's contribution to the approach of some of the so-called "neorealist" filmmakers. As Calvino's contemporaries, the *Neorealists* found in the Sicilian author's approach a potentially fruitful sense of what might serve as the initial elements through which to define national character: its diversity and apparent decentralized sense of itself.

While on the surface Calvino appears to put some distance between himself and Verga, his technique finds correspondence in Verga's own adoption of the "bozzetto" (literary snapshot) approach. The episodic terms of Calvino's style are snapshot iterations of particular situations or actions that link him to Giovanni Verga. Calvino's innovative addition to the "bozzetto" is that he adds a photographic or cinematographic dimension to it by revisiting and re-viewing the narration and its writing almost obsessively over and over again, almost as if he were shooting the same scene from different angles. Both depend on or hint at the function of an oral tradition as the basis of their work. Verga reports that which he hears "along the paths and byways of the countryside," while Calvino recounts the stories spoken in and around the partisan camps, around the campfires (Verga's *focolare* or hearth).[17] Calvino recalls that "anyone who started writing, then found himself handling the same material as the nameless oral narrator. . . . Some of the pages of this novel originated in that new-born oral tradition, in those events in that language."[18] This repetitive technique hints at how stories might change when told again and again, as they are passed on from person to person. This undermines the notion of "getting it right" and further accentuates a collective participation in the telling of history.

The correspondence between Calvino and Verga, separated by a little less than one hundred years, is more than coincidence and influence. It is the result of a socio-cultural and linguistic history, which determines certain lines of approach that cannot be discounted or overlooked. Even though it is aimed at a more national agenda and is conditioned by twenty years of Fascism and a sense of urgency in renewing a culture, Calvino's writing retraces some of the paths that Verga himself had stumbled upon. It is the almost impossible task of finding a collective voice of expression, of the tentativeness of taking on the task of speaking for those who cannot or will not speak, of seeing one's self as the product of a collective culture, that cannot be rooted in any singular sense of identity, collective or otherwise.

The snapshot of such an identity can only be the blurred image of a story in constant flux. Calvino writes about the sense of "remorse" that he feels toward reality, resulting from his description and distortion of it in an attempt to make it more immediate and dilute any sense of ideological partisanship that it might express. Even as his desire was to write a book situated within what could be termed a literature of the Resistance, this necessitated a rebellion against the conformism of Fascism and the residues of "right-minded respectability."[19] Calvino's attempt was to reduce the obviousness of an ideological point of view. His was an attempt to write through an anonymous persona that was above all a reflection of a collective identity. As he describes it in his preface, Calvino's approach was to issue forth from a snapshot the interpretation of a potentially expansive sense of identity:

> I will have to start this preface once more, from the beginning. I have not yet got it right. From what I have said, it would seem that, writing this book, I had the whole thing quite clear in my mind: the reasons, arguments, the adversaries to combat, the poetic to sustain. . . . Instead, if all this was there, it was still in a confused, shapeless stage. Actually the book came forth as if by chance; I started writing without a precise plot in mind. I set out from that urchin character, from an element of direct observation of reality, a way of moving, of speaking, of establishing a rapport with grownups.[20]

While he was rather successful in his approach, the process was also a discovery of the impossibility of the task at hand. His "remorse" vis-à-vis reality could possibly stem from this experience, which could almost be interpreted as a betrayal of his basic initial task. Yet, these we must take not as the failings of a writer, but rather as the failings of representation.

I have chosen to comment upon Calvino's writings because he is a writer who unmistakably links the visual to the written. He identifies images and their repetition or progression as the basis of the written word like few others have. The fact that Calvino applies the same sense of decipherability and interpretation to reality and its written narrative that he does to photography is a demonstration of the latter's terms of physiological function. Memory, or the stimulus that we call memory, is where the blurred images of experience reside. Since we depend on memory for our recollection of events and images, we are doomed to reconstruct falsely even as we place all our faith in the dependability of language and images:

> Memory—or rather experience, which is memory plus the wound it has left in you, plus the change it has worked in you that has made you different—experience, first nourishment also of literary work (but not only of that), true wealth for the writer (but not only for him), now, as soon as it has given shape to a literary work, declines, is destroyed. The writer finds himself once again the poorest of men.[21]

Such a sense of memory leads Calvino to the notion that what is represented is partially destroyed through its expression. A contemporary expression of this in photography is to be found in one of the digital formats in which images are saved, the *jpeg*. As one of the most commonly used formats in which photos are stored, viewed and reviewed, the *jpeg* is resampled every time it is accessed. The process of resampling and reorganization of the pixels into a discernible image results in a degradation of the file data so that what is represented is partially destroyed through its expression a little more each time.[22] As the preface to *The Path to the Nest of Spiders* illustrates, Calvino's interests lay not in a detailed realistic accounting of the world but, rather, in a more subjective representation of people, events and perceptions, all of which add up to structure our own individual sense of reality. The terms of this type of realism are quite incisive and revelatory in their application; they constitute a sort of theory of relativity of literature and culture that has influenced much of Italian society since the immediate post-World War II period.

"L'avventura di un fotografo" (A Photographer's Adventure), from the collection *Gli amori difficili* (Difficult Loves) (Einaudi, 1970), is the story of Antonino Paraggi, employee in a small firm, unmarried, decidedly not a photographer, and a careful observer of life's trials and tribulations. He is, for all intents and purposes, and "by intellectual proclivity, a philosopher."[23] Seeing as everyone around him appears to live only to view the photographs they have taken during their weekends, the images that will give them "tangible possession of their days," Antonino begins to feel a growing sense of isolation.[24] So as to understand both his isolation and the drive that leads his friends to document their lives, Antonino undertakes the task of analyzing the situation. He comes to the conclusion that the "secret" of everyone's fascination with photography must lay somewhere beyond their mere personal ability or the technical advancements that yield increasingly better results.[25]

As time goes by, Antonino comes to notice that as his friends marry and start families, so their interest in photography grows. The connection between the two is undeniable for Antonino, who, by linking photography and paternity, also identifies in the medium the only means by which life's changes might be documented and preserved. By drawing a line between photography and paternity, Calvino intimates that the desire to photograph is an almost physiological response ("the passion for the lens is born naturally and almost physiologically, as a secondary effect of fatherhood").[26] This brings about an interesting relationship by which the declaration and signification of fatherhood is also a manner by which photography declares authenticity. Paternity and photography are both modes of reproduction that must in some way be controlled in order to fix them within our traditional social spheres. The restricted manufacture of images, ensuring that the father and photographer are identifiable, is a way to counter a potentially uncontrolled and uncontrollable relationship.

Photography = creation; Antonino's rejection of photography works as a distraction from the fact that he is not married and not involved in the creation of a family. It is a way to veil the tact that Antonino lacks not only the photographs that document the stages of his life, but also the very subject matter by which the stages are marked by his friends: a conventional life. While Antonino despises what he considers to be vain attempts at self-preservation, he appears to be frustrated by the underlying fact that without procreation he is headed for extinction.

As the only bachelor in his circle of acquaintances he is often asked to shoot a photograph of his friends' family groups. His subconscious resentment, toward what he sees as foolish attempts at halting reality, emerges as an act of sabotage in which his photographs cut off the heads of his subjects. Antonino also takes it upon himself to warn his friends that their attitude can only lead to the insane notion that "all that is not photographed is lost, as if it had never existed."[27] Calvino's equation of photography with a physiological function by which a means of mechanical reproduction parallels the natural one, determines Antonino's eventual failure and his friends' (ephemeral) victory.

## THE SHOWN AND THE SAID: LEONARDO SCIASCIA'S BLINDNESS

Calvino's guarded yet critical enthusiasm for photography is but one among many meditations by literary figures on the medium. And, while Calvino's own peculiarities and interests color his approach to photography and images in general, others are in turn influenced by their own proclivities as writers in their view of the uses of it. One such writer is Leonardo Sciascia, the Sicilian intellectual whose literary career has always been at the service of Italian and, more specifically, Sicilian society as a watcher and moral commentator. His themes range from emigration, to the workings of the Mafia, to analysis of the Italian political and judicial systems, to discourses upon popular and traditional cultures.

While agencies and organizations such as the Alinari brothers performed a national role in defining the newly emergent nation, the unstated dimension of their task included the unveiling of imagery that might be considered dissonant with the standards they otherwise set. In other words, while Florence, Tuscany and Renaissance culture were fixed as standards of Italian culture, their photographs of life in other regions, as well as Tuscan peasantry or popular culture, were meant to contrast the imaged community they were constructing.

In the essay "Verismo e fotografia" (Verismo and photography), collected in his *Le Opere 1971–1983* (Works 1971–1983), Leonardo Sciascia appraises the uses of photography and its validity as a tool or representation.[28] While recognizing the valuable contribution to the dialogue on photography by Valéry, Alberto Savinio, Roland Barthes and Henri Cartier-Bresson, Sciascia also states his doubts regarding it. So as to illuminate photography's inadequacy in representing the truth, or its tendency to distort it, Sciascia recalls a joke made by Nabokov regarding the use of photography on the part of "communists" as one of the means of airbrushing away the existence of those who had fallen out of favor with the regime.

One of the most famous such cases is from the 1920 Congress of the Communist International. A photograph which in its first version shows Lenin surrounded by a number of Internationalists, in subsequent versions makes clear the eventual progressive removal of individuals from the picture as they fell into disfavor.[29] Of course, this manipulation is not limited to "communists" and today we are well aware of such manipulations, the possibilities of which are made especially simple and effective by digital image manipulation programs such as Photoshop.

Though Sciascia does not summarily dismiss photography for how easily it might be manipulated, he does make his doubts clear. The photographic image can only render something for not more than a momentary truth, or "the truth of a moment that contradicts other truths of other moments."[30] Sciascia then turns to Valéry's stance on photography, stating that "the instant generates the form and the form generates the instant," as a way to support his own denial of photography's influence beyond what is recorded in and of the instant.[31] Unfortunately, even in this, and with the additional support of the example of manipulative chemistry, Sciascia inadvertently exculpates the use made of the medium toward the construction of systems of oppression and social determinism.

Sciascia's assessment of Luigi Capuana and Giovanni Verga's relationship to photography is disappointingly simplistic. He assumes that given the relative novelty of the photographic process at the time (the authors "are born during the same years as photography"), that it could be nothing more than a mere "diletto" or entertainment for the two writers.[32] Sciascia is of the belief that, if Capuana and Verga had chanced to assign to photography the objectivity and distance that they had sought in Verismo, it would not have supported their experiments. He in fact goes so far as to say that photography would have instead resulted in the authors' questioning of their own realist premises.

> But I don't think that they thought about it too much, taken as they were from the "fun" and "play." In fact, it is most likely that they considered it to be not "verist" enough, given the required pose, that hint of fiction that it suggests, and the lack of color.[33]

Sciascia's central critique revolves around the notion that, rather than document a subject, photography constitutes a moment of its crisis. Recalling Roland Barthes, Sciascia writes that photography "is the advent of myself as another: an astute disassociation of the conscience of identity."[34] This may well be true for Barthes and Sciascia, bourgeois intellectuals whose status allows them the privilege of considering these points and to manifest the desire to be something other than whom they might be. But did Verga's peasant subjects, or for that matter those in his own family who posed for the writer/photographer, conceive of the photographs as doubles of themselves?

Did they in fact sense the disassociation that Barthes describes? And, in the end, can these be considered negative manifestations of the effects of photography? It is not completely clear whether Barthes takes his stance in the negative. It seems to me that his use of images, his commentaries on *mythologies* and the publication of his own photographic memoir, *Roland Barthes by Roland Barthes* (1978), all play on the ambiguous and fluid nature of identity rather than decry the loss of a certainty. At the point of disjunction, where an individual is set against the image of himself and is brought to question the status of all that defines him, Barthes finds a fascinating point of departure for his work. He defines and emphasizes photography's literary limits and value, rather than its literalness, a contrast that I believe is further supported in his outline of the *punctum/fulcrum* distinction made in the essay *Camera lucida* (1981).[35]

As supportive of his objections, Sciascia further quotes Barthes' assertion that "a photographs is the meeting ground for four types of imaginary. It represents what one believes one's-self to be, what one would wish others to see, what the photographer sees, and the means by which the photographer is able to express his or her art."[36] None of this however makes clear what might be behind Sciascia's resistance to, and dismissal of, photography. I imagine that his must be a purely ideological necessity, framed as it is by the Nabokovian anecdote. Sciascia's literary, intellectual and social commentary aims, at least in his own telling, to demarcate the limits between good and evil, right and wrong, reality and illusion as dependable categories.

The binaries Sciascia champions would appear to be dictated by his ideological stance within the Italian context and, as a Sicilian, necessitated by a politics of location. This might be the place of disjunction for Sciascia himself, where the "crisis of the subject" could be situated as something that finds resonance in the work of the other Sicilian writers. I would suggest that regardless of class or social status, any human subject feels a sense of disorientation and disassociation when a camera points its lens at her. Further, I also believe that this disassociation or identification takes place when the photographer notices his subject becoming aware of being photographed. This is possibly the moment of crisis that Sciascia detects, something similar to what leads Verga and others to write as they do in the representation of moments of social self-consciousness.

Luigi Pirandello's groundbreaking work in the analysis of subject/object relationships, the ambiguity of the congruent spheres of reality and fiction, certainly addresses the question. In relation to such a moment he had much earlier described the strangeness that an actor feels before the camera, in the process of having to isolate instances of representation and make them the focus of recitation.[37] An actor energizes the isolation and extraction of a moment and not the documentation of a complete and whole truth, whatever that may be. Therefore, by contrast, the non-actor subject is more directly representative of a moment rather than its isolation and extraction. The photographer's task is, in such a case, to isolate moments or assume that all moments are of equal value in the historical continuum. Could we not accept that all moments are of equal value in remembrance of what Gramsci suggested as the answer to the question "what is man?":

> Knowledge is power, but the question is complicated by something else: namely that it is not enough to know a set of relations existing at a given moment as if they were a given system, one also needs to know then genetically—that's to say the story of their formation, because every individual is not only a synthesis of existing relations, but also the history of those relationships, which means the résumé of all the past.[38]

## LE DICERIE DELLE IMAGINI: GESUALDO BUFALINO

Any moment is an instance of historical import that, even in its isolation, has a relational connection to other moments. Gesualdo Bufalino, also a Sicilian writer, states as much in his book *Il tempo in posa* (2000). The volume is an expanded version of an essay that accompanied a set of photographs discovered by Bufalino and Gioacchino Iacono in the attic of Iacono's grandfather's abandoned country home.[39] The finding provided Bufalino with the energy to write a piece in which he considers the function of photography as a medium that constitutes a sort of "archeology of the modern."[40] The writer argues that, even with all its inherent inadequacies, photography nevertheless "possesses an unequalled dramatic value: the sentiment that the moment portrayed *has been*, and it was just *like* that, with a ray of sun on the hedge, that long beard, and that triangular shadow on the wall."[41] These moments Bufalino sees as the constraining action to the assumed primitive beliefs and customs associated with the Italian South; the superstitions by which images of particularly laden icons of an unchanging social order are turned upside down by the subject matter represented. Even while the social hierarchy and class distinctions are evident, Bufalino associates the photographic act and choice of subjects as a trait of modernity and, as such, a potentially progressive act: ". . . this attention to *lowly* subjects is after all an insight into obvious intellectual courage and a modernity of choices that are not at all amateurish."[42]

The figurative grammatical system constructed by these moments finds resonance also in the photography of the previously mentioned writers/photographers, Capuana and Verga. It is by accentuating the potential expression of those moments through a system of their own making, that photographers and subjects are cast out of the mere elegiac and "into history."[43]

The finding of Iacono's photographs led Bufalino to the work of other amateur photographers of the Comiso region. This occasioned the writing of other short pieces to comment upon their contribution that, in turn, led to the book. The photographs of Iacono, Francesco Meli Ciarcià, Carmelo Arezzo and Corrado Melfi become representative of the need to express a modality of life that projected existence externally, toward a community that at the time was more imagined that real. Paradoxically, it is with the passing of time that such a community has become more apparent as it has disappeared materially. Moreover, these photos are illustrative of the customs that the pre-Risorgimento Giacomo Leopardi had considered to be lacking or un-manifested at the national level in his *Discorso sopra lo stato presente dei costumi degl'italiani* (Treatise on the present state of the customs of Italians) (1824):

> More than customs, Italians have traditions and habits. Few of these could be said to be national, but these few, along with the more numerous one that might and should be said to be provincial and municipal . . . public spirit in Italy is such that, aside from what is prescribed by law and ordinances of principles, it leaves everyone almost completely free to behave for all the rest how they might please, without any interference. . . . Customs and traditions in Italy generally amount to this, that everyone follows their own customs and traditions whatever those might be.[44]

Given this, and it could be argued that the situation persists to this day, it is therefore not surprising that photography might come to be viewed and used as a repository of diversity. By documenting and museifying the diversely defined body of the nation it also defines in contrast a way to visualize an invisible and idealized national body; one that concentrates first and foremost on the ambient before focusing its lens on those who move within it.

It is of course possible to assert that costumes are in fact an invisible aspect of culture. How can one represent patriotism, generosity or their opposites through photography if not by depicting attitudes, actions and populations that we have already come to associate with such traits? Quite incisively, Leopardi states that "Italians lack society," which might be translated as meaning a lack of associative traits.[45] The aim of Leopardi's *Treatise* is to provide a snapshot of Italy that suggest a photographic literariness. Bollati has us note that in his *Zibaldone,* Leopardi's great book of thoughts and meditations, the poet of Recanati suggests that "the image always stimulates," leaving us to imagine a possible society beyond the one that is represented and literal.[46]

Leopardi leaves his readers to ponder a sense of national identity that he considers to be a fictional construct that finds little correspondence within Italian society. Though he is clearly not alone in his critique that precedes the events of nation building, Leopardi adds yet another layer to the question, making of the *Treatise* a document that is perhaps as important today as when it was first written. Leopardi's argument goes directly to the question of the fictional aspects of nationhood, to how its narrative is established, maintained, represented and remembered. Leopardi of course could not foresee the events of the Risorgimento and Unification, nevertheless he lived at a time when a certain national fervor was in the air. The *Treatise* is therefore not concerned only with unveiling the fictions of national character but mostly in elaborating the mechanism of fictional representation and the construction of the *believable fictions* of nationalism. The ideals of the Risorgimento were being elaborated during his lifetime. The writer's keen intellect, his powers of social observation and commentary made it possible for him to conceptualize what later came to be represented visually with the invention of photography. Leopardi suggests where one might finds examples of these fictions in a very "visual" letter from Rome:

> These immense factories, and as a result these infinite streets, are so many spaces thrown among men, instead of being spaces that contain men . . . men's sensitive faculties are limited in these places to the purely visual.[47]

Leopardi's suggestions toward how one might define a sense of the national take us directly toward an inevitable point of convergence to suggest that the visual might possibly be the singularly effective realm for the representation of a disparate national ground such as Italy. This is not to say that everyone might see, appreciate or interpret the landscape in the same manner, but it lends a starting point from which to propose at least a common visual referent. If, on the one hand, Leopardi sees a unifying factor through which to begin to describe Italian nationalism, on the other he is fully cognizant of the fact that the Italian character continues to carry with it those negative traits he previously described.

Leopardi's criticism is aimed at that social class, economically elevated class representative of a very strict minority, that defines the terms of "being Italian" and holds the power to express itself. It is in this class that the lack of "vision" is predominantly obvious, so much are they concerned only with their own point of view: "Every single Italian city and each single Italian makes its own thunder and blows its own horn."[48] The self-centered gaze undermines every possibility of expressing a collectivity and foregrounds a preoccupation with cutting a *bella figura*, a good appearance, that conditions and determines a mode of seeing that could be considered particularly Italian.

Leopardi's description of the visual as the only possible manner by which to relate a sense of Italian nationalism links directly to the effort of cataloguing "national treasures" that will be eventually undertaken by the Alinari Brothers in Florence. The narrative exposition of Italian nationalism is thus constructed through an accumulation of "things" (monuments, palazzi, works of art, archeological ruins, and so on) that find general approval exactly because of their *thingness*. In other words, they don't appear to be directly or specifically connected to any one cultural resource. The *believable fiction* of the Risorgimento rests solidly on other *believable fictions* such as the Renaissance, the Enlightenment and Roman antiquity.

This tendency toward the literary, the interpretative, the imaginative and innovative, rather than the literal, is most likely also the trait that has made Italian design, the "Made in Italy" iconographic reference to an imagined identity, such a widely traveled, accepted and successful export. Giannino Malossi refers to this phenomenon in his anthology on the place of "the icon of Italy in global pop culture":

> What is it that makes today's Italy so different, so appealing? While the overall popularity of Italian style is certainly generated by Italian fashion, which involves references to specific cultural features, the content of the Italian spectacle is written on the surface of objects, as it were.[49]

Malossi goes further in identifying within these objects or things an inherent sense of openness of meaning and reproducibility that is globally available:

> there exists a cultural specificity of that which is—or which is depicted as—Italian that extends well beyond the place of industrial manufacture ("Made in Italy"): Italian products are successful because they incorporate the depiction of the icon of Italy, that is, they contain an emotional quality, they are signs of a desire produced by the image of Italy.[50]

All well and good, this stretch of a claim of a globally valent emotional link with Italian products. However, since Malossi does not actually identify any specific element as representative of the "image of Italy," it would appear that we are yet again in the grip of another *believable fiction* that we are asked to accept without question. Most certainly, while the "Made in Italy" pedigree finds a connection to the expressed desire for national identity and unity of the Risorgimento and the eventual Unification of Italy, it is presented as a continuation of the earlier Renaissance. Not surprisingly then, the desire for nationhood, found its direct referents in the figuration of the Italian landscape and its peoples within the signifying field provided by images produced through the Florentine lens of the Alinari.

## NARRARE NARRANDO

Arguably, the most visually interested and active contemporary writer in Italy today is Gianni Celati. Celati's publishing career begins in the 1970s, thereby placing him in what might be considered an older generation, yet even among the multi-layered, multi-medial and omnivorous "cannibali" generation of writers or their younger manifestations, it is hard to find anyone who actually engages visuality so thoroughly. The "cannibali" and others who might reflect the contemporary strategies of dubbing, quoting and collage, and whose hip-hop tinged world includes tagging and graffiti as well as an expansion into the realms of trance, house and dance, are not so much visually aware as visually intoxicated.[51]

Although Celati would probably be the first to deny a long-term attachment to any one place, his geographical relationship is to the central region of Italy that is Emilia-Romagna, and the cities of Bologna and Reggio-Emilia. The former as a result of his association with the University of Bologna, and the latter through his friendship with the photographer Luigi Ghirri. Nevertheless, even while his writings, projects of all kinds, including filmic collaborations (the latest in Senegal), displace him all over Europe, England, the US and Africa, he has had a long and close working relationship with the geographic area traced by the River Po.

His writing career began in the context of the exciting cultural period that marks the 1960s. That post-Fascist, post-war, post-neorealist period that is traversed by Italy's "economic boom," heavy internal migrations, and the profound cumulative effect of these phenomena, provided the stimuli to re-envision Italian society and culture. The neo-avant-garde movements of the time, from *I novissimi* of Alfredo Giuliani and Antonio Porta, to the Gruppo '63 conferences and public debates (which included intellectuals the likes of Nanni Balestrini and Umberto Eco), to the activist presence of writers and intellectuals "in piazza" (in the streets) alongside workers and students, gave Celati the opportunity to test his theoretical and critical writings in the trenches.

His first publication of a work of fiction is the 1971 *Comiche* (Funnies). That book carries an introduction by Italo Calvino, with whom he shares a sense of the visual dimension of writing, and who was to remain a life-long. It was also during this period that Celati began to publish Italian translations of Celine, Barthes, and Swift among others. Gianni Celati's works of the 1970s show the writer at his experimental best. Given Italy's eternal struggle with "la questione della lingua" (the language question), and the tense conditions brought about by the meeting of dialects, standardized Italian, the language of mass media and the technological language of industry, linguistic experimentation was at the forefront of many writers' preoccupations. Celati exploited the comic aspects of language, developing what has been termed "verbal slapstick," a device extrapolated from comic silent movies. Within that cultural context, Celati's work began to play with notions of unknowing and uncertainty that necessitated a shift away from conventional realist forms and literary genres. It is through his exploration of other, more culturally appropriate forms of expression, that the term "avventura" (adventure), as "what will come in the future," begins to insinuate itself into his story telling.

The 1985 publication of *Narratori delle pianure* (Voices from the Plains) represents a move away from linguistic experimentation toward a much closer engagement with particular landscapes and their inhabitants. It is obvious by the map that accompanies the book, and the paths traced upon it, that Celati has come to find in those places a treasure map of untold stories. The writer lends his ear to the geography for its narrative, dedicating the book "to those who have told me stories, many of which are transcribed herein."[52] Interestingly enough, here we have come full circle in that Celati's positioning as a "transcriber" of stories told to him parallels somewhat Verga's reporting of stories he hears along the "paths and byways" of the Sicilian countryside. We are left to consider, of course, what this might mean in the context of the arch of time, approximately 150 years, during which photography and the written word have alternated or corresponded in their declarations of faithful representation of facts, peoples and events.

Landscape offers a more than effective place from which to begin an exploration of knowing and unknowing, seeing and observing, belonging and non-belonging. Staking much of what we profess to know about ourselves on landscape and the demarcation of territory, we fall into the trap of associating our being *in a place* with being *of a place*. Celati's interest in this conundrum finds just the sort of unstable ground he can appreciate in the kindred work of the photographer Luigi Ghirri.[53]

Just as Celati's writing travels toward and within a narrative of what he calls "believable fictions," Ghirri's photography sets out to narrate the spaces of Emilia Romagna. Due to the lack of it, space in Italy is the expression of a contradiction, and a fiction. And yet space, or at least the appearance of it as a demarcation of territory, culture, belonging and citizenship has acquired value even as it has in certain terms been undermined or redefined (for example by immigration and the European Union). In general terms, appearances define cardinal points by which we orient ourselves within a place. It is through the thread of appearance, through the suturing of appearances as narrative, that we experience space and define it.

It is Celati's assertion that stories and cinematographic or photographic images should mirror each other, that they should be regarded in a similar manner, as randomly scattered journal pages. Celati the writer shies away from any suggestion of authorship, offering that nothing can be authored, only subjectively observed and reported. Narrative, as a relationship to the world is in his opinion, is meant to give *sollievo*, relief, a word that contains feeling, up-liftedness that generates an image of flight and lightness. And so we find in Celati's writing a hint of the presence of a border between adventure (what is to come) and familiarity (what is); but it is a border that is not trespassed and retains a sense of ambiguous in-betweenness rather than division. The writer/observer takes the time to attempt to make apparent that which is *celato* (unapparent) in that border.

My pun on Celati's name is meant to be more than just a clever instance of fortuitous correspondence; it actually points to the writer's approach to writing as a mode of photography and thereby his close relationship to Ghirri's work. The approximation of Celati to *celato* is indicative of his view of language as a place in which

> We do nothing more that quote our belonging to a common terrain, that of the spoken, of linguistic ties, and of the said of words in which we are submerged. And that which constitutes us, the obvious, which we could also refer to as habit, habitus, terrain or tradition.[54]

Celati makes the above observation in the context of a conference on Italo Calvino that took place shortly after the latter's passing. There and on other occasions Celati reads Calvino's *Palomar* (1983) as an expression of writing that has reached beyond the point of knowledge, a writing that becomes a point of observation and re-narration, rather than authoring.[55] The main character, Mr. Palomar's observations of common-place events situate him only as an observer and not a participant or instigator of the events he witnesses. Those familiar events or occurrences add up to be the world in which Mr. Palomar is situated, but a world that only becomes apparent when one stops to look. Celati seems to suggest that in the familiar we find the obvious, and that the obvious appears as a novelty when we finally open our eyes and pay attention. What is hidden is right there before our eyes, it only requires a direct engagement with the present moment and the present situation in order to be seen.

The above-quoted passage from Calvino's "Visibility," in which he ponders "how the imaginary of an era [might be] formed in which literature does no longer look to an authority or a tradition as its origin or end," is fruitful for a reading of both Calvino and Celati and their emphasis on the visible as a place in which to situate a culture that seeks to establish itself in relation to the authoritative voice of tradition.[56] A place where language loses its primacy and the visual becomes a point of reference that carries all the hidden but obvious messages that the literal might well seek to rhetorically veil. Of course, the idea that language is unimportant for a writer is merely a commentary on the notion of Italian language and the Italian literary tradition as points of reference, as normative forces, as instruments of coercion. Celati and Calvino both attempt to distance themselves from those cultural impositions that they see as conditioning of their vision of place, language, literature and citizenship. It may not be a coincidence that both writers chose at some point in their lives to live outside of Italy while continuing to write in Italian.

Celati's own statements regarding place are quite interesting in how they also delineate his writing. His novels, stories, commentaries and documentaries author place only as they disappear from his perception. Having formed a temporary bond with them and then broken it, by either removing himself or being removed from them, words become the residue of a meeting, the echo of experience much in the way that some words might be particularly evocative of a place (geographical or otherwise).

> In order to think of a place you have to be able to think of its borders and its differences, and then have some images of what might happen within those borders. . . . The moment in which something that I see as a place begins to lose its traits, the essence of it reveals itself to me as a space for encounters, with an atmosphere, with certain faces, with certain habits, that will never again be the same. . . .
>
> Those who are fanatically territorial would have us believe that someone is planted in his natural place, and speaks his natural language, with roots that go deep into some land of origin, like in some sort of limbo where nothing every changes.[57]

This last statement offers an opportunity to extract an exemplary statement of Celati's relationship with photography, and provide a further sense of what might constitute and distinguish literal from literary photography. Celati identifies the moment in which things begin "to lose [their] traits" as the opening for a more incisive and in-depth relationship with them, as a "space for encounters." This aperture, unhindered by labels and well-defined "traits," is where the possibilities of meaning and being are amplified, where the literary resides. Contrast to this the literal, well-defined and rooted expression that Celati relates to "fanatical" territoriality. This extension, even more expressive of the writer's preference for things "that will never again be the same" and are therefore unencumbered by definition, is also what brings him closer to the photographer Ghirri, whose photographs Celati declares "never document anything specific, they merely *enable one to see*."[58]

We might indeed ask: *what do they enable one to see*? Conveniently enough, Luigi Ghirri's sense of photography corresponds to Celati's sense of the function of literature. Ghirri states that "to photograph a place makes one conscious of being always at the border between the known and the unknown, and this signifies the end of a sentiment of belonging."[59]

Though we cannot work retroactively to interpret photographic practice during its early days with the ruminations of those who have had over a century to consider its uses and observe its evolution, it is possible to collapse time when ideological terms constitute an obvious part of the equation in the use of the medium. What I have wanted to show in this chapter is a wide range of the possible relationships one might have to photographic images and how these relationships have emerged in the context of Italian literary history. I take Campanella's image wall to be photographic in nature by its tautological exposition that makes it similar to a photographic record of the items whose products are displayed. Though a limited set of samples, they are, nevertheless, among the most significant. In particular, I have also wanted to illustrate how in a sense the visible becomes an important refuge for writers who become distanced from their so-called homelands or "places" of culture: Dante, Campanella, Calvino, Celati.

Perhaps it is the instability of images that is attractive to these writers, whose sense of place depends both existentially and politically on the impermanence of narratives or on the "open" (in Umberto Eco's sense of an interpretational open work) aspect of their meaning:[60]

> [Ghirri] says that every photograph . . . actually recalls another photo, either existing or yet to be made, or other images one might have seen. The situation is the same as for a story, which is made up of contingencies, passages from one moment to another. However, if every moment is a choice made in relation to the preceding one which renews expectations, every moment renews how the story will be perceived.[61]

This perception of the workings of photographs and images is detrimental to their use within a unifying rhetoric, such as we might find in their use as promulgators of national character. Again, while this might appear to take a retrospective approach to the issue I will, in upcoming chapters, address the national rhetoric fixed within the images of the Alinari Brothers enterprise and provide, specifically in the figure of Giovanni Verga, a sense of image making that is similar to that of the more contemporary examples I have alluded to herein. I will demonstrate how Verga's literary activity in language and photography counter the Alinari's more literal exercise.

Again, Sironi cites Celati as someone who can lend us the words through which to reconsider the uses of photography in the establishment of national or cultural origins: "To find the origins again does not mean finding the point from which everything began but, rather, to find that movement that perpetuates beneath or within every natural social or familiar stability."[62] In other words, we may do well to look for the stories photography has to tell in its erratic moments, in the motion we might discern within and beneath the apparently stable pictured moments, in the belated images of blurred subjects.

The image of Campanella's *City of the Sun* is the image of the world and a pedagogical proposal that expresses itself through the real, the uses made of the materials in the world once they become apparent and not representations of it. Photography, on the other hand, is a representation of some aspect of the real that is intangible for the way that it marks a distance from what we call reality by the reduction of its dimensional and material aspects. Though this may not be of much concern when photography is used as a mode of recording objects, our relationship to the medium is quite different when the lens is turned toward the human body.

## NOTES

1. Greenberg as quoted in Lucy Lippard, *The Lure of the Local: Senses of Place in a Multicentered Society* (New York: The New Press, 1997), 54.

2. Pasquale Verdicchio, "'O Cuorp' 'e Napule: Naples and the Cinematographic Body of Culture," in *Italian Neorealism and Global Cinema,* edited by Laura E. Ruberto and Kristi M. Wilson (Wayne State University Press, 2007), 261.

"In the bowels of the historical center of Naples, marking a small piazza that in contradiction of its size is known as the "Largo Corpo di Napoli," is a not-so-monumental statue of the river-god Nile. This sculpture depicts the Nile comfortably reclining on one arm, a cornucopia in hand and surrounded by little *putti* as personifications of the Nile's tributaries. Unearthed in the 1400s and restored in 1657, this statue known as *'o cuorp' 'e Napule* (the body of Naples) remains as an artifact of Alexandrine influence in the city, and a direct referent to this locale's renown as one of the city's "locations of power." This status is related to Naples' Egypto-Greco-Roman heritage, its pre- and extra-Christian cultures, and the associated ritualistic baggage. The "Largo Corpo di Napoli" sits within an area in proximity of which once ran the *vicus Alexandrinus,* where the temple to Isis was situated. As such, it is closely related to the Isiaic mysteries, the most important and secret in Naples' "esoteric" history, and to an aspect of Naples that lends this city its fascinating and of contrasting character."

3. Lucy Lippard, *The Lure of the Local: Senses of Place in a Multicentered Society* (New York: The New Press, 1997), 54.

4. Tommaso Campanella, "Appendice della politica *La città del sole* di Tommaso Campanella," a.c. di Laura Barbieri, http://www.liberliber.it/biblioteca/c/campanella/la_citta_del_sole/html/la_citta.htm

5. Ibid.

6. Italo Calvino, "Visibilità," in *Lezioni americane: Sei proposte per il prossimo millennio* (Milano: Oscar Mondadori, 2003), 89–110.

7. Ibid., 3.

8. Dante Alighieri, *La divina commedia* (Milano: Hoepli, 1991), 271–72.

9. Calvino, *Lezioni*, 93.

10. Ibid., 97.

11. Ibid., 100.

12. Italo Calvino, *The Path to the Nest of Spiders* (New York: Ecco Press, 1985), xv.

13. Ibid., v.

14. Ibid., vii.

15. Ibid.

16. Roberto Rossellini, *Rome Open City* (The Criterion Collection, 2009).

17. The hearth or campfire is used extensively to signify the place around which stories are told and recounted, a place where the imagination is given free reign. It is also a place where histories are passed down from generation to generation.

At the opening of "Nedda," Giovanni Verga states: "The domestic hearth served as a rhetorical figure with which to frame the mildest and serene affects . . ." In *Le novelle*, 3.

18. Calvino, *The Path*, vi.

19. Ibid., xiii.

20. Ibid., xv.

21. Ibid., xxiv.

22. Sue Chastain, "Screen Shots of JPEG Save Options for Various Software," *About.com: Graphics Software*. http://graphicssoft.about.com/od/formatsjpeg/ss/jpegoptions.htm.

23. Italo Calvino, *Gli amori difficili* (Milano: Oscar Mondadori, 1993), 50.

24. Ibid., 49.

25. Ibid., 50.

26. Ibid.

27. Ibid., 52.

28. Leonardo Sciascia, *Le Opere* (Milano: Bompiani, 1989).

29. Ando Gilardi, *Storia sociale della fotografie* (Milano: Bruno Mondadori, 2000), 207.

30. Sciascia, *Opere*, 1127.

31. Ibid.

32. Ibid.

33. Ibid., 1128.

34. Ibid., 1129.

35. Roland Barthes, *Roland Barthes by Roland Barthes* (New York: Hill and Wang, 1978).

Barthes revolutionized criticism by the completely self-conscious insertion of his biography and first person, subjective observations that in their elaboration outline a critical methodology rather than a biography of the writer. *Roland Barthes by Roland Barthes* is illustrative of this methodology. The book includes reminiscences, photographs and other autobiographical referents that are engaged as incisive critical tools in Barthes' reading of Barthes as text.

36. Sciascia, *Opere*, 1129.

37. Luigi Pirandello, "Pirandello Luigi: *Quaderni di Serafino Gubbio operatore*" *Liber liber biblioteca*, 19 dicembre 1998, http://www.liberliber.it/biblioteca/p/pirandello/quaderni_di_serafino_gubbio_operatore/pdf/quader_p.pdf

38. Antonio Gramsci, "What is Man?" in *The Modern Prince and other Writings* (New York: International Publishers, 1967), 76.

39. Gesualdo Bufalino, *Il tempo in posa* (Palermo: Sellerio, 2000).

40. Ibid., 31.

41. Ibid., 40.

42. Ibid., 51.

43. Ibid., 53.

44. Giacomo Leopardi, *Discorso sopra lo stato presente dei costumi degl'italiani* (Milano: BUR, 1998), 75–76.

45. Ibid., 79.

46. Giacomo Leopardi as quoted by Giulio Bollati, *L'italiano: il carattere nazionale come storia e come invenzione* (Torino: Einaudi, 1996), 137–39.

47. Ibid., 136.

48. Leopardi, *Discorso*, 57.

49. Giannino Malossi, *The Icon of Italy in Global Pop Culture* (New York: The Monacelli Press, 1999), back cover.

50. Ibid., 29.

51. "I cannibali" (cannibals) was a group of young Italian writers who looked to the American pulp novel genre as an inspiration through which to express their dissatisfaction with the state of affairs of the world and the prospects for their generation. Called "cannibali" for the raw and explicit imagery of their works. Some of the most successful and prolific writers of this group and their novels are *Woobinda* (1995) by Aldo Nove, *Occhi sulla graticola* (1996) by Tiziano Scarpa and *Destroy* (1997) by Isabella Santacroce.

52. Gianni Celati, *Narratori delle pianure* (Milano: Feltrinelli, 2000), epigram.

53. Luigi Ghirri was a photographer deeply steeped in the culture of Emilia Romagna whose images Gianni Celati regarded as parallel explorations to his written work through which both writer and photographer attempted to make obvious and apparent the mechanisms by which culture (and in particular national culture) is constructed, packaged and rhetorically presented. This is where the "believable fictions" of Gianni Celati's books could be regarded as the "negatives" of Ghirri's photographs and, vice versa, Ghirri's photographs be seen as the images that make possible the imagi(ni)ng of scapes in words.

54. Marco Sironi, *Geografie del narrare: Insistenze sui luoghi di Luigi Ghirri e Gianni Celati* (Reggio Emilia: Edizioni Diabasis, 2004), 30.

55. Italo Calvino, *Palomar* (Torino: Einaudi, 1983).

56. Calvino, *Lezioni*, 97.

57. Gianni Celati, "Qualche idea sui luoghi e il lavoro con Luigi Ghirri. Intervista con Marco Sironi," in Marco Sironi, *Geografie del narrare: Insistenze sui luoghi di Luigi Ghirri e Gianni Celati* (Reggio Emilia: Edizioni Diabasis, 2004), 226–27.

58. Ibid., 227.

59. Gianni Celati, "Discorso di Fontanellato," in Sironi, *Geografie*, 2004, 201.

60. Umberto Eco's *Opera aperta* (Milano: Bompiani, 2000) proposes that cultural texts are fields of meaning, that are best understood as open, internally dynamic and engaging and that, as such, result in a much more satisfying and ongoing effect on the reader and their use in society.

61. Gianni Celati, "Commenti su un teatro naturale delle immagini," in Sironi, *Geografie*, 2004, 178.

62. Marco Sironi, *Geografie*, 50.

# 3

# Looters, Photographers, and Thieves

## *Stolen States of the Image/nation*

### THE ALINARI BROTHERS

Among the many practices to emerge with, and as a result of, photography was the accumulation and organization of images into repositories that would amount to national archives. These image banks stored troves of photographic images meant to define the geographical, cultural and anthropological characteristics of the nations that prepared and preserved them. Among those who carried out this exercise in Italy, the Alinari Brothers stand out as undisputed masters and innovators. Their self-assigned task comprised the cataloguing of the particularities of the Italian nation as it formed out of the struggles of the Risorgimento, when Italy rid itself of foreign governors and moved to unify the disparate regions of the peninsula.

However we might want to define our own present period, as postmodern, postcolonial, post-postmodern, post-ideology, post-history, or any number of other labels, all of these locutions generally reflect the power relations that have contributed to their conceptualization. Hierarchies are recognized as emerging and established through the institutionalization of practices in which we all have or will become participants. Under the banner of a variety of media that appear to democratize image-making and consumption, photography participates in what Antonio Gramsci might have called the *apparatus of ideology*.[1]

The coercive forces at work in societies that the Italian Marxist identified as the mechanism by which hegemony is articulated by dominant cultures, are not always outwardly violent and oppressive. In fact, much of the influence we experience today and the sway we allow ourselves to live through is carried out through a comforting rhetoric of individual freedoms and choices. This finds confluence with Canadian intellectual Marshall McLuhan's subtle prodding to recognize the less than neutral effect of images. Recognizing the process by which one is "mass/aged" into collusion also points to an understanding of photography as a mechanism through which knowledge, and therefore a notion of "reality," is produced. Photography, for its efficient spoon-feeding of easily recognizable and referenced images, is easily classified among various other means that establish and maintain power relations. The primary mode for doing this is the creation of an apparent familiarity with its subjects. Foucault's lesson that power engenders or produces knowledge sheds light on what we come to know about the production, use and reproduction of photographic images; that these cannot be considered innocent, neutral or disinterested.[2] As part of its development, photography is rooted in an historical dimension that can help us achieve an understanding of its workings and intricacies. Part of that history is steeped in anthropological determinism.

Early on, photography became a useful tool for imperialist and colonialist powers that used portraiture not only to emphasize class, stature and other differentiating characteristics, but also to establish terms of correspondence to, or difference from, some idealized national type. Further, portraiture was engaged, in a less formal and possibly more "scientific" sense, as a means to define dissimilarity and support the construction of anthropological hierarchies. The historical imprinting of types and characters has directly or indirectly given photography an enormous role within the constitutive resources that formed modern nation states, and to a great extent continues to define *us* vs. *them* alignments. It is at this very effective and powerful level that we must understand, through and beyond Foucault, the mechanisms that might facilitate or hinder the entry of individuals or populations onto the playing field of the production of knowledge.

When the camera is pointed at a subject, that action represents an extension of the physical body's selection and isolation of it through the mechanism that is the eye and all its associated physiological, cultural, social, intellectual and ideological parameters. An act akin to reading, where the eye peruses a text and isolates within it a place at which it will linger, photography also relates a sense of physicality. By the time a camera records a photograph, the body of the viewer/photographer has already "captured" the subject and related it to her own body. This function has been brought into active prominence by the major and popular camera manufacturer Canon Inc. One of Canon's innovations is its "eye controlled focus" system, which puts into function what I have just described above even more emphatically. The "eye controlled focus" takes a step toward the marriage of physiological and mechanical processes. As the Canon website explains:

> Use the ELAN 7ne's exclusive Eye Controlled Focus™ for instant, intuitive AF in almost any situation. The Eye Controlled Focus System tracks the glance of the eye, integrating composition and focus into one uninterrupted step. Canon's fastest Eye Control system to date, it works whether the camera is oriented horizontally or vertically.[3]

This process is merely a technological update of the selective editing made on a broader scale in the establishment of national archetypes. The Alinari, as foremost capturers of images in Italy, created one of the most extensive national archives of photographic images. While an actual visit to the Alinari Museum is always preferable, today we can at least partially access its holdings through www.alinari.com. Situated in Florence, in the newly renovated palace delle Leopoldine (Santa Maria Novella), the *Museo Nazionale Alinari della Fotografia* offers all who visit it a glimpse of the imagery that helped shape much of what the mind might conjure up at the mention of Italy and Italians.

Though not alone in their endeavor, the Alinari were the primary force on Italian territory to carry out an encoding of images into a nationalist repertoire. Their dominance in this respect is well recognized. The historian Giulio Bollati refers to the Alinari mobilization abilities as "an army of photographers." One might imagine them marching up and down the peninsula "composing a mosaic of visual stereotypes so tenacious" that they will forever "replace" the actual places themselves in the national and international imaginary.[4] The Alinari were unquestionably a well-orchestrated organization at the forefront of a truly national task. That they might represent the pinnacle of such a nationalist integrationist movement at the visual level is a result of their industrial monumentality, organization, commercial know-how and cultural effect.

Alinari photographers did indeed travel the length and breadth of Italy collecting images of people, places, objects and events. Many of the images became postcards, others sold as prints, and still others were created purely as documentation. Most importantly, a good portion of them found their way as illustrations into books about Italy and Italians, both in Italy and abroad. As such, Alinari images contributed to the formation of a visual stock of the country and its inhabitants that to a great extent still holds its place in the imaginary of peoples around the globe.

The Alinari Brothers photographic house and archive is the oldest of its kind in existence. Founded in 1852, the Alinari photographic venture and its activities represent a fundamental point of reference for Italian photography since its beginnings; its Archive accumulated from their extensive cataloguing of Italian life, culture and art treasures. Alinari activities were centered around, but not limited to, Florence and they in effect acted in creating a conservation archive out of a living one. Through their success as a commercial venture, by the production of photographic souvenirs and postcards, the Alinari also became the referents for many of the accepted types and characters that to this day represent the Italian national community. The Alinari Archive introduced, instituted and propagated their images in formats that would travel the world over.

The Alinari's art begins amidst the artisan shops that populate the section of the city of Florence known as the *oltrarno* (beyond the Arno), on via Cornina. In other words, they initially inhabit a section of the city that, while rich in tradition, culture and history is nevertheless regarded as a lesser Florence when compared to the aristocratic and overwhelmingly patrician historical center of the city. The brothers Romualdo, Leopoldo, Giuseppe and sister Antonietta are born of the marriage of Sebastiano Alinari and Scolastica Paganori. The boys enter a variety of apprenticeships at an early age. Leopoldo, the eventual founder of the photographic enterprise, works with the engraver Giuseppe Bardi from a very early age. It is with Bardi's influence that Leopoldo Alinari begins to establish a small laboratory of his own that will mark the beginning of the Alinari venture.

While Leopoldo is responsible for initiating the photographic studio, it would be his first son, Vittorio to take the activities of the family business toward a larger and more industrial presence. Leopoldo's brothers, Romualdo and Giuseppe, managed the business for a number of years, but it was eventually Vittorio who would firmly root Alinari's premier status. It may be only by mere coincidence that activities at the Alinari studios reached their most productive and influential peak during the period in which Florence was, from 1865–1870, the capital of the emerging Italian nation, before its eventual establishment in Rome. The latter's historical position as capital of an empire and its geographical location made it a more appealing choice, yet the Vatican's alliance with France made Rome a tactically difficult conquest during that period. A case could also have been made for Florence to remain as the capital for a number of reasons however. The city was arguably the most successful example of the communal system that flourished in the area during the Renaissance; something that presented a good model for the establishment of the new national infrastructure. In addition, Florence in the late 1800s is not only the capital of Italy but also a booming city for the arts, literature and philosophy. It is a city that thrives on its Renaissance past and on the legacy of that period as it lingers in the small artisan shops and specialty decorative arts.

Most appropriately, Leopoldo Alinari's initial activities were centered around making photographic reproductions of his native city's vast art treasures. Eventually, he also establishes himself as a portrait photographer and situates a sitting-room/studio within the confines of the small apartment that housed his photography laboratory. The demand for photographic reproductions of Florentine art and portraits soon proved to be too much for the small premises on the via Cornina, and a move to larger facilities was soon under way. The Alinari family moved lock, stock and barrel to the via Nazionale palazzo where the Alinari Archive and all its associated ventures remained until their most recent move to the Leopoldine in 2001.

The Alinari's activities were so respected that they were commissioned by a number of aristocrats and noblemen, Italian and not, to document a variety of monuments and works of art. Among England's Prince Albert's commissions were a trip to Vienna and an order for reproductions of drawings from Florence's Uffizi Galleries and from the Gallery of the city of Venice. The Duke of Luynes commissioned the documentation of the frescoes of Santa Croce in Florence, and of the Sistine Chapel in the Vatican. These were not small endeavors, given the technical know-how and skill required in making such reproductions on large plates (approximately two by three feet), all of which had to be prepared and processed *in loco*. The inventiveness and skill of the Alinari and their staff enabled them not only to carry out such work but, most importantly, to develop the technical apparati and ability to make them also innovators in the field.

By no means the only photographers active in Tuscany or in the rest of Italy, the Alinari shared the nation's image-making tasks with Ugo Bettini, Pietro Semplicini and the Brogi family in and around Tuscany, the Anderson brothers in Rome, and Giorgio Sommer in Naples, who also worked as the king's photographer. Yet, not one of their colleagues came even close to the organized and orchestrated documentation projects of the Alinari, nor could anyone match the archivalist sensibilities that the brothers demonstrated both in archiving their work and in the publication of catalogues, the first of which dates from 1865. As briefly mentioned above, their interest in experimenting with new products and techniques drives the brothers beyond the mere job of documentation, whereby the media, the processes, and their accurate exploitation and manipulation, establish the Alinari photography laboratories among the top in Europe. It is Giuseppe who becomes a photographic technician of the highest order, while Romualdo leads the company as a top-notch administrator and public relations man.

As might be expected, not all received the Alinari photographs well. The brothers, and especially Giuseppe, who is the first to produce full size reproductions of famous paintings from the museums of Florence, are strongly attacked and denounced for what is seen by many as a disservice to the cultural patrimony of the city. The Alinari were sourly criticized for their reproductions, which were said to diminish the value of immortal works of art by sapping the soul from them with a mechanical contraption, and for the dissemination of "artistic mediocrity."[5] Little did their critics realize that the Alinari's activities were going to be instrumental in influencing the global imaginary. It is a not oft-noted fact that possibly, as a result of the Alinari enterprise (and design?), to this day most references to Italy are closely associated to Florence and its Renaissance period.

Despite such opposition, photographic documentation was nevertheless considered by many to be a useful instrument for the preservation of artistic treasures and/or the documentation of supposedly vanishing ways of life. As for the photographic image itself, its apparently subversive and mysterious processes project a somewhat less than legitimate aura and, during its early days, photographic reproductions seemed to have had an intense effect upon those that viewed or possessed them.

Wladmiro Settimelli, writing on the Alinari's activity in the catalogue for the exhibition "Gli Alinari: Fotografi a Firenze 1852–1920," emphasizes that, even through the potentially blinding commercial success of the firm and the widespread desire for its products, the brothers never for a moment forgot photography's status "as instrument for communication and documentation."[6] It is this very awareness on their part that led the Alinari to participate fully and deeply in the many photographic projects that spread throughout the Italian peninsula more and more as photography took the imagination of those who could most give it standing. For example, the criticism that branded photography a "mediocre" instrument was quickly undone by the passion that the princes of the Royal House of Florence held for the novel medium. And, as the effort to document the events that made of the fragmented Italian peninsula a modern nation state involved many nascent photographers, the Alinari themselves had a-priori demonstrated their ideological affinity to the national project by the contents of the archive.

As Florence had briefly been the capital of the new Italian nation, so it became the Italian capital of photography. On the 25th of June 1887, the city held the first Italian Photographic Exposition. It was during this event that the Italian Photographic Society gathered its initial membership, which in turn led to its inauguration on May 26, 1889. While the Alinari were notably absent from the administrative body of the Society, most likely due to their disagreeable relationship with its president, Professor Senator Paolo Mantegazza, they nevertheless ranked in its higher echelons among the elite members of the Society.

The Alinari's importance and innovative spirit is clearly evidenced through the pages of the *Bullettino della Società fotografica italiana* (1889–1911), which in its November 1889 issue carried the news of the Alinari's receipt of a Gold Medal at the Paris International Exhibition. The *Bulletin* becomes not only a compendium for the Alinari's photographic exploits but also comes to carry more personal news of the family, such as the deaths in 1890 of Romualdo and Giuseppe.

With the disappearance of the two brothers, the Alinari venture comes to rest on the shoulders of Vittorio, Leopoldo's nineteen-year-old son. He would be the one to take the photographic house to new heights in their photographic expeditions to every nook and cranny of Italy, in their experimentation with new materials and processes, and with an increase in their publishing activities. Under Vittorio the Alinari house of photography would also become more engaged in the political dimensions of photography. Vittorio wages an all-out battle in the pages of the *Bulletin* against the proposed taxes that would be levied on photographic reproductions of works of art held in national museums and galleries.

What sets the photographs of the Alinari apart from those of other individuals and studios is the consciously innovative effort by which the operators of the house do not limit themselves to merely capturing images through single frontal shots. Whether they are landscapes, architectural or artistic subjects, Alinari photographers and photographs tend to read their subjects through a variety of angles that offer up their most intimate details and information. In other words, Alinari photographs represent both the fruit of the creativity of the photographer and a certain attitude and ideology on the part of the house of photography. In such a manner, the Alinari image becomes almost a trademark for its easily recognizable traits of approach and angles of rendition of a subject.

The success of Alinari photographs is exemplary of the terms discussed extensively in Walter Benjamin's "The Work of Art in the Age of Mechanical Reproduction." The ability to mobilize a large corps of technicians, to process and reproduce the images in their own facilities, situates the Alinari squarely within the scope of Benjamin's essay. "The Work of Art" traces various modes of reproduction through their historical succession and some of their effects on society. In the case of photography, Benjamin identifies a shift not only in the mode of production and reproduction, but also in "artistic function" and modes of perception:

> Photography freed the hand of the most important artistic functions which henceforth devolved only upon the eye looking into a lens . . . pictorial reproduction was accelerated so enormously that it could keep pace with speech."[7]

And

> "The mode of human sense perception changes with humanity's entire mode of existence . . . the medium in which it is accomplished is determined not only by nature but by historical circumstances as well."[8]

The work of art itself, that which is photographed and reproduced, undergoes a series of changes, among which is that even though the reproduction "may not touch the actual work of art . . . the quality of its presence is always depreciated."[9] In other words, the work of art is altered not physically but in our perception of it and in its fundamental place as an object of cultural and traditional value. No matter what Benjamin's ideological affinities might have been, his insights into the workings of image making and processes of production and reproduction are important for his speculations on the meaning of multiple reproductions of a single work for its maker as well as for the subjects represented. And, while these meditations could be said to be flawed for their emergence from a linguistic rather than visual paradigm, it cannot be denied that, when dealing with photography in the context of defining a new cultural language for an emerging nation, Benjamin's insights are more than coherent and relevant.

An enterprise such as the Alinari depends on this force of reproducibility for their activities. The diminishment of the original work's authority in effect enabled the Alinari to construct their own reproductions' sense of authority. The firm's photographic project and eventual archive became situated as the sole holder of existing remnants of a disappearing, hidden, and often inaccessible world of masterpieces. Benjamin's observation that "even the most perfect reproduction of a work of art is lacking in one element: its presence in time and space, its unique existence at the place where it happens to be" would seem to almost contradict the Alinari's activities.[10] Yet, if we take the archive's function to be a repository that s(t)imulates space out of time in an almost virtual recapitulation, in the very least archival preservation could be said to put into action an ordering of history according to particular patterns that in this case satisfies a narrative for the modern Italian nation.

By this reasoning, and as pioneers in the usage of a number of photographic processes, the Alinari go a step further toward constituting their own authority. Their use of enlargements, diversified camera angles, and other manipulations to emphasize and augment the original's initial impression, establish an Alinari "language" in the reproduction of cultural patrimony. This translation of Italian culture and landscape will go that extra length to become aspects of an Italian culture that will travel and insinuate themselves into the "living" environment of those who purchase the photographs and carry them back to their homelands.

It should be obvious that I am here less concerned with how the presence of an original is "depreciated" than with how the reproduced object is "reactivated" within a newly defined context.[11] The traveling image, the residual effect of the displaced or de-contextualized (reproduced) image, for a traveling audience, marks one of the Alinari's fundamental effects on the national(ist) imaginary. Their production of photographs and postcards for a touring/tourist public becomes more than an incidental agent in the generation of Italian character, culture and, finally, nationhood. As "testimony to history," the Alinari's photographs constitute an important component within the formative/normative scheme of the new Italian nation.[12] Tactically, Alinari photographs are more useful than the original subjects they portray, exactly because they lead to that "shattering of tradition" that will serve to initiate a new context, history and tradition through newly familiarized cultural signs.[13] In turn, these will go toward establishing new relationships for the creation of what Roland Barthes might well have designated as "mythologies."[14]

Lucia Rodler, in her exciting study *Il corpo specchio dell'anima: Teoria e storia della fisiognomica* (The body as mirror of the soul: A theory and history of physiognomy) (2000), recounts the variety of theories of perception that have sought to describe our habits of seeing.[15] Rodler recounts how, according to Gestalt theory, when we see something, what we register is not the single details but rather "only a few simple and schematic elements . . . innate and formed in infancy."[16] This way of seeing is what leads one to "recognize rather than know the phenomenological data, through a sort of perceptive constancy that interprets the unusual through the familiar."[17]

Whatever the power of the original image or object, those remain mostly distant and inaccessible on the walls of museums, or frescoed on the plaster walls of palazzi, chapels and churches both public and private. Photography closes the gap by making accessible and palpable such art, thereby creating an intimacy heretofore unavailable. Photography further makes available the illusion that, either personally or as the signifier of national territory and heritage, it is possible to hold and possess any desired object that photography has rendered familiar.

## MAKE ROOM FOR A VIEW

Among the many literary works that document the meeting and contrast of cultures, E. M. Forster's *A Room with a View* provides a glimpse into the power of imagistic suggestion as the carrier or translator of particular cultural traits and effects. Forster's analysis of class and cultural hierarchies, both within the British circles it scrutinizes, and in their relationship to an external "other" as provided by the characters' Italian sojourn, includes another incisive and instructive peek into the temptations of exploring beyond one's areas of social and cultural comfort.

Forster's novel is full of exemplary illustrations of the impact of cultural products when they are translated, read, interpreted and often misinterpreted outside of their context. Chapter 5 of *A Room* is particularly pertinent to my argument for it just so happens that a set of Alinari prints are used to represent cultural disconnectivity.

The character through which Forster chooses to test British mores and limits is Miss Lucy Honeychurch, a young woman who visits Italy with her very proper cousin Charlotte as chaperone. The following excerpt quite clearly notes Lucy's desire to go beyond the behavior expected of a young lady and feed the desires of her adolescence in a land that provides openly and freely for it in its art, culture and social norms:

> Lucy does not stand for the medieval lady, who was rather an Angelico's "Coronation," Giotto's "Ascension of St. John," serious. Nor has she any system of revolt. Here and there a restriction annoyed her particularly, and she would transgress it, and perhaps be sorry that she had done so. This afternoon she was peculiarly restive. She would really like to do something of which her well-wishers disapproved. As she might not go on the electric tram, she went to Alinari's shop.[18]

Miss Honeychurch purchases a number of images at the Alinari Brothers Photography shop situate at Via degli Strozzi 1. Aside from what will come to pass in association with these prints, it is quite interesting that her visit to the "Alinari's shop" is considered somewhat transgressive. Its presentation in relation to the electric tram, as another expression of dangerous modernity in a land whose fascination is almost exclusively otherwise described as primitive, is startling. But what is even more potentially startling is the proximity to which modernity and primitiveness are drawn together through a set of images captured and reproduced by the Alinari's cameras and laboratories. The photographers' images (and by extension Italy) insidiously challenge *Britishness* and all that is proper, good, and civilized.

> There she bought a photograph of Botticelli's "Birth of Venus." Venus, being a pity, spoilt the picture, otherwise so charming, and Miss Bartlett had persuaded her to do without it. (A pity in art of course signified the nude.) Giorgione's "Tempesta," the "Idolino," some of the Sistine frescoes and the Apoxyomenos were added to it. She felt a little calmer then, and bought Fra Angelico's "Coronation," Giotto's "Ascension of St. John," some Della Robbia babies, and some Guido Reni Madonnas. For her taste was catholic, and she extended uncritical approval to every well-known name.[19]

Alinari photographs were ubiquitous and popular among Grand Tourists of that period. Available as postcards, prints and posters they traveled the world, exporting the fascination of Florentine and Italian art and culture. Forster recognizes the seductive power of the photographs and their transformative potential, a magical potency that makes "unfamiliar things" real.

> "Nothing ever happens to me," she reflected, as she entered the Piazza Signoria and looked nonchalantly at its marvels, now fairly familiar to her. The great square was in shadow; the sunshine had come too late to strike it. Neptune was already unsubstantial in the twilight, half god, half ghost, and his fountain plashed dreamingly to the men and satyrs who idled together on its marge. The Loggia showed as the triple entrance of a cave, wherein dwelt many a deity, shadowy but immortal, looking forth upon the arrivals and departures of mankind. It was the hour of unreality—the hour, that is, when unfamiliar things are real. An older person at such an hour and in such a place might think that sufficient was happening to him, and rest content. Lucy desired more.[20]

Miss Lucy Honeychurch's purchase of photographic reproductions of great works of art made by Florence's own Alinari Brothers represents an attempt to isolate and possess images that capture the eroticism and exoticism of a stereotyped Italy. Since the photographs are themselves fashioned through the selective and editorial eye of the Alinari camera, they are a double-edged representation of Italy in all its exotic, erotic and therefore illicit glory, as well as in its Renaissance and historic splendor. The effect of photography in this case is exactly that of making "unfamiliar things . . . real" by giving the Grand Tourists what they sought to absorb during their sojourn, as it also provides the Alinari themselves with the desired effect by which to disseminate their notion of national representation.

The reproduced images appear to be even more real than what they represent, making them that much more palpable as national icons and signifiers of alterity. These transgressive images and situations cannot be possessed by Miss Honeychurch either by culture or nationality, and neither can they be directly touched, felt, sensed and lived. What she desires is available through the photographs, since a closer proximity to the things themselves may in fact be too "real," too intense and dangerous. In fact, Honeychurch gets even more than she bargained for as she strolls through Piazza della Signoria. While crossing the living monument that is the Piazza the light begins to fade from it, the buildings and statuary begin to take on a ghostly appearance, a semblance of "unreality." Even as she strolls through this completely foreign and otherworldly experience,

Lucy finds herself thinking "Nothing ever happens to me."[21] No sooner has the thought crossed her mind that Florence begins to swirl around her with plenty of opportunity:

> Then something did happen.
>
> Two Italians by the Loggia had been bickering about a debt. 'Cinque lire,' they had cried, 'cinque lire!' They sparred at each other, and one of them was hit lightly upon the chest. He frowned; he bent towards Lucy with a look of interest, as if he had an important message for her. He opened his lips to deliver it, and a stream of red came out between them and trickled down his unshaven chin.[22]

Almost as a way of giving life to what appears as inanimate and hinting at the residual power of photographs, blood splatters as a result of the altercation, blood splatters on the photographs Lucy has purchased. The incident directly connects the "unfamiliar" with the "real" and comes to constitute an instance of literal experience. Such photographs could in a very real sense be considered almost pornographic, by their suddenly have become directly connected to a real-life situation that had, up to that point, remained hidden. There to rescue Miss Honeychurch and re-establish a sense of order, propriety and respectability is Mr. Emerson.

> "Where are the photographs!"
>
> He was silent.
>
> "I believe it was my photographs that you threw away."
>
> "I didn't know what to do with them," he cried, and his voice was that of an anxious boy. Her heart warmed towards him for the first time. "They were covered with blood. There! I'm glad I've told you; and all the time we were making conversation I was wondering what to do with them." He pointed down-stream. "They've gone." The river swirled under the bridge. "I did mind them so, and one is so foolish, it seemed better that they should go out to the sea—I don't know; I may just mean that they frightened me."[23]

Lucy Honeychurch's fainting spell, brought on by a more direct experience than she could have hoped for, is illustrative of a condition that has been reported as apparently overtaking even contemporary tourists to Italy. The psychosomatic condition that has been named "Stendhal Syndrome" brings on rapid heartbeat, dizziness, confusion and even hallucinations. Named after the nineteenth-century French writer who described his experience in response to art in Florence during his residence there, the "illness" is testimony to the intoxicating residual power of Renaissance imagery. Miss Honeychurch receives the full brunt of its effect by carrying reproductions of the art within the bounds of its original context.

Emerson's own reaction to the incident shows a particular awareness and knowledge of this power. He testifies to this as he rids Miss Honeychurch of the photographs and confesses to his own aversion for whatever spell Italian culture may hold over its foreign visitors ("they frighten me"). The recognition of this power is frightening for it represents a potential shift in how and through whom knowledge might be constituted. Seen in larger terms, it is a direct challenge to an established and familiar power/knowledge relationship. Even for a person of less prestigious class such as Emerson, it is more comfortable and reassuring to support a power he knows rather than one he does not.

Lucy Honeychurch's purchase is a rather transgressive act by a Victorian straight-laced English woman made in an attempt to experience the open and unmediated physicality of Renaissance art. While she has avoided Botticelli's more explicit "Birth of Venus," Lucy is nevertheless affected by the pictured representations she holds in her hands. The images are made more real by the bloody altercation that takes place as she crosses the piazza. Their mysterious hold on the foreign sensibility is brought to life by a spilling of blood and a mixing of sensuality and passion that can only be described as "frightening" to those whose culture, upbringing and sense of propriety has struggled to conceal them.

What is threatening in this case is that by potentially weakening an individual's groundedness in themselves in relation to the culture "contained" by the photographs. The disparaging comments and opinions expressed by the characters in relation to Italy and Italians could be construed as a defensive response to a perceived undermining of the validity and assumed superiority of *Britishness*. At this point, the contrast with the more primitive and animalistic Italians fails. Hierarchical categories are put into question by the approximation of images of Italian national treasures and the immediately available performance of Italian quotidian events. The result of this potent expression of (Italian) nationality is that it comes uncomfortably close to undermining British imperial and colonial prowess. The challenge is of course something that is posed by what some have defined as a particularly "Italian way of seeing."[24] Though this might in some manner sound essentialist, it nevertheless should pique one's interest toward speculating what it might indeed mean. Admittedly, every culture has its own particular way of "seeing" or perceiving the world; the result is the great variety of cultural diversity in the world. In the case of Italian culture and its highly visual tendency, it could possibly be a result of the eye being called or distracted by visual elements and the mind wandering off on its own, through associations, justifications, and culturally conditioned extrapolations. Such moments could also allude to the recognition of the distractive instance that indicates what is at work in the image to produce its effect. Therefore, as a photographer generates an image that solicits a response by which the viewer begins to speculate as to a particular way of seeing, it expresses what is seen in a preconditioned context of what might be called recognition.

Recognition and memory are elements that photography foregrounds, stimulates and simulates, thereby causing the mind to fabricate beyond the represented subjects as they begin to acquire a sense of "familiarity." Photography, as representative of a moment extracted from a series of moments, makes it difficult to define a series as sequence. Life itself is only a series of events unified by an individual, whereas the expression of an individual's activity or role within a collective could be read as a series of moments. As such, the extracted moment finds confluence within each viewer's series by constructed strands of signification that may or may not meet within a social, historical or cultural fabric. Rather than deny the historical value of photography, this view of it tends to expand it through a multitude of inclusions and differentiations. Therefore, rather than a particular way of seeing, we might consider viewing photographs as a particular *representational* mode that is specific to national, political, social and cultural contexts.

The image of an archaic Italy that emerged in much of the pre-unification literature was strongly supported by the first daguerreotype images. It is an Italy still rooted in an ancient peasant rural culture contrasted to the few large urban centers through which proponents of modernity and supporters of a national ideal view the new nation. Carlo Cattaneo expressed a certain impatience regarding Italy's slow progress toward modernity, and tended to view the pictographic representation of antiquities and the archeological landscape as a negative anti-modernist trend.[25] This slowness, however, is a very apt reflection of the very processes by which the Italian nation came to be politically, socially and culturally.

When contrasted to France, where the centralization of culture, language and identity is historically enacted early and with more conviction, the Italian situation appears, even today, as a scattering of decentralized cultures and languages that strongly reflect regional associations. France recognized the power of photography as a tool of centralization and "nationalized" the invention by providing its innovators with a status unmatched in any other country. In Italy, the unveiling of a sense of the uses of photographic nationalism was mostly left up to individual practitioners. They, in turn, put it to the disposal of a national scheme meant to correspond to a State that, at least initially, had neither recognized its potential nor granted it status. Adolfo Mignemi's *Lo sguardo e l'immagine: La fotografia come documento storico* (The gaze and the image: Photography as historical document) (2003) emphasizes that "the photography studio is the place in which an image of the [national] territory is concretely constructed. The Alinari are among those who undoubtedly have the merit of having traced the stereotypes of the national landscape . . ."[26] As a result, the activities of these individuals in recording and collecting images, as well as establishing photography studios, became prototypes of a national archive. Through their own private sense of organization and preservation, these photographers and their assistants became the "organizers of images of the communities in which they operate."[27]

Carlo Cattaneo, in "Sulle scoperte lucigrafiche di Daguerre," and Macedonio Melloni, in "Relazione intorno al Dagherrotipo," among the first commentators on the subject in Italy both write in 1839 the praises of the daguerreotype as a dependable technique even in low light situations.[28] Such adaptability convincingly situates photography to supplant the need of the painterly arts as a medium through which to represent Italy's landscapes.[29] Since the national territory is strewn with the ruins of a glorious classical past, such photo-historic representations begin to provide a support system for a positivist approach to the representation of the nation and its archeologically based eternal beauty.[30] Both Cattaneo and Melloni exalt photography for its ability to reproduce, via the use of technology, imagery superior to any other manufactured representation "so as to make art's rescue impotent and empty."[31]

Their ever increasingly popular point of view gives unlimited gain to the notion that the photographic image is indeed representative of "a way of thinking, a characteristic trait of western figuration."[32] Assigning photography status as an infallible technology corresponds to the needs of those who would want to represent Italy as a modern state solidly situated on its historic greatness. The latter effect is achieved and made undeniable through the apparent elimination of the human, and therefore fallible, artifact whose motion and presence is denied by the photographic technology of the day. The importance of this particular trait will be made clearer below.

## *IMAGED COMMUNITIES*

Benedict Anderson's thumbprint has remained heavily evident in most discussions of nationalism since the publication of his *Imagined Communities* in 1983. Anderson's critique tends to isolate the imagined constructions within a state that go to govern the formation of imagined communities or nations within a state or nation itself. While I would agree with this to a great extent, as my concentration on the activities of the Alinari and other herein would seem to suggest, I would propose that much of what was imagined and imaged as a coherent community of types, characters and socio-political scapes was, in the case of Italy, in large part external to the nation itself. The imagined Italian community served external interests as much as internal ones, and presented the opportunity to project on the European front a pre-legitimized formulation of that nation. Once it was idealized by the likes of Camillo Cavour and Giuseppe Mazzini, albeit differently by each of the two, the existing imaginary of Italy abroad provided the political support to make the nation a reality.[33] Again, this is not to say that Italians did not participate in the propagation of the image, or that the precepts were not followed in turn by Italians themselves. But, once a fairly standardized and acceptable image had been proposed, the task of making Italy part of a European reality was that much easier. It became a way in which to insert Italy within the appropriate hierarchical situation to properly accommodate and reassure the major powers. In such a way, the tracks were laid for a further application of instruments such as photography to establish the parameters of more subtle categories and notions such as equality and citizenship.

Before returning to the Alinari Brothers and their explicit creation of a national photographic image, I will work through some other instances that were undeniably fundamental in illustrating how photography came to participate in the process of nation building. The first instance in which photography becomes a useful tool in the representation of the nation is in the struggle for unification. During the battles of the Risorgimento, the struggle for freedom and independence aimed toward unifying a collection of disparate regions, photography acquired an important role by becoming an instrument through which to interpret the pre-unification period.[34]

To reiterate, that photographic technology of the time required long exposure times, in other words posed situations, meant that it could not register movement except as blurred movement. This means that it did not allow for a properly adequate "epic" documentation of the battles of the Risorgimento. The resulting landscapes of the battles and wars of the Risorgimento are therefore much like any other photograph of those same landscapes. The record shows only the before and after of battles, with group photos, barricades, tents and halted convoys all with the usual background of ruins, some ancient, others more recent, which stall Italy in a visual continuum of "perennial archeology."[35] This is also true of the photographic record of the American Civil War. Mathew Brady and his associates, among them Alexander Gardner and George Barnard, produced an impressive photographic record of Civil War battlefields, camps, towns, and civilians affected by the war but, in all their diversity, the images most obviously absent are those of the battles.[36]

While the accuracy of what might have taken place on the battle fields was in part defined by the technology, the results lent themselves to revisionist efforts by which first republican and then monarchist interests had wanted to instrumentalize the wars. Bollati points to these shifts in the representation of the battlefields. During the early Risorgimento, the 1849 battles in defense of Rome, there had been an attempt to represent the wounded as heroes and proud fighters in photographs that were in a sense more journalistic. Later, during the 1859 campaign, there is the imposition of an out and out censorship by which photographers are kept from the battlefield by the Piedmontese and French commanders in order to conceal the true costs of war.

The rhetoric constructed to prevent pictorial testimony by limiting access to the battle fields was presented as a restriction necessary to prevent "the desecration of the military field by thieves, looters and photographers."[37] This edict, by which photography is equated with theft and desecration, and which in turn robs and defiles the realities and costs of war, begins to firm up the ground upon which the Italian nation will soon be founded. Today, we might liken this type of censorship to "embedded journalism" and the reluctance to show civilian or "our" side's casualties while making more than visible the enemy's. While it is represented as a protective strategy, both for embedded journalists and against enemy propaganda, the imposed restrictions amount to nothing more than censorship on the free collection and dissemination of information from contemporary war regions. Then, as now, the ultimate goal of the restrictions was indeed primarily meant to manipulate public opinion.

The quiet, still landscapes of the wars were meant to represent the struggle for independence and national unification as an almost effortless and victimless process. This eventually gave way to a more brutal and direct approach when it came to enforcing the achievement of Unification among the not-always cooperative peninsular populations. The Risorgimento battles were fought against foreign governors of Italian regions with the goal of bringing together all italic territories under one national government. However, the post-unification period had to confront a different and more potentially destabilizing struggle against its imposition from within.

*Briganti*, brigands or outlaws, were not uncommon in the southern regions of the peninsula. Their opposition to the central Bourbon power structure was well established; there exists extensive documentation of wars and legislature directed against the *briganti* by the Bourbons prior to unification. The *briganti* in effect came to represent an expression of rural resistance to any and all established powers, even though it may have only partially coincided with peasant struggles for land reform.[38] While, undoubtedly, the *briganti* have been mythologized by some as glorious revolutionary figures, their instrumentalization by those who would present Unification as a globally supported achievement is no less innocent. Indeed, there is a history of conflating criminal bands with resistance groups in order to diminish the effort of the latter, for whom Unification was merely another invasion by a foreign power.

Those who would define the activities of the briganti during the period immediately following unification only as criminal are merely reiterating the familiar litany by which the South is representative of poverty, fatalism and banditism. Such a population could hardly be thought of as one that might offer resistance in a more coherent political sense. Social scientist Pier Paolo Poggio strongly suggests that it is "necessary to give attention to the brigand emergency, especially during the period 1861–1864, when it assumes the dimensions of a peasant social war, and is fought and repressed as a delinquent/eversive phenomenon. Brigandage and its destruction coincide so strongly as to connote in negative terms the relationship society-State in the decisive phases of the construction of the unificatory order."[39] When the Piedmontese, with Garibaldi and the Savoy Royal House, replaced the ousted Bourbons, the *briganti* merely refocused their dissatisfaction on the new rulers, necessitating a repressive strategy that made use of pre-standing notions about the South and its inhabitants: "there is no doubt that the stereotypes utilized to describe southern society, and in particular the peasants who rebelled or were accomplices of the *briganti,* were already available and were later projected beyond that historical period."[40]

The indigenous resistance to unification in the South of the peninsula found confluence and correspondence with the already existing *brigantaggio.* To counter this potentially harmful presence, the newly established parliament implemented the Pica Law, which instituted a "state of brigandage" in the South. The result was to grant full repressive powers to the generals leading the fight. It is hard to believe that, if the *briganti* had been merely scattered bands of criminals, they would have attracted so much attention and expenditure of resources. The brutality of the repression under general Cialdini is legendary, but it was to pale against the impositions of general Emilio Pallavicini under guide of the new Law. Pallavicini and a military force of well over 10,000 covered the southern peninsula in an intense fight from 1863–1865, during which they were able to noticeably reduce the presence of the *briganti* in many areas. That these post-Unification wars against brigands were a pretext to eradicate a resistance movement is a well-documented trend by a number of historians and social scientists, among them Vito Teti, who in the book *La razza maledetta* gives an enlightening updating of some of the trends that led to the justification of such actions.[41]

As the newly established nation flooded the South with its military, adding new conscripts from the annexed areas as it progressed, photography became a particularly useful tool used to sway public opinion regarding the new battles. Annexed southern populations make an entrance onto the national stage not as one might expect, in a celebratory manner in photographs that depict the local customs, dress, and achievements. What prevails in how southerners are depicted sharply in contrast to photographs of Risorgimento battles. A choice is made to portray resistance to annexation in a very specific manner. Southern presence in national photography is made visible as neatly arranged rows of bodies executed by firing squad, formations of decapitated bodies, heads and posed cadavers. More insidiously, many of the images show apparently harmless, middle-of-the-road individuals that would not on a first glance appear to be criminals. The illusionary element of the images is to be found in the bourgeois attire of some and in the traditional costumes of others. By giving an initial sense that these are "normal" people and then, through the use of captions, make them known as southerners, the viewer's prejudices, backed by "scientific" evidence, find justifying grounds. The photographs seem to suggest the insidious nature of the *briganti* who might dress and look like "normal" people but are obviously not, thereby creating an overall air of suspicion and fear in certain areas. What is fascinating here is that this sort of photography rhetorically suggests its own fallibility in recording fact, only to turn to itself to establish its representational infallibility. As an added bonus, such photographs functioned quite well as an effective warning against sedition, a crime punishable by death (Figure 3.1).

Bollati identifies in the photographs of *brigantaggio* a first instance of a national pedagogy.[42] There is little doubt that in the effort for unification

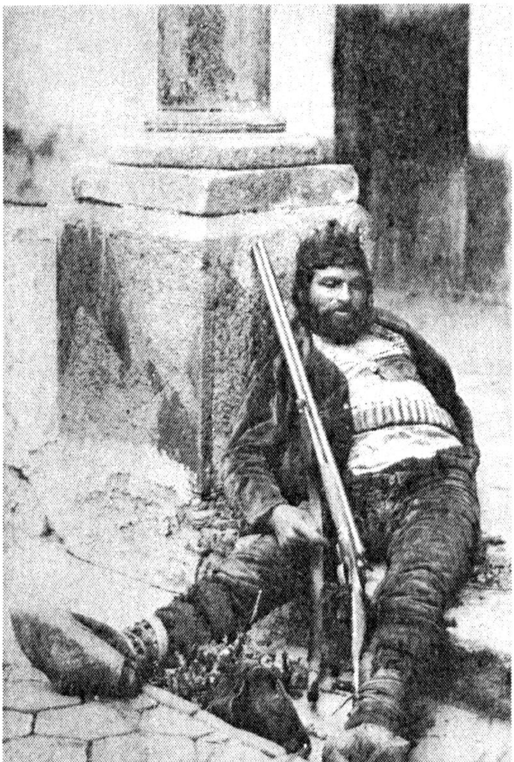

Figure 3.1. ***Post mortem portrait of a brigand, lying on the cobblestones.*** **Salvatore Lo Cascio, c. 1870. Fratelli Alinari Museum Collections-Palazzoli Collection, Florence. Credit: Alinari Archives, Florence.**

these photographs were instrumentalized as propaganda. As an aside, I would go a little further and suggest that these representations in concert with others, such as the ones Teti, Marselli, Poggio, Germinario and others document, led to a prejudiced view of the South that aided in the institutionalization of a very particular national pedagogy. I am referring to the positivist racialization of peninsular populations meant to define a sense of "Italianness" through anthropological categories. Since so much has been written on the subject, and I myself discuss aspects of it in *Bound by Distance: Rethinking Nationalism through the Italian Diaspora*, I will leave it to the reader to explore it further, except to say that such a skewed image of the Italian south is still rampant in some regions of northern Italy today.[43] Its continuance, made painfully evident in the politics of the Northern League, hints at the radical conditioning and sustained power of images.

With the founding of the Italian nation, and as it continues to coalesce, a veritable visual dictionary begins to take shape. Illustrations and postcards representative of the new nation proliferate at a high rate beginning at this time. The Vesuvius, the Coliseum, the Pantheon, spaghetti eaters and spaghetti factories, fruit-vendors, washer-women, street urchins, all come to constitute *topoi* of a landscape that by its illustration represents a field of anthropological knowledge that firmly holds the diverse identities of the peninsula in its grip. These images, meant as much for exportation as for domestic consumption, define an image of Italy and its populations that continues to hold currency.

## CUTTING A BEAUTIFUL IMAGE

All of the propositions and tendencies, trends and fashioning of a national image within the context of Italian cultural habits, as I have outlined so far, could be viewed under the canopy of the popular Italian expression *fare una bella figura* (to cut a beautiful image). This is a centripetal and centrifugal trope around which the forces of image-building and imagined community might be considered. Predominantly perhaps understood as an aesthetic reflection, this idiomatic expression also contains a moral/civic normative sense that touches upon its influence on national behavior and character. Aesthetically, the attitude could be taken to be, in classical terms, a referent to the representations of the figure (not only human) in Italian art, design and architecture. Taken in its normative sense, to "cut a beautiful image" reflects a concern with self-pride and civic duty, in the sense that it is suggestive of the actions, behavior, and care for appearance of an ideal citizen.

Further, this popular figure of speech also proposes a normative way of looking or seeing. It excludes that which is not deemed proper or adherent to an idealized national character. The valence of the terms "looking" and "appearing" suggest this very conformism and exclusion:

looking can be understood as a way of casting one's gaze toward others, as well as how one might appear to others; and appearing can be read as the positive term of the result of not looking right, disappearing. When one looks well and good, one is able to discern normalcy and distinguish or associate one's self from/with others. The normative elements of citizenship work somewhat within these parameters, especially when it is assumed that the citizen might be distinguished from the non-citizen by physical appearance. Racism and ethnicism often lead in categorizing certain sectors of national populations as "second class" citizens by visual distinctions that I believe are related to the issue of "cutting a beautiful (or proper) figure." Our contemporary struggles with defining citizenship, or even merely residency, when racial or ethnic parameters are applied, are an apt instance and reminder of the failure of the application of visual distinctions. And certainly, what we have come to know as "profiling" in the application of law enforcement is similarly flawed.

That the official forces of Italian bourgeois society perceived photography as a normative instrument is made obvious by writings such as Carlo Brogi's 1895 publication on practical tips for portraiture. In *Il ritratto in fotografia, appunti pratici per chi posa* (Practical notes on posing for the photographic portrait) (1895), from which I will quote later, Brogi's advice is aimed at both subjects and photographers. His guidelines propose a way of posing and a set of photographic techniques to ensure the proper figural representation of bourgeois cultural norms that would help conserve that class' status as it stands before the photographic eye.

If we literalize the Italian expression *fare una bella figura* we arrive at what Frederic Jameson has engaged in his definition of post-modernity, in other words, the infinite proliferation of images that has come to influence, define and construct our view of the world in which we live. We live today the result of that consuming production of images that goes into representing over and over every aspect of our lives. Given Italy's historical, social and cultural context, the image of what might constitute an "Italian" is particularly problematic. It could be said in fact that the image of what is Italian is tightly bound in what *fare una bella figura* contends. The fabrication of (*fare* or to make) images to define Italianità, a term that suggests an "essence" rather than a history, begins early in the nation's history, and is aided in its formulations by the almost contemporary emergence of photography.

## THE FLORENTINE SCHOOL OF ANTHROPOLOGICAL PHOTOGRAPHY

During the latter part of the nineteenth century, Florence grew to be an important center for the study of anthropology and ethnography. Anthropologist and photographer Paolo Mantegazza founded the Florentine school, with E. H. Giglioli, C. Letourneau, and Paolo Cipriani; Mantegazza was appointed as the first Chair in Anthropology in Italy, in 1869. Given his convictions regarding the affinity of the disciplines, Mantegazza brought them to bear on the ideology that defined the Florentine School of Anthropological Photography.

As an avid "Darwinian," Mantegazza's interests in photography as an instrument to facilitate the collection of data were fundamental to his practice. Mantegazza's involvement with photography was so great that it led to his election as first president of the Photographic Society of Italy. As a result of his conviction regarding photography's ability to "document first and foremost in a faithful manner" he elaborated a methodological approach by which the new medium might serve the field of anthropology.[44] While photography had been widely used by many in the collection of anthropometric data, Mantegazza and the Florentine anthropologists are credited with having expanded that use to the development of "a methodology that would allow anthropologists and ethnographers to collect photographic data according to scientific and not merely casual criteria."[45]

E. H. Giglioli and A. Zannetti published a "manual" for the collection and evaluation of anthropological and ethnographic data in 1880. The authors suggested that "[art] and particularly photography will remedy the difficulties of collections."[46] Most importantly, they propose that in addition to the frontal and lateral views generally used for the collection of measurements, "another, artistic type of photography should be associated with the scientific in order to properly represent the natural attitudes, almost the character of the individual or race."[47]

Mantegazza et al. had already published a manifesto in 1873 in which they outlined their intentions for what the "Florentine School of Anthropology" might become. Central to their approach was a heavy emphasis on the cultural dimensions of anthropological research:

> Anthropology must legitimate the examination of all the great branches of human activity; one day the psychologist, the legislator, the economist and the philosopher will be able to ask of anthropology a collection of facts that have been well observed, coordinated and which are destined to serve as a substrate to all their scientific specializations.[48]

Mantegazza's manifesto and the observations brought forward by Giglioli and Zannetti found rich correspondence in the notion of "artistic" photography which was nothing more than ethnographic photography or, in other words, the "representation of man in his own habitat."[49] The Florentines tend to regard ethnographic photography beyond its function as an instrument of scientific research and more as a method "that would permit to fix the 'visual' memory of events, cultural traits, populations that the flow of history condemns inevitably to being transformed and, often, to disappearance."[50]

The methodology they outline points to a holistic consideration by which ethno-anthropologic observation is to be undertaken within three delineated sections:

> 1) industries and commerce, in other words material culture, technology and modes of production; 2) everything that has to do with emotion and the legislation that makes reference to it, in other words familial and social organization, moral norms, social sanctions, etc.; 3) everything that is related to the expression of the intellect, therefore religion, fine arts and science.[51]

Especially interesting is the emphasis on portraiture as a modality that might more clearly unite the more traditional anthropometric photography to one that is more obviously demonstrative of cultural traits such as "tattoos, hair styles and other codified bodily manipulations."[52]

Whether this is directly significant or not might be purely speculative; however, the emergence and significance of Mantegazza's anthropological photography at an historical junction that corresponds with the definition of what might constitute Italy and its inhabitants should at least set one thinking. The fact that both these currents find commonality in Carlo Brogi's activities and prescriptive norms for portraiture, such as his suggestions regarding the "proper" manner in which to take and pose for a portrait, I take to be of extreme significance.

Brogi and Mantegazza became influential for their dissemination of methodologies and styles within the realm of the Photographic Society of Italy. As a result, the application of the prescribed technical and "artistic" know-how in photographing "subjects" upon the Italian national landscape became ensconced as the norm. Brogi's guidelines for successful portraiture were a directive toward picturing a truly effective and representative image of what could be declared proper "Italian" types. This was limited of course to those who had access to portraiture as privileged subjects and not as subjects caught informally in the throngs of every-day life, labor and struggle for survival. We might then assume that those who came to be the example of *bella figura* and the ideal of an essentialized *italianità* were these same privileged subjects. Those photographed in the realm of the everyday, outside of the studio and unposed, we could in contrast consider to be subjects of a more "artistic" and properly ethnographic representation.

As I have previously intimated, due to their rather antagonistic relationship with its president Mantegazza, the Alinari were not among the executive of the Photographic Society. This is not to say that they did not find in the proposals of the Florentine School of Anthropological Photography a useful set of parameters to augment their own set of methodological approaches. It is more than possible that the Alinari formed their own brand of idealized Italian *bella figura*, much as they had devised new techniques and modes by which to re-present Florentine and Tuscan works of art.

It probably goes without saying that the most immediate and obvious use of photography was most likely in the realm of portraiture. Handed a camera, the choice of subjects are initially fairly limited to pointing the apparatus out toward what surrounds us: the landscape, another person or persons, or one's self. The Alinari did not shy away from placing themselves and their families in front of the lens, and we have quite a number of images from those familial photographic sessions. Aside from the simple portraits of Leopoldo or Giuseppe Alinari, of the Signora Scolastica Alinari and other members of the family, we have other, more intimate family scenes. For example, there are photographs of Giuseppe Alinari and his son at the age of three, in which there is an obvious show of love between father and son; and a later set of photographs of Giuseppe Alinari and his wife, the first quite obviously posed and the second discovering the couple during a moment of affection.

Beyond the meaning of an image fixed upon the medium, these images also beg the question of what the function of such self-portraits might be for individuals involved in an enterprise such as the Alinari's. I believe that the answer to this cannot but return us to the notion of *fare bella figura*. The Alinari's concerns and preoccupations with creating a unified and recognizable national image leads them to propose their own family and self-portraits as representative of what might stand as the exemplary *bella figura*. Their poses, their cohesive and prominent family structure, the Alinari's social status, are thereby presented and offered as properly Florentine, Tuscan, and Italian standards (Figure 3.2).

Not meaning to be hyperbolic, I would say that photography is in this case illustrative of the representation of representation. The Alinari activities and archives provide a matrix by which their images do not simply represent Italians and their emerging society. Their accumulative image bank prepares an ideological space that enables the creation of more images that will be more emphatically and clearly nationalist in their expression.

Submitting one's self and one's family to the lure and embrace of the new medium also becomes an extremely effective way in which to project the value of photography. By casting themselves as the first family of the photographic portrait, the Alinari proposed it as an enviable yet clearly obtainable object. Anyone who happened to cast their eyes upon Alinari portraits, and was of the means to participate in the documentation of their own class privilege, was encouraged to join the ranks.

The Alinari Archive is rich in portraiture, an activity that begins for them in 1870 and continues with great fervor for thirty years thereafter. Although the numbers drop off slightly thereafter, portraiture remains a major activity throughout the Alinari history. The important place held by portrait photography is made clear by the publication of the above mentioned

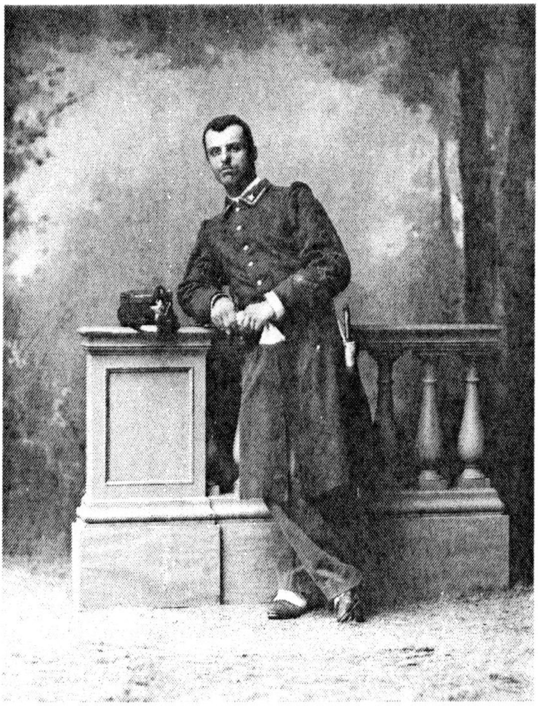

**Figure 3.2. *The engineer Arturo Alinari.* Alinari. c. 1890. Credit: Alinari Archives, Florence.**

guide by Carlo Brogi, which testifies to its function as more than just a fashionable trend. *The photographic portrait* outlines a number of precautions and preparatory ideas for those who might consider becoming subjects of a portrait. Brogi's practical advice suggests how one might appear composed and natural for a portrait. One should avoid being in a hurry so as not to appear preoccupied, and definitely guard from walking too fast to the studio lest one might perspire or become red in the face. Brogi also suggests that one should not invite too many observers along, so as to avoid becoming distracted during the session. Most important however are Brogi's intimations as to how one might appear "normal" in expression and pose and not artificial. He thoroughly believed that a portrait should represent a normalcy that has not much to do with a personal look or realistic rendering. The suggestions regard posing as a behavior that is representative of one's social status. Therefore, while a portrait might at first appear to be a manner in which to preserve one's own or a loved one's image, it is also touched by a class consciousness that generates a set of rules to enable the appropriate presentation of class credentials. The following excerpt and its admonitions make quite clear the intentionality of Brogi's rules:

> After all is said and done, the photographic portrait never strays far from certain constant rules that one might call conventionalism and of which the public can no longer do without. Aside some very rare exceptions, portraits have the same lines and more or less the same poses; and if it might happen that a photographer chances to stray from this direction, to break what might be a monotony, by infusing a bit of life and imagination in the pose . . . he will surely not satisfy his customer. Everyone likes to see such portraits in shop windows, but no one wants them for themselves.[53]

The Alinari participated quite fully in the documentation and legitimization of the Florentine and Tuscan leading classes as examples that might be adopted in the establishment of an exemplary and national citizen type. Their portrait work was not limited to the bourgeoisie. Their portraitists for the Italian aristocracy, kings and queens, as well as their specialized reproductions of Italian art, gave them the leading edge among Italian and European photographers of the period. Thusly, the Alinari lens defined to a great extent the appearance of what has come to be known as *italianità*. This definition of what is or is not Italian, within a nationalist conception of individual characteristics, became further idealized, and extended to racially root its parameters in the decades that followed, by Mussolini and the Fascists.

The emergence and practice of engaging positivist anthropology as a selective filter for the designation of desirable "national" typologies and less desirable types find coincidence with the unfolding of the Risorgimento, the eventual Unification of the country and the struggles to consolidate it. As a matter of interest, there is a notable correlation in the emigration flux that grows incrementally after Unification, particularly marking a loss of population for the southern regions of the peninsula.

Speculations regarding a national image have always dominated Italian culture in all its manifestations. Whether regarding language, customs, the validity of traditions or the italic origins of its populations, the creation and emergence of a nation state generated a perceived need for the standardization of all these categories. Nevertheless, and possibly in part as a response to these normative movements, expressions of diversity have not been lacking. Chronologically we could begin by listing the Verismo of Luigi Capuana, Giovanni Verga and others; and the emigration stories of Maria Messina during the late part of the nineteenth and early twentieth centuries. During the second half of the twentieth century Elio Vittorini, Cesare Pavese, Elsa Morante, and Carlo Levi wrote of their preoccupations with travel, migration, social, and political issues and the mostly conflicting and contradictory images of the "Italians" that populated their society. And Italo Calvino, in his contemplations on the personal and societal habits of his characters express this diversity also in a variety of narrative and representative modalities, photography among them. While the "realistic" images of the Italians that some of these writers propose come from fairly circumscribed regional situations, they go to sustain a counter-current to what is suggested by institutionalized national habits.

We could jump from these narratives to the great tradition of Neorealism in cinema, which in certain cases looks back to reflect on the literary tradition that the previously named early writers represent. It is well documented that a number of filmmakers at the Centro Sperimentale Cinematografico during Fascism gathered under the moniker *the Verga Group* as a way of looking back to the works of the Sicilian writer as an example of "realistic" representation.

That the rise of Neorealism takes place in the post WWII period is of course of major importance. At that historic juncture, Italians were optimistically concerned with creating a new nation and a newly diversified tradition to replace essentialist and reductive notions that had taken hold during the Fascist period. There is no need to review the role of photography in this instance, but the names of those photographers who influenced cinematic representations and those who were in turn influenced by Neorealism makes for a long list.[54]

As far as an external or foreign gaze cast upon Italy, there are plenty of examples, but I have limited myself to citing Forester's *Room with a View* as a way to make a point that also directly makes reference to the Alinari. The books in this category range from the many writings of the Grand Tour period, to more recent views such as Paul Hofmann's *That Fine Italian Hand* (1991), Tim Parks' *Italian Neighbors* (2003), and Frances Mayes' *Under the Tuscan Sun* (2003). Outside of that, among the myriad photographers whose images have fixed and defined the Italian body, perhaps the best-known non-Italians who settled and worked in Italy were Giorgio Sommer and the Baron von Gloeden. Their images are particularly important because they tend to contradict the image/nation proposed by the Alinari, Brogi, and Mantegazza. These foreign photographers highlighted the other side of a national mirror that their Italian counterparts had recorded as quaint aspects of the Italian population (Figure 3.3).

Sommer and von Gloeden in essence structured an economy of Italian imagery aimed mostly at the expectations of a foreign public in search of idyllic landscape peopled by uncivilized yet obsequious race. This is an image that still finds currency in the global imaginary.

As with any cultural interaction and interpretation, when the foreign eye casts its gaze on the Italian body the results are fascinating, even in their most demeaning manifestations. Ranging from semi-social commentary, to Sommer's images of landscapes, customs and trades (intriguing for the foreign traveler), to von Gloeden's romanticized, fetishized nude bodies of Sicilian adolescents, when trained on Italy photography's lens seems to have been mostly drawn to the ethnographic and artistically

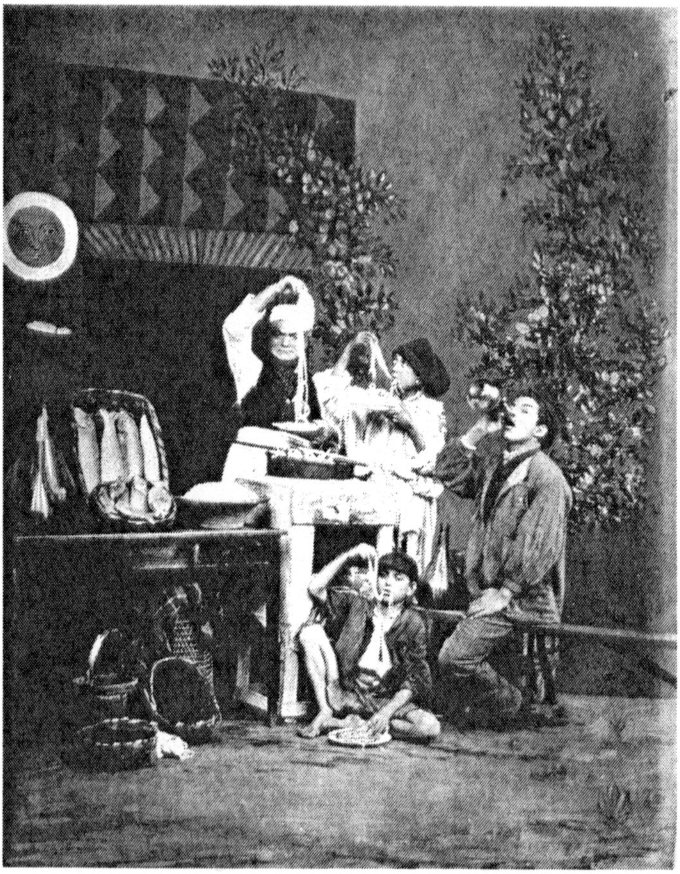

**Figure 3.3.** ***Genre scene of folk life in Naples.*** **Giorgio Sommer, c. 1870. Fratelli Alinari Museum Collections-Palazzoli Collection, Florence. Credit: Alinari Archives, Florence.**

picturesque. The result was a view of the country firmly rooted in images that counter the attempts of the Italian photographers I have discussed so far to offer up a more bourgeois, if not more "European," image of Italians. This does not exclude, of course, that during that same period there were Italians who found photography an interesting tool through which to explore the diverse landscape that Italy offers in ways similar to the foreign photographers. Among them was the already mentioned writer Giovanni Verga, whose work I will discuss directly.

The resulting storehouse of figural references is what stands as a fragmented paradigm of appearances that in actuality offer a greater spectrum of choices and direction. Pier Paolo Pasolini's writings on cinematographic images suggest that the vocabulary of the figural is not as well established as the verbal. The signifying networks of the figural represent a language in constant construction that appears to withstand reconfiguration into a settled vocabulary. An image, the same image repeated *ad infinitum,* can theoretically elicit a different response every time it is shown/seen. What this suggests is that paradigms of national figuration and representation are not as indelible or fixed, as it is often represented, and that they might indeed be penetrable and alterable. To this end, I would like to quote Pasolini regarding the value and function of bodies within context that pretend to represent, shape and enforce a sort of national behavior, prescriptive and exclusive notions of citizenship:

> A "body" is always revolutionary; because it represents what is uncodifiable. In it we live codified situations, both old and new, making them unstable and scandalous. If then a "body" lives a life deemed "unworthy of being lived" (a person of color, a Sardinian, a Gypsy, a Jew, a transsexual, a poor person) it is also manifestly revolutionary (this is a function that is not manifest in the "body" of a manager, a politician, etc.). A poor person, a downtrodden person, is always eroic, whether they are resigned or rebellious (even when they might act criminally) since they are always without any real alternative. . . . To be a good citizen of which nation?[55]

Photography's own qualities of representative breadth would appear to prevent it from being a completely dependable and sustainable instrument of nationalism, even if the medium's power to suggest an undeniable "reality" continues to seduce. Given the temporal changes that photography and cinematography make evident, their usefulness to nationalist discourse differs. The former seems a less efficient tool, given the fact that cinematography creates an illusion of temporally sustained images and representations through visible action. This is not to say that photography has not been put to efficient use by propaganda machines such as those involved in colonialism, imperialism or commercialism. Photography is extremely functional and practical in those enterprises that are often dependent on the effect of potent, incisive and convincing fleeting images that have no temporal historical legitimacy except in their immediate application and rhetorical success.

The objects, goods or products of colonialism, imperialism and trade depend on creating an immediate desire and demand, a precise effect and response to the represented images. The residual impression of the images is counted upon to linger in the receptor's mind and infect any sense of objectivity that may linger there. The viral dissemination of photographic images at the service of national enterprises, of which the Alinari are strong representatives, begins in the early days of the medium and continues to our day.

## NOTES

1. Antonio Gramsci and Louis Althusser identify in the ideological state apparatus a social mechanism that engages ideology to constitute human beings as subjects. The variant I propose throughout this book is a resistance to such manipulation by which the object of photography and other reproductive media is not only the produced image as a formal or aesthetic thing but, more importantly, is the total reproductive apparatus, including the spectator, and the human subject as spectator, who participates in generating meaning and through his or her experience informs the application and eventual uses of the photographic apparatus and the images it produces.

2. Michel Foucault's work is widely recognized as the most explicit investigation into the relationship between power and knowledge. Discourse, in the case of this study photography as aimed toward certain ends that might be political or otherwise, but always in defining a hierarchy, joins power and knowledge in the creation of what I have called (borrowing Celati's term) *believable fictions*. The creation of identities through the medium of photography has resulted in national, ethnic, racial and gendered characteristics that we as observers absorb and rely on to negotiate our societal structures.

In the case of photography, even as it appears to have become a widely available and "democratic" sort of discourse, the heavily influential dissemination of mediatic images is controlled and perpetuated by those who have the power and means of communication. According to Foucault, truth, morality, and meaning are created through discourse that is generated and controlled by a dominant group and lived by others as a "truth." The creation of a body of photographic work by enterprises such as the Alinari is an excellent example of how national typologies might be created and disseminated in order to propose an idealized form of citizenship that by appearing "natural" or "real" becomes all encompassing.

3. "Canon USA Consumer Site," http://www.usa.canon.com/consumer/controller?act=ModelInfoAct&tabact=ModelFeaturesTabAct&fcategoryid=138&modelid=9831&pageno=1

4. Bollati, *L'italiano*, 150.

5. Vladmiro Settimelli and Filippo Zevi, *Gli Alinari: Fotografia a Firenze 1852–1920* (Firenze: Edizioni Alinari, 1977), 18.

6. Ibid., 19.

7. Walter Benjamin, "The Work of Art in the Age of Mechanical Reproduction," in *Illuminations: Essays and Reflections* (New York: Schocken Books, 1987), 219.

8. Ibid., 222.

9. Ibid., 221.

10. Ibid., 220.

11. Ibid., 221.

12. Ibid.

13. Ibid.

14. Roland Barthes, *Mythologies* (Norwich: Granada, 1980) is a collection of essays by the French philosopher in which he examines the processes by which contemporary society creates modern day teleologies that reflect and uphold its

value systems. Barthes expands on the basic elements of linguistic semiology devised by Ferdinand De Saussure by proposing a second level in the significatory chain where signs are elevated to the level of myth.

15. Lucia Rodler, *Il corpo specchio dell'anima: Teoria e storia della fisiognomica* (Milano: Bruno Mondadori, 2000).
16. Ibid., 10.
17. Ibid.
18. E. M. Forster, *A Room with a View* (New York: Penguin, 2000), 38.
19. Ibid.
20. Ibid.
21. Ibid.
22. Ibid., 39.
23. Ibid.
24. Bollati, *L'italiano*, 124.
25. Ibid., 135.
26. Adolfo Mignemi, *Lo sguardo e l'immagine: La fotografia come documento storico* (Torino: Bollati Boringhieri, 2003), 57.
27. Ibid.
28. Carlo Cattaneo, "Sulle scoperte lucigrafiche di Daguerre," in Carlo Bertelli and Giulio Bollati, *Storia d'Italia. Annali 2 L'immagine fotografica 1845–1945* (Torino: Einaudi, 1979), 210.
29. Macedonio Melloni, "Relazione intorno al Dagherrotipo" in Ibid., 229.
30. Bollati, *L'italiano*, 134.
31. Ibid.
32. Diego Mormorio, *Una invenzione fatale: breve genealogia della fotografie* (Palermo: Sellerio, 1985), 20.
33. Giuseppe Mazzini and Camillo Cavour are regarded as the two main architects of Italian unification. Mazzini's dream of a republican and centralized form of nationalism was possibly a little too early in its inception. Based ideally on a popular uprising, Mazzini's plans manifested in a short-lived Roman Republic in 1849 only to pretty quickly fade. The ex-Mazzinian General Giuseppe Garibaldi eventually became the instrument to bring unification about at the service of Camillo Cavour, the parliamentary liberal leader of the Sardinian-Piedmontese region, who after obtaining initial assistance from Emperor Napoleon III of France in 1859 eventually orchestrated the "liberation" of Italy and its (partial) "unification" in 1860.
34. Bollati, *L'italiano*, 140.
35. Ibid., 141.
36. George Sullivan, *In the Wake of the Battle: The Civil War Images of Mathew Brady* (New York: Prestel Verlag, 2004).
37. Bollati, *L'italiano*, 141.
38. Paolo Morello, *Briganti: Fotografia e malavita nella Sicilia dell'Ottocento* (Palermo: Sellerio, 1999), 12.
39. Pier Paolo Poggio, "Unificazione nazionale e differenza razziale," in *Nel nome della razza: Il razzismo nella storia d'Italia, 1870–1945*, edited by Alberto Burgio (Bologna: Il Mulino, 1999), 88–89.
40. Ibid.

41. Vito Teti, *La razza maledetta* (Milano: Il manifesto, 1990). Other writers who have recently revisited the terms of Italian nationalism and investigated the "racialized" historical nature of North/South relations are Salvo Fallica, Marta Petrusewicz, Massimo Salvadori and John Dickie.

42. Bollati, *L'italiano*, 142.

43. Pasquale Verdicchio, *Bound by Distance: Rethinking Nationalism through the Italian Diaspora* (New Jersey: Fairleigh Dickinson University Press, 1997).

44. Brunetto Chiarelli and Paolo Chiozzi, *Etnie: La scuola antropologica fiorentina e la fotografia tra '800 e '900* (Firenze: Alinari, 1996), 9.

45. Ibid., 15.

46. Ibid.

47. Ibid.

48. Ibid., 17.

49. Ibid., 15.

50. Ibid.

51. Ibid., 18.

52. Ibid.

53. Settimelli, *Gli Alinari*, 206.

54. Perhaps the most interesting collaboration in this case is that between Cesare Zavattini (the famous "neorealist" theorist, writer and collaborator of, among others, Vittorio De Sica) and the American photographer Paul Strand. The work represented by the book *Un paese: Portrait of an Italian Village* was done in the early 1950s and was eventually published by Aperture in 1981. The project was driven by a desire to shed light on subaltern cultures both in America and Italy, and to generally use these images to generate interest and respect for populations that were regarded primitive, secondary and certainly "unproductive" within the national ideal that drove both countries toward modernization and an industrialized society.

55. Pier Paolo Pasolini, "Interview," in Tommaso Anzoino, *Pasolini* (Firenze: Nuova Italia, 1970).

# 4

# Giovanni Verga

## *Photography and Verismo*

### GIOVANNI VERGA'S "THE SHE-WOLF" AS VISUAL NARRATIVE

Giovanni Verga's precepts for the school of Verismo, a particular evolution of Naturalism in Italy, are stated clearly and unambiguously in Verga's own literary works. Verga, who with Antonio Capuana can be described as one of the founders of Verismo, has long been the subject of critical attention for his suggestions that writing could represent reality directly and unobtrusively. The rhetorical introductions to some of his works, such as "Nedda" and "L'amante di Gramigna," set the theoretical ground for his supposedly unmediated representations of Sicilian life. The author takes great pains, in both short stories, to position himself as an objective *raconteur* of "found" stories:

> To Salvatore Farina
> Dear Farina, here is not a story, but the sketch of a story. It will have the merit of being short, and of being historic—a human document as they say—interesting perhaps for you and all of those who study the great book of the heart. I will repeat it for you just I heard it along the byways in the fields, more or less with the same simple and colorful words of popular narratives. You will no doubt prefer the fact of being face to face with the naked fact without having to look for it between the lines of the book, through the lens of the author. Simple human events will always cause one to ponder,; it will always hold on to the efficacy of *having truly been*. . . . What I am recalling for you today, I will only tell you the starting point and that of arrival; that will be enough for you,—maybe one day it will suffice for everyone.[1]

Thus begins "L'amante di Gramigna," a short story about a young woman's love and passion for an outlaw. The romantic story is merely a pretext for the rhetorical plan that Verga lays out at the story's outset under the guise of a letter to a journalist acquaintance, Salvatore Farina. Verga suggests that as author he has taken no liberties with the story that will follow the letter. The story, reportedly heard "along the paths and byways of the countryside," is said to be retold more or less "in the same simple and picturesque words of popular narration . . ."[2]

"Nedda," on the other hand, begins with a description meant to situate the source of imagination and story telling in a very specific place within a peasant home environment, the hearth:

> The domestic hearth has always been in my view a rhetorical figure, useful as a way to frame the most humble and serene affects, like a moonbeam that kisses blond tresses; but I would smile every time I hear it said that the fire of the hearth is like a friend. It seemed to me a friend that was almost too necessary, at times boring and despotic, that would eventually want to grab your hands or feet and pull you into its smoky den, to kiss you like Judas. I did not know the pastime of playing with the firewood, nor the voluptuousness of feeling inundated by the trembling flame; I did not understand the language of the log that bursts spiteful, or grumbles by flaring up; my eye was not taken by the bizarre designs of the sparks that run through the blackened charred wood like fireflies, by the fantastic figures that the carbonized wood assumes, by the thousand gradations of chiaroscuro of the blue and red flame that flickers shyly, gently caresses, and then spreads with petulant forwardness.[3]

Enveloped by the magical and hypnotic effect of the fire, the mind is freed to make associations between the natural world and a more mystical dimension. Verga the writer confesses that he has no direct experience of this and suggests that what he narrates is part of someone else's experience, creation and legacy.

But the rhetoric and theoretical slant of any particular approach is quite different from the actual exercise an author might carry out and its final product. However, since Verismo is representative of an approach in which the reporter supposedly writes from a removed situation, about a class he has nothing in common with, describing a situation that requires a certain amount of interpretation, its claim to objectivity must be examined closer.

The cultural anthropologist Alberto Mario Cirese makes a distinction between Verga's Verismo and that of other authors in his book *Intellettuali, folklore, istinto di classe* (Intellectuals, Folklore, Class Instinct) (1976). Cirese proposes that Verga's "reporting" of events takes place in the

> necessity to view the popular world "from a certain distance," remaining within the bounds and the activities of much larger world; in that significant mention of the "angle of vision" necessary so that things may take their significant place and relevance; in that explicit declaration that the eyes must be substituted by the mind, and that the "essential, in order to be clearly and efficiently real" rests in the "work of intellectual reconstruction."[4]

It is of course important that Verga regards the intellect as a necessary instrument in the reconstruction of an essentially mythic world, one to which he was a stranger. Given the inherent objective distance required for such an operation, as readers we must seek out the *veristic* elements of Verga's stories somewhere other than in the recounted stories themselves. I would go far as to say that the elemental aspects of what constitutes Verismo are not to be found in the hearsay and proverbs picked up "along the paths and byways of the countryside."[5] The proverbs and stories recounted are certainly part and parcel of a mythic self-representation of the peasant world from within, but they are also expressive of the conception of the Sicilian peasant class by bourgeois readers. "Nedda," "L'amante di Gramigna," "La lupa," and "Fantasticheria," short stories from Verga's first *verist* collection, *Vita dei campi* (1880), stand out among others as works that simultaneously present and misrepresent reality. These stories are steeped in the myth and superstition that define a certain type of folklore assumed to be that of peasant culture. What they do not actually represent is an objective assessment of the peasantry as a social class and its function within a larger social sphere. Antonio Gramsci's thoughts on folklore are useful in this context to provide some initial bearings:

> Gramsci contrasts traditional studies of folklore as a bizarre or picturesque element with the necessity of "studying instead as" a concept of the world and of life implicit in large measure of determining strata (in space and time) of society" (Q p. 2311). This reevaluation of folklore as the object of science does not at all mean an exaltation of it (as some might believe). Actually, folklore is in a strict rapport with "common sense" or "philosophic folklore" and constitutes with it a "concept of the world that is not only not elaborated and asystematic . . . but in fact multiple" (Q., p. 2312). It in fact includes different stratifications and presents itself like an "undigested agglomeration of fragments of all ways of conceiving the world and life that have succeeded each other in history, the majority of which, in fact, find only in folklore the remnants of documents truncated and contaminated" (ibid.). Within the complex and in contrast to all that is national "the folkloristic is close to the provincial" (Q, p. 1660). A new culture will have to suppress "the break between modern and popular culture or folklore" (Q, p. 2314) so as to have that same culture become relevant to the masses at the level of a critical-systematic concept. Gramsci is anything but a populist![6]

Among Verga's most visually active short stories, I have chosen "La lupa" as an example from which to draw a reading that might better inform Verga's Verismo and his activities as a photographer. The collection *Vita dei campi* and the story "La lupa" represent a period of transition for Verga the writer, and *Vita* situates his initiation of Verismo and his own personal initiation into a little seen or known Sicilian reality. As I have already suggested, "La lupa" contains various linguistic and cultural contradictions and paradoxes that could be said to undermine Verismo's own claims at objectivity. The result, or artifact of such a reading, reveals an attempt at grounding otherwise marginal characters within an expression of linguistic rebellion against constructed conventions of difference. This attempt is repeatedly countered by reciprocal negations that emerge from within the text along linguistic, cultural and visual strata. The result is a series of negations and negotiations that develop into a concatenation of frustrating trials that go to undermine the main premise of Verismo. The works put into prominence the "other" side of Verismo, one that is also related to Verga's own interests in visual representation and photography. The impossibility of achieving a readily definable and describable reality in writing is made clear when re-explored by Verga through the medium of photography mostly in the years that follow his Verismo period (after 1887). The results of the author's photographic work make even more evident, and only completely in retrospect, the status of the Lupa as an individual subjected to both linguistic and visual representational conventions.

"La lupa," set in a small village in Sicily, is the tale of gnà Pina, a widowed woman regarded as a savage being who will stop at nothing to subdue men. For this she is given the animal name, and the story suggests that she victimizes a young man, Nanni. The name given her by the villagers is a result of their belief that "nothing could truly satisfy her."[7] Not only is her hunger insatiable but, as town testimony would have it, her power overwhelms men even when they are in church: "[she] made them follow behind her skirts with only a look from those devilish eyes, even had they been before Santa Agrippina's altar."[8] The popular gossip, in association with gnà Pina's physical description, creates a figure endowed with magical and supernatural powers, whose demonic aspects excuse the male inhabitants' own actions or intentions.

During the process of reading her story, one becomes aware of the nature of the Lupa as a simulacral being who differs from the "popular voice," creating in the disparity between the two the space in which the narrative develops. Verismo's reality could be said to lie in that unattainable dimension that is the simulacrum, a deception situated somewhere between the "popular voice" and the observer's eye. The Lupa as a popular construction becomes a sign without referent, a body whose only essence is what has been projected upon her. The hearsay reproduced at the beginning of the story as conversation among townsfolk is an appearance that the narrative unfolds to reveal a contradictory more self-possessed image of the woman. The attraction men felt toward her may be attributable to a desire for something that is absent in their lives. Gnà Pina, with "a firm and vigorous breast," represents not herself but a perceived absence in the lives of the townsfolk; some type of myth whose incarnation becomes a destabilizing force as it is used in an attempt to fulfill that same absence.

Carefully considering gnà Pina's relationship with Nanni, it soon becomes clear that it is the woman who falls in love with the young man: "one time the Lupa fell in love with a handsome young man . . . but love in the strongest sense of the word," which for Nanni represents an obstacle in his planned acquisition of material wealth.[9] He does not want her, but only her possessions and her land. When the Lupa makes her desire known to him, Nanni contrasts it with his materialistic wants disguised as a desire for her daughter, Maricchia.[10] The result is a compromise marriage between Nanni and the daughter that is founded upon two negations: Nanni's rejection of gnà Pina's desire, and the negation of matrimony's true meaning (which supposedly cannot survive such a compromise). These negations in turn give rise to a whole series of abnegations, both of which constitute some of the basic fabric of this short story.

## WOLF-SPEAK

Since a large part of the negations in this story are linguistic and directly associated with the negation of a referent for gnà Pina, I would like to briefly examine some of the many linguistic expressions employed by Verga in "La Lupa." The expressions concerned serve to demonstrate that gnà Pina's life is nothing more than a series of exclusions: "she was no longer young . . . nothing could truly satisfy her . . . alone like a wild bitch . . . she never went to church . . . no one would have taken her [daughter] as their wife. . ." These expose the undercurrent of rejection that characterizes the relationship gnà Pina/society. The negatory lexical material that shrouds gnà Pina thickens in the last part of the story with: "she did not step back . . . she did not lower her eyes . . ." These examples put into evidence the deprivation found in the predominant semantic structures directed at gnà Pina, who is denied not only an identity but also a self-defined life. In order to work within the interstices of the "popular voice" and the simulacral appearance, we must see how these negations, including those gnà Pina engages as a response, block the existential movement of both the Lupa and those who come into contact with her.

Gnà Pina's actions during the story delineate a negation of rest and quiet; this is because the character is engaged in a compromise she has suggested, and which in turn represents a negation of the realization of her true desire. The other element that blocks progress is the absence of a self-procured identity, the result being that the Lupa sinks into uncertainty and solitude, increasing her love and isolating her further. At the beginning of the story gnà Pina is alone, as she walks "like a wild bitch" through the countryside.[11] In the fields too, she works as if she were alone, with anxious and unbridled movements, expressed in descriptions that qualify her activity with great clarity ("she gathered bundles").[12] The agitation is complicated by the falling in love, due to which the woman loses her sleep as well ("[it] kept her awake all night").[13] Love progressively develops into not only a negation of external, physical movement, but also into internal negative movement manifested as depression. Gnà Pina becomes introverted and appears to fall ill: "the Lupa was almost ill"; "she no longer moved about"; "she no longer sat at the door step."[14] These hint at the internal turmoil caused by love, and at a mediation after which is revealed a more decisive and decided gnà Pina—but always a slave of love, to Nanni—that moves in a wider and definitive manner toward the threshing floor, a place of differentiation by definition and, as such, representative of the possibility of fulfilling her desire. Her new resoluteness could also be understood as a clear declaration of identity but, in the conflicted encounter of contradictory sentiments, her determination falls short. Even if Nanni lets himself be seduced, and gnà Pina feels a certain satisfaction from it, as "the Lupa went away retying her proud tresses . . ." suggests, he attempts to nullify her self-proclamation by the use of the proverb "no good woman walks about in the hours between vespers and nones."[15] Such a pronouncement goes further to define gnà Pina as less than a woman and more as a wild animal. The following expression of her division from the surrounding world is directed at her identity as a woman:

> gnà Pina was the only living soul that could be seen roving about the countryside, over the burning stones of the paths, among the scorched shrubs of the immense fields, that lost themselves in the suffocating heat, far away, toward the foggy Etna, where the sky was heavy on the horizon.[16]

Gnà Pina's realization of her total alienation, of her inability to obtain and/or maintain her own identity, and of the impossibility of possessing Nanni, translates into the staticity of the story's conclusion. Gnà Pina makes no attempt whatsoever to subtract herself from Nanni's fury, further increasing the series of multiple reflective negations in which she is immersed until the very end:

> As he noticed her from far off, among the green fields, he stopped hoeing the vineyard and went to pull the axe from the oak. The Lupa saw him coming, pale and wild-eyed, with the axe shimmering in the sun, and she did not take a single step back, did not lower her eyes, continued to walk toward him, with her hands full of red poppies, devouring him with her black eyes.[17]

This brilliantly visual description represents gnà Pina's liberation from a life denied and her outright refusal to live an imposed role. The axe that Nanni takes to kill gnà Pina becomes a liberatory symbol for both characters. It is up to Nanni, who upholds the values of the community, to find a sacrificial victim to maintain them. The choice is problematic in that his sexual attraction to gnà Pina leads to a very direct identification with his victim. This is recognizable by his actions, similar, and attributed, to the Lupa in other instances: his hands through his hair, the panic that overtakes him, and the anxiety he feels as he awaits her coming.

Nanni's intended victim however is not the Lupa, a sacrificial animal, but a woman, a mother and a lover. In the final act of violence the differentiation between woman and animal is ambiguous, and there is a moment in which a division takes place in the image of the creature that both Nanni and his community have created. This division reveals the unique nature of the two characters; it sinks Nanni into a crisis by which, at the moment he raises the axe to kill the Lupa in an act of differentiation, he negates its possibility by showing indifference in the act.[18]

The photographic nature of Verga's writings presents the final act of the story as sort of Kodak moment. The apparently static moment also plays out as one of the most alive episodes of the whole story. Colors, physical and environmental details come to the fore in their clearest and sharpest delineations, forming a photographic frame that contains the mythic representation of the Lupa along with the character and values of the community that have defined her in such animalistic terms.

## TWO SIDES OF THE SAME ANIMAL

Other explicative signs within the story where many negations are rooted can be found at a cultural level. The presence of an attractive, non-conformist widow, who owns land and other material wealth, could be a cause of conflict in the given setting. Gnà Pina is represented in the local imaginary as a form that is then perceived as a threat to extant cultural norms. When the narrator speaks of Maricchia he confirms that "no one would have taken her as their wife" and exposes a typical cultural negation caused by the "perverse" nature attributed to the mother.[19] Gnà Pina fights back on this regard with negations of her own. Foremost among them is the unconventional rapport mother-in-law/son-in-law that breaks up the basic family nucleus. But she also engages the negation of accepted norms through the denial of the above-cited proverb, which pits her directly against the superstitious/religious foundations of her community. The proverb is shown to be ineffective even through repetition: as it is quoted by the story Nanni gives in to the seduction; he then personally cites it, to no avail. Such proverbs are shown to be its inefficient, and their negative power demonstrates that, contrary to popular judgment, gnà Pina may not be a "bad woman" after all, and that she may in fact be victim to a scheming Nanni. The Lupa's oppositional challenge to the proverb can be read as another instance of self-definition. In the chapter "I personaggi" (Characters), in *L'officina del racconto* (The Short Story Laboratory), Paolo Marchese isolates a specific movement in this passage of the story. Having previously identified the voice representing the townsfolk as the "popular narrator," and the voice of the writer as the "implicit author," he further uses these to demonstrate that the "implicit author" (theoretically absent in Verismo) emerges here to take the place of the "popular narrator":

> Right here it seems that the inevitable emergence of the implicit author takes place, that it takes its distance from the popular narrator, while quoting a proverb that summarizes the woman's ideological emargination. The woman protagonist is in fact represented like an enigmatic character with her own air of solitary greatness, in a landscape without borders, where existence seems to rejected by the unbearable aridity and can be allowed only to a ctonious being of overflowing vitality, such as gnà Pina.[20]

Gnà Pina's "solitary greatness" is very evident indeed, but not as a direct expression of the "implicit author's" opinion. Indeed, it seems that the movement is not from "popular narrator" to "implicit author," but from "popular narrator" to gnà Pina as auto-narrator. It is in fact possible to read the reflective "si" in the passage "gnà Pina was the only living soul to be seen wandering the countryside" (see Notes for Italian) not only in its impersonal sense, but as self-referential.[21] Again, an attempt on the part of the Lupa to undo the identity created for her by others and substitute it with her own tentative identity. Gnà Pina views herself in the landscape in opposition to the prejudiced sense of the uttered proverb.

To further expand on the possible cultural implications of "La lupa" it might be useful to briefly consider its theatrical version. In it, Verga describes Nanni as a "lupo" or wolf: "Nanni Lasca . . . wolfish teeth, and beautiful hunting dog eyes."[22] In the theatre piece, gnà Pina's position as a slave to love is much clearer; she is a woman undeniably and incurably in love. Her murder would serve the function of protecting the stability of the family/social situation in which Nanni has been able to situate himself, thanks to a deceptive compromise that resembles the one in the short story. Ironically, the townsfolk find it necessary to protect themselves from the disorder caused by the men's transgressive attraction to the Lupa by isolating her as the problem and by overlooking the men's own actions. It could well be that over a distance of sixteen years Verga may have thought it useful to render more evident Nanni's questionable nature.

Finally, this story expresses a succession of negations that undermine the attempts of two characters to realize their respective desires through the description of the relationship between society and the "diverse" within it. The negations are initiated on the surface of the text by its lexical reality, and end in the nullity of death suggested as a way of suppressing desires unrealizable in a given cultural context. The Lupa becomes a scapegoat as a result of the monstrous nature assigned her, which, in turn, is interpreted directly as the cause of the crisis suffered by the community in which she lives. What I would suggest distinguishes Verismo from other Naturalist or Realist expressions is Verga's denial of the author's intervention via his rhetoric of form. The "implicit author" identifies with the excluded elements of the story, here "La lupa," but each story has its own. In this manner he opposes the accepted and stereotypical views of that less privileged class held by the bourgeoisie, to whom the work is directed, as a way to present facts to be considered with the mind and not merely the eye. In other words, he incites his readers not to judge prematurely on first impressions, or first sight. Cirese's consideration of such an approach by Verga is consistent with this and is supported by the fact that author's reading public initially did not receive his Verismo work well.

The doubling evident in this short story (Lupa/gnà Pina) is not uncommon in Verga's narratives, it is connected to diverse individuals quite often victimized by prejudice and injustice, whose lot is to function as a moral escape valve for the actions of others. The doubling is a rhetorical device that does not and cannot describe reality but one that causes readers to question it. Violence undoes every attempt at differentiation and contradicts the sequence of events that promises a definitive end. Such a turn of events cannot but lead the reader back to the text in order to search for the point of articulation where a tentative expression of identity may be discernible. That place is where the story calls itself by name, in other words the title itself. It is evident that the story continually quotes its title, as if eventually it should present the reader with a clear image of the simulacrum that it contains. The title itself, in its identification with a negated referent, undermines the possibility of a definitive conclusion and exalts its ambiguity. Mythic or symbolic classifications/representations function to institute differences or similarities that Verga, by presenting them as a truth, urges us to question. Proverbs and hearsay are the sediment of myth, attempts at describing an ungraspable reality. Stories such as "La lupa" more often than not demonstrate that "the story is there but it is hidden and, what's more important, negated."[23]

## TRANSITIONING TO A NEW MEDIUM

Following such a reading of "La lupa," that Giovanni Verga might find in the then nascent photographic medium the potential to expand his artistic horizons should come as no surprise at all. Verga shared his enthusiasm for photography with his friends, the other Sicilian "veristi," Luigi Capuana and Federico De Roberto. When gifting Capuana a copy of his book *I malavoglia*, Verga dedicates it to "Luigi Capuana fotografo." Photography was called into action not only as a parallel to the writings of these authors, or as an after-the-fact collection of images to match their characters in writing, but as an aid in representation, as the following letter by Verga to Capuana makes clear:

> You must absolutely make for me or procure me the sketches and photographs of the landscapes and customs for my volume of Sicilian short stories, peasants both male and female, priests, and gentlemen, and some landscapes of the countryside around Mineo, that's what I need, but it is of the utmost necessity. You could take them yourself with your camera from S. Margherita. (December 26, 1881).[24]

And again, in occasion of the theatrical production of Verga's *Cavalleria rusticana* in Turin, in 1884, he writes Capuana:

> Now please do me a great favor, right away, and know that everything depends on you, the success of my play; and know that it also depends in part not only on the perfect synchronicity but also on the strict particulars of scene, costume, etc. Now, please send me, right away, I beg of you, photographs of peasants (and you know the main characters well), two young women wearing a short mantle, one without and older, also to help me visualize their hair style, and some kind of cart driver and peasant. In other words, have a look at the short story and you decide. If you could also get me a photograph of a village interior, street or square, it would be a great help. For the costumes, please make a note as to the color and possibly the material used in making the clothes. (October 29, 1883).[25]

The interest that the masters of Verismo share for the new medium generates a lively correspondence and dialogue on the validity of photography as a means of documentation and art. The discovery of this is a fairly recent development in Verga scholarship, and almost accidental in its revelation. Verga scholar Prof. Giovanni Garra Agosta had been cataloguing the photographs in Verga's archives since 1966 with the possibility of a publication in mind. But it was not until 1970 that the photographs were "discovered" in a more general sense when two television producers included a brief segment on Verga's photographs in a tourism segment on Sicily. What was done more as a novelty than the unveiling of a new discovery attracted the attention of the critic Francesco Crispolti, who in turn contacted the 3M Communications Society. 3M sent the art scholars Wladmiro Settimelli and Fridel Geiger to Sicily to meet with Garra Agosta and assess the collection. During the course of that same year, 3M opened an exhibition of Verga's photographs in Catania, curated by both Settimelli and Garra Agosta. It would then take a full six years for Settimelli to edit and publish the book *Specchio e realtà* through Magma Editions of Rome.[26]

Settimelli's introductory essay to the book, "Ipotesi per una ricerca su Verismo e fotografia" (Theory for a Study of Verismo and Photography), begins by questioning the neglect that Verga's photography has suffered. He quite rightly suggests that Verga's photographic works, along with those of other writers of the period, represent underappreciated treasures that may, in their unearthing, open new and exciting horizons for Italian culture.[27] One possible reason for such neglect is that the work of these writers, which could be thought of as interdisciplinary, has been studied under the strict and limiting categorizations of genre and discipline. Verga's photographs are viewed only as what a literary figure might have produced during a brief distraction from his usual activities as a writer. As such, they are deemed secondary, casual, hobbyist and amateurish, if at all. The isolation of modes of production and genre distinction have guided scholarship in an overwhelming way, often in clear contradiction to an artist or writer's own production and stated intention, toward specialistic renderings and expanding into ever more artificial categories. What is exciting about more inclusive approaches and critical trends such as Cultural Studies is that they offer the possibility of receiving and perceiving work such as Verga's photography in direct relationship to his writing. How satisfying to approach Verga's photography aided by this new set of circumstances, and to begin to think of it not merely or only as a parallel activity or passing interest, but in and of itself as a potential other dimension to writing.

In Giovanni Garra Agosta's own book on Verga's photographs, *Verga | Fotografo*, Sipala's preface touches upon the fact that most of Verga's photographic production follows his Verismo season (1870–1890).[28] Verga's silence in writing during the last thirty years of his life does not mark the end of his activities. New interests and activities dominate his life, among them are photography and cinematography, two new media through which he continues to explore the contradictions inherent in the representation of reality. The move beyond the page into photography, cinematography, and theatre inspires new angles and new perceptions of already tried themes. In order to adapt a subject to a different medium the author must himself shift his point of view and question the way in which he has previously perceived his subjects. The dimensionality gained by characters such as those of "La lupa" when shifted into photography are representative of possibilities that dovetail into each genre's limitations, and unfold into new terms of interpretation for their viewers or readers.

The attraction of photography and its associated media is of course that they appear to provide what language struggles to attain. While language can express a sense of temporality through its grammatical structures, narrative modes and in a selective use of syntax and vocabulary, photography assumes for itself the task of setting the captured moment into a temporality that is apparently unquestionable. This notion has been debated continuously since the invention of photography. O. W. Holmes and Balzac, among others, have argued that photography functions partially to capture or disclose some sort of "essence" of the objects it registers; this "essence" is transferred onto the image thereby making the object visible as what it is. While this "essence" can be interpreted to mean an objects' luminosity, its reflective qualities, which may or may not satisfy the more metaphysical among us, it comes closer to a consideration of the chemical and physical functions of the medium.

While seductive, the proposition that photography might be able to record a precise moment and establish a sense of temporality through its mechanisms seems dubious. In fact, the only temporality that can be established through the photographic medium is that of its own processes. Speed, exposure, aperture: these are the elements that in their manipulation provide the photographer with a sense of the time frame that must be exercised in order to generate a reproducible image of the subject before the lens. The nature of light and the camera's ability to translate and capture it, the time element involved in photography is flexible rather than constant. In other words, the time of exposure is related to the aperture, which in turn is related to light availability and the desired effects related to focus and depth of field. Temporality and photographic concepts such as Henri Cartier Bresson's "decisive moment" school of photography are not fully achievable unless one purposely defines them as external to the passing of historical time.

What makes Verga's photographs valuable is that they bridge the very evident and extant gap between normative bourgeois portraits, proposed and produced by Brogi, Alinari and others, and the unposed, snapshot type of photography common to individuals interested in recording daily life and events in an as unfiltered manner as possible. Gordon Baldwin's *Looking at Photographs: A Guide to Technical Terms* (1991) defines the snapshot as a term that "applies to an informal and apparently unposed and instantaneous photograph, usually made by an amateur, without artistic intention and as a keepsake of persons, places, or events."[29] While I may be generalizing somewhat, it is not hard to see that photographs of those classes deemed to be representative of a nation's character are set in highly controlled situations. The photographic environment of the bourgeoisie and aristocracy is hardly "natural," it is neutral, undisturbed, calm and filled with recognizable symbols of status and privilege. The ambient photography that instead represents the populace is on location, spontaneous and "natural"; what seems to be important in such photographs is not so much the individual as the dissonance of the framed moment, a representation of the "inferior" class and all its inadequacies. We therefore see blurred faces and bodies in motions, perplexed stares, clothing not quite properly arranged and unkempt hair (since many of the photos depict people at work and in movement).

Giovanni Verga's own photographs fall within the range of the second type of photograph. Photos of peasants, workers and common people, all of whom populate the end of the spectrum most distant from the "norm." Verga photographs these individuals and groups in a manner to attempt to level the field of representation by closing the gap between social classes. There is not much difference between Verga's photographs of his family and those of the people he meets in the fields and along "the paths and byways" of the Sicilian countryside. The former are not quite posed or prepared as they might be in a professional studio, and the latter may be photographed in a spontaneous manner or they may be slightly posed. Blurring, that in the photographs of so-called professional photographers appears as an effect of the disinterest for the lower classes, has a different meaning in Verga's photos. Blurring and movement in Verga does not signify hierarchy, it cuts across class distinctions, and is the result of the photographer's own surrendering of complete control of the situation.

Once again, Verga's photographs, set side-by-side with those of Hine and Riis, could be said to represent a before and after of migration. The difference between their images is to be found in the depiction of the people they record. Verga's potential emigrants are photographed as themselves, identified with their role in their communities as fishermen, peasants, workers, families, and individuals (Figures 4.1 and 4.2). Hine and Riis photographed their subjects as people without a country in search of one; people whose potential to become Americans can be read in the photographs that captured questioning faces and displaced bodies. Hine and Riis' immigrants are a generalized lot to be molded into something that would eventually be unrelated to the places and cultures from whence they came. Compared to Hine and Riis, or almost any other photographer of the lower classes, Verga's photographs stand out as figural representations of a subalternity not to be molded or erased but as a viable class in and of itself, and as an expression of a cultural alternative to the dominant one.

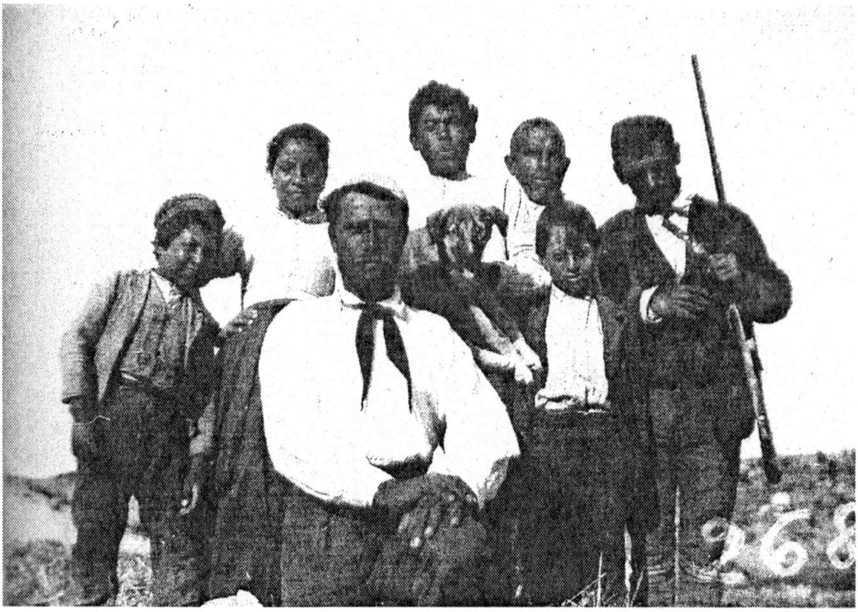

**Figure 4.1.** ***Tébidi, 1897: gruppo di contadini.*** **Tav. 72; cat. 248. Giovanni Verga, in** ***Verga | Fotografo.*** **Permission granted by Maimone Editore.**

It may be useful at this point to return to "La lupa" for a final consideration of how the figural in Verga finds a plausible manifestation in the written word as well as in the photographic image. Verga manages to elicit a correspondence between the media in which he worked. The imagistic strength of gnà Pina makes her live beyond the page. She is described as a living, breathing person whose actions are incisive, decisive and colorful. From beginning to end, the short story offers a she-wolf that is a cabinet card portrait of an individual. "La lupa" is definitely not a posed portrait; it is the spontaneous portrait of a living body that acquires the sort of dimensional materiality that one might find in a stereoscopic image. Verga's photographs are a step toward rendering visible that which normally is not. While his writings succeeded in giving a previously unknown dimensionality to Sicilian peasants, his photographs added yet another aspect to his attempts at approximating that reality. Visibility as a result of technological advances makes knowable what was previously invisible. At this point I am tempted to paraphrase Vico in saying that what is made visible is made knowable, keeping in mind of course Foucault's warnings regarding the proximity of power and knowledge and the obvious questions we must consider regarding the mechanisms by which individuals are inserted within diverse systems of knowledge. Following Sipala's suggestion that "photography can be

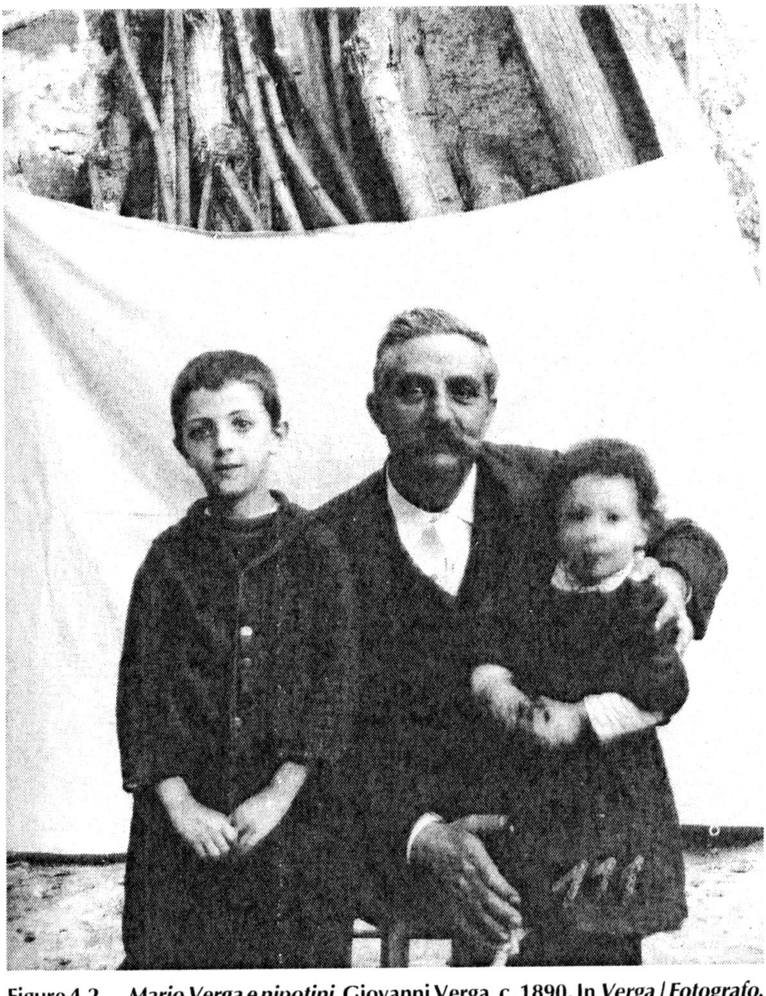

**Figure 4.2.** ***Mario Verga e nipotini.*** **Giovanni Verga, c. 1890. In *Verga / Fotografo.* Permission granted by Maimone Editore.**

art; but verist art is not a 'photography' of the real,"[30] I would offer that photographers like Verga make of the photographic image a possible site where the relationship between power and knowledge might be reassessed. Differently from those who seek to establish "characteristic" images at the service of institutionalized notions of citizenship and nationality, Verga's photographs present a knowledge that, even though it may be mediated to some extent by the technology and its user, can begin to be defined away from its supposed status and dependency as a reflection of hegemonic power structures.

## NOTES

1. Giovanni Verga, "L'amante di Gramigna," in *Le novelle* (Milano: Garzanti, 1980), 212–20.

2. Ibid.

3. Verga, "Nedda," in *Le novelle*, 3.

4. Alberto Mario Cirese, *Intellettuali, folklore, istinto di classe: Note su Verga, Deledda, Scotellaro, Gramsci* (Torino: Einaudi, 1976), 9.

5. Verga, "L'amante," in *Le novelle*, 212.

6. Umberto Cerroni, *Lessico gramsciano* (Roma: Editori Riuniti, 1978), 22.

7. Verga, "La lupa" in *Le novelle*, 206.

8. Ibid.

9. Ibid.

10. Ibid., 207.

11. Ibid., 208.

12. Ibid., 207.

13. Ibid.

14. Ibid., 208.

15. Ibid., 208–9.

16. Ibid., 208.

17. Ibid., 211.

18. The sacrificial distinction, the distinction between the pure and the impure, cannot be obliterated without obliterating all other differences as well. One and the same process of violent reciprocity engulfs the whole. The sacrificial crisis can therefore be defined as a crisis of distinctions—that is, a crisis affecting the cultural order. This cultural order is nothing more than a regulated system of distinctions in which the differences among individuals are used to establish their 'identity' and their mutual relationships.

See "crisis of difference" in Rene Girard *Violence and the Sacred* (Baltimore: Johns Hopkins UP, 1977), 49.

19. Verga, "La lupa," 206.

20. Angelo Marchese, *L'officina del racconto* (Milano: Mondadori, 1983), 191.

21. Verga, "La lupa," 208.

22. Verga, *La lupa* (1982), 3.

23. Cirese, *Intellettuali*, 17.

24. Paolo Mario Sipala, "Prefazione," in Giovanni Garra Agosta, *Verga | Fotografo* (Catania: Giuseppe Maimone Editore, 1991), 13.

25. Ibid., 14.

26. Wladmiro Settimelli, *Giovanni Verga: Specchio e Realtà. 84 foto inedite dello scrittore siciliano* (Roma: Editrice Magma, 1976) precedes Giovanni Garra Agosta's own volume on Verga the photographer cited above, *Verga | Fotografo* (Catania: Maimone, 1991).

27. Ibid., 13.

28. Ibid., 14.

29. Gordon Baldwin, *Looking at Photographs: A Guide to Technical Terms* (Los Angeles: J. Paul Getty Museum, 1991), 76.

30. Sipala, "Prefazione," in *Verga | Fotografo*, 16.

# 5

# Imaging America

## *The Photography of Lewis Hine and Jacob Riis*

Early on in its history, photography began to receive the critical attention of intellectuals and cultural critics concerned with various aspects of social, political, and technological change. Between 1859 and 1863, Oliver Wendell Holmes, journalist, writer, photographer and critic, published three articles dealing with the photographic image and the stereographic genre in *The Atlantic Monthly*.[1] Throughout, Holmes champions the stereographic format based on his conviction that the dimensionality achieved through this process is a most important representational achievement. The reasoning behind Holmes' preference for the stereograph is based on the notion that, while a photographic work offers viewers "concrete" images of the world, the stereograph records and gives dimension to the most minute details.

Indeed, while any photograph can claim detail, the appearance of dimensionality is only achievable through the stereograph. However, the same sort of critique that would be applied to any photograph regarding figural representation must also be applied to the stereograph's virtual dimensionality for its lack of the materiality that might render it "concrete." From our historical vantage point we must give O. W. Holmes his due credit as an astute critic and photographer for having intuited certain horizons within the realm of photographic representation and for having theorized their potential extrapolation. Holmes' meditations on photography represent one of the most advanced speculations on the medium to this day; they approximate the concept of virtual space/representation as we have come to know it today.

By donning the stereoscope, and isolating one's vision toward the card carrying two identical photographs placed upon the instrument, the viewer steps into the illusion of depth and dimension. But it is by this act of separating one's self from the surrounding world, of allowing one's gaze to be directed exclusively at one image, that stereographic images betray the supposed materiality that Holmes assigns to them. The materiality is only an optical illusion, and the image remains to be found solely and singularly on the flat surface of the stereoscopic card. Further, it is an image whose decontextualized landscape lacks both historical dimensionality and any link to personal experience that might be had by visiting and photographing the place directly.

A medium such as photography valorizes detail and stimulates thought to push beyond the image, provoking yet more detailing of what remains invisible but is nevertheless related to its representation. History is one of the invisible details of photography that conditions the visible ones. Walter Benjamin has argued that the historical value of a work of art and its reproduction "in the age of mechanical reproduction" is to be considered alongside other pertinent issues, such as the authority of the work in question and its market value.[2] Historicity therefore become a complex and intertwined set of circumstances that, far from merely being declared present or altered, takes on the tonalities of the period in which a work is re/produced and disseminated.

The works of Lewis Wickes Hine (1874–1940) and Jacob August Riis (1849–1914) are often uncritically taken as historical documents. It is not unreasonable to suggest that their photographs were conditioned by the stories they were eager to tell about their country and the events that they witnessed, which they sought to incorporate into their view of an evolving "America." Though they worked mostly in New York during a very specific period, the stories of that city intersect with each other and the stories of the world to such an extent as to have bestowed upon their works historical authority. Given that they form a visual/historical data bank, these are stories for which, in one way or another, many generations of Americans share a certain amount of interest. Those who migrate hold within themselves worlds that do not always find explicit expression, but are narrated in many different ways. Those who receive immigrants share in those same stories by how they are appended to stories recounting the construction of national histories. The "truths" of a nation include beliefs and stories that go to form communal *believable fictions*. Difference perceived as something un-assimilable into the history of a nation is shunned, suspicious, and thought to be of doubtful value. Difference perceived as an inferior trait, available to be altered or bettered by integration into a "civilizing" system, is readily highlighted and foregrounded.

The processes involved in constituting the concept of nation and citizenship have been the subject of many studies. At the cultural and anthropological level, a nation defines itself through the embodiment of a belief in its anthropological identity (in Italy expressed as *italianità*, which also carries with it an essentialized notion of behavior); a belief in its own tongue (in Italy, Italian as a standardized language in contrast to regional "languages"); and a deep belief in civilization, customs, and creative art (both the Roman Empire and the Renaissance are the commonplace referents for Italy at home and abroad). While ideally these conditions might be fluid they are not always manifested as such, in which case the stories of immigrants tend take second place to the needs and tendencies within a preexisting and inflexible national ideology. The United States, though not always following through on the ideals to which the country aspires, has been able to integrate a variety of extra-national stories within the construction of their own national narrative.

The constitution of one Italian nation in 1861, by declaiming in negative terms the presence of internal cultural and "ethnic" differences, well documented in the writings and correspondence of its architects and activists, becomes in part responsible for its massive emigration. Today, having become a major economic power, and itself a destination for immigrants, Italy again moves to take halting measures as a way to emphasize its national standards against what it considers an invasion. The results of a series of recent electoral victories, including the 2000 regionals, the 2001 and 2008 nationals, and the most recent 2010 regionals, the right-wing alliance that includes the Northern League, National Alliance, and Forza Italia (which has now become Popolo della Libertà), can be understood as an expression of xenophobia, even more so if one considers the continuing exponential gains of the League. The language that surrounds isolationism and makes swings to the right possible is common to all exclusionary rhetoric, whether it be Italian, American, Quebecois, or Kenyan, and its meaning always translates into suffering.

The invention of photography roughly coincides with the "great migration" to the Americas of the late nineteenth century. Being also a hot period in colonial enterprise, the era is one in which social positions are defined, determined and solidified to facilitate exploitation. Through them, the formation of nationalist ideals and the creation of national characters takes form. By virtue of these coincidences, the photographic image becomes embroiled in history as it aids in the documentation of the changing face of the world.

The almost immediate bleeding of photography into anthropology, tied to that science's positivist developments, produced images closely tied to the intentions of colonial determinism, consolidating the categories necessary for its success. The medium came to constitute an unsurpassed instrument for cataloguing the human cargo of imperialism and the inventory of colonial enterprise. With travel and tourism photography further enriched the archival knowledge of population types, racial and ethnic categories, and cultural representations that came to support and re-enforce colonial rule by the unilateral interpretation of the images produced. Aside from direct collectionism, in the form of removal of objects and peoples, photography could be categorized as the principal element by which cataloguing takes place in the institution of storehouses of geographical and scientific knowledge and in the accumulation of anthropological data.

Along with these more obvious uses of photography, we must also consider that this period includes the expansion of capitalism. As the anthropological uses of photography helped sustain colonialism by designating the colonized as different and inferior, and inferior because different, in the case of capitalism photography aided the processes involved in the selection of laboring bodies. The control of immigration and the exploitation of particular populations according to the needs of economies generates a sort of kinetic and infinite colonialism that directs the import/export of bodies toward its economic structures while continuing to exclude them totally or in part from its social and political ones. The interactive aspects of colonialism, capitalism and nation building therefore become imbricated with the imagery produced by photography. The names we have come to give the results of these processes include among them *emigration* and *slavery*.

The American photographers Lewis Hine and Jacob Riis became principal actors in the documentation of the immigrant influx to the US through New York and Ellis Island. An extension of both photographers' concerns with social matters, photography represented a valuable medium through which to document their era. Because they partook of a representational mode that carried with it the ambiguity of realist representation and the ambivalence of the figuration of foreign bodies, their photography acquired and maintained value beyond the simple inventory it might have remained. The effectiveness of their work was aided by the fact that not only did they engage a new medium, but that they were also among the first to catalogue laboring bodies and immigrant populations. Their activity engaged America at a scale and level of populist social involvement never before seen.

Trained as a sociologist, Lewis Hine considered photography as a tool through which to bring social ills to public attention. Hine began to photograph the immigrants who crowded onto New York's Ellis Island in 1905. He also photographed the tenements and sweatshops where immigrants were forced to live and work. Hine's "Child Labor in the Carolinas" and "Day Laborers Before Their Time," the first of his many photo essays documenting child labor, were published in 1909. These essays included pictures that showed children as young as eight working long hours in dangerous conditions.

Hine was hired by the National Child Labor Committee in 1911 to explore more extensively child-labor conditions in the United States. He traveled throughout the eastern United States making pictures of exploited children and the slums in which they lived. During World War I he served as a photographer with the Red Cross, and after the Armistice he remained with the organization in the Balkans. As a result of that, he published the photo essay "The Children's Burden in the Balkans" (1919). Later, in 1932, again in New York City, Hine was hired to record the construction of the Empire State Building, after which he published *Men at Work* (1932).

American social reformer, photographer and journalist Jacob Riis was born in Denmark and arrived in the United States in 1870. In 1877 he became a police reporter for the *New York Tribune*, and in 1888 he began working for the *New York Evening Sun*. Riis strove to use photography as an instrument through which to achieve reforms in tenement housing and schools. His *How the Other Half Lives* (1890) was one of the earliest popular social documentary books to be published in the United States. The volume instigated reform legislation in New York City by attracting the attention of Theodore Roosevelt, then police commissioner, who cooperated with Riis on reform programs such as introducing parks and playgrounds into congested neighborhoods. Roosevelt offered Riis further opportunities to work with him, but the photographer preferred to continue his creative work, producing books on the plight of poor children, immigrants and tenement dwellers. Among his photographic innovations, Riis is credited with being one of the first journalists to use flashbulb photography to record nightlife in the streets.

Socially minded photography during that era was thriving not only in America but also found many practitioners in Europe. Englishman John Thomson's work documented London street life in the 1870s, and German Heinrich Zille made photos of the Berlin underclasses. There is however a distinct difference between those photographers and Hine and Riis, at least in the Americans' series concerned with new immigrants. The primary difference lies in the fact that the Americans are involved in the documentation of foreign bodies whose images were destined to construct and inhabit the American imaginary.[3] The documentation of bodies considered foreign and threatening in Europe was mostly, but not only, restricted to the spaces of colonialism. I say mostly, because in Italy, while the work of Giorgio Sommer and the Baron von Gloeden, and even that of the Alinari Brothers, could easily be classified as anthropological, their aesthetic claims tend to indicate otherwise. Large scale documentation of foreignness and an expression of dis/ease with difference in Europe would not be seen until the assiduous documentation of Jews, Gypsies, homosexuals, and other "undesirables" in Nazi Germany.

My interest in the work of Hine and Riis gravitates around its function as a pedagogical tool (with potentially both positive and negative implications) for their contemporaries and for future generations. Their photography constitutes what could be considered the creation of an archive of the future. Without doubt, the cultural legacy of these two pioneers must be considered in view of their contribution to the accumulation of historical information vis-à-vis the development of the American nation. However, their true socio-historical value can only be gauged through the construction of a continuum that goes beyond national borders and participates in the documentation of populations toward ends not always humane. In addition, through evaluations relative to our contemporary understanding of photography, Hine and Riis can be helpful for understanding the medium of photography itself and its relationship with what may be termed its "subjects."

## PHOTOGRAPHY AS STORY

Even though Hine and Riis proposed to tell the stories of immigrants and workers, we must ask if their stories were in fact those of individuals meant to be inserted into a larger general story or history, or if they could be categorized as something other. Given that the photographs were neither controlled (commissioned), nor made or kept by the subjects themselves, leaves room for speculation. The idea of an archive of the future acquires currency when we consider that these images became the referents for stereotypes of American difference and diversity. No matter what their creators' intentions, these photos are first and foremost an anthropological catalogue and function within the scopes of that category and its uses. That such photos could be taken to delineate a historical period and document moments of an unknown or future national percourse and strategy rather than express an essentialist figuration, and also fold to the service of exclusionary practices in immigration, illustrates the ambiguous and multivalent nature of the medium itself.

The breadth of the two photographers' involvement in the documentation of immigrant communities, and the labor and social issues that were swirling around them, is of insurmountable importance and has influenced social photography through the decades. Admirably, Hine and Riis made it their business to immerse themselves in the situations they sought to illustrate. However, that this was sometimes done with what might be considered force and disregard for the private aspects of the lives of those they documented is offensive to say the least.

The now mythic Ellis Island is of paramount importance as an entity that allowed the two photographers access to their subjects. The doors to the future were a clearing-house of population types. Ellis Island was where the typecasting for the future nation took place, where the process of inclusion and exclusion continued for those who had made their way there after enduring in the places they had left behind.

Within such a context, photography becomes an aid to a process of selection by which the image of a nation is created. In this sort of imagistic phrenology, types are cast in patterns similar to those already selected through other criteria, for which the correlation through photographic evidence becomes an easily supportable term of differentiation, exclusion, and descriptive of the terms of citizenship.

While it may be said that Hine and Riis helped put into evidence the plight of those they photographed, it could also be said that they issued a potentially damaging anthropological catalogue. The terms by which Hine intended to present his images of workers and immigrants are similar to what came to be one of the tenets of Italian Neorealism cinema: "to show poverty and suffering is to protest against them."[4] But, in fact, the work of selection and exclusion that immigration authorities carried out on Ellis Island was indirectly based on traits that the photography of Hine and Riis highlighted and documented.

Believing that Americans had no idea of who these new arrivals might be, Hine sought to make them "known."[5] At the same time, the physical/pictorial representations of immigrants instilled in the American mind a set of details by which immigrants, or any individual matching them, might be recognized as foreign, different or non-American. Think of the "profiles" used by immigration authorities and police to halt, detain and investigate "suspicious" individuals. An American expression ripe with racism states "they all look alike to me," which references all aspects of difference to a normative WASP standard, thereby denying an individual's distinctive distinguishing racial or ethnic traits and value as individuals.

It may be in fact interesting to think about the representation of inter-immigrant differences themselves. I have often thought by looking at Hine and Riis' photographs that the national/ethnic origins of the subjects could almost be interchangeable. It is at times rather hard to distinguish an Italian immigrant from a Polish-Jewish immigrant from a Greek immigrant from a Slavic immigrant, unless the photographer makes evident a particular piece of clothing or accessory to aid in that distinction. Even in that, however, it would take a certain amount of knowledge of those specific cultural elements to make the identification possible. The 1924 Immigration Exclusions Act designated all the above-named groups as undesirable for immigration into the United States. The dominant traits that rendered them all excludable had been extrapolated from so-called scientific evidence, including photography, which proposed to give proof of the threat they were perceived to pose to "the American way of life."

The relationship of the facelessness of immigrants and their apparent interchangeability within a capitalist structure is indicative of trends in the labor market. The desirability of one or another laboring body is dictated by a person's resistance to exploitation toward overcoming economic hardship and their ability to remain an amorphous presence, at least through the work-day. The anthropological catalogue from which these bodies are extracted seems to remain fairly consistent; so much so that the history of labor, social and emigration politics could be told through photography as a visual narrative. Nevertheless, when shared across cultural realities, visual narratives need translation as much as any linguistic text.

I see photographs of Russian-Jewish gentlemen wrongly identified as Italian by one photographer, and I wonder if Hine and Riis themselves faced this difficulty in naming their subjects. It might explain why the titles of many of their photographs are more generic than specific, such as "Immigrant children at play" or "Immigrant women in sweatshop." There is no doubt as to the well-intentioned activity of Hine or Riis, in illustrating social injustices and inequalities, as well as documenting the diversity that was reaching American shores. However, questions remains regarding their "aestheticization" of immigrants and their erasure of those individuals' lives and cultures as they were entered into a neutralizing catalogue of types. I also find it interesting that while he is quite critical and argumentative regarding the uses of photography in Italy toward the establishment of a "national pedagogy," Giulio Bollati is not as inquisitive regarding the work of a photographer such as Lewis Hine. He seems to miss altogether how the American photographers feel a need to shape a national physiognomy out of what they see as an amorphous mass that is reaching the American shores at the turn of the twentieth century. Bollati's view is that "those who really want to know the people who were our peasants forced to emigrate" have to go to Lewis Hine.[6] It would seem that the power of inscription as proposed by Benjamin has provoked an opposite understanding in this case, by which the images of Hine and Riis have been solidified into "truth."

As an aside that I deem to be an important expression within the American landscape of a similar work and attitude, I would like to remember the work of Edward Sheriff Curtis as another great photographer whose self-appointed mandate was similar to Hine and Riis'. Curtis' unfinished multivolume catalogue of the American Aboriginal Peoples, then termed "the vanishing race," is a highly valuable document. It too, however, given the history of U.S. and Native relations, cannot be considered wholly objective and disinterested. It becomes quickly evident through careful scrutiny that Curtis adorned his subjects with accessories that he himself carried as part of his photographic studio. Without much regard being given to tribal differences or customs, Curtis would ask his subjects to wear pieces of jewelry and other accessories that he had used in previous photographs.

Curtis' imprinting of Native life and his manner of defining American Natives as a "vanishing race," though no doubt well-intentioned, could be considered just as influential in making Aboriginal Peoples invisible as it was in immortalizing their images. The "race" was vanished through an aestheticization that rendered the photographer's subjects noble and distant. Since their most recent history is one that was written by "White" men in "Red" men's blood, pitting their savagery against white civilization, the memory of a noble Indian could only represent a fiction to most Americans. We might also alter the old saying that "the only good Indian is a dead Indian" to say "the only good Indian is one photographed by Curtis." Curtis' depictions of Aboriginals at work fishing, hunting, gathering, weaving, and in general taking care of the everyday were veiled behind the scalping, raping, looting and killing that was regarded in general as more likely activities that they might undertake.

What we might consider is that Curtis' photographic documentation was meant to rescue and preserve what Western culture holds important, not the people themselves but their cultural artifacts and the objects of a past presence. The objects the photographer took with him on site and makes present repeatedly in photographs are ones that were deemed important referents of Native life. The objects are what has remained of that "vanished race." North American Native culture has today been fully inscribed as a culture of objects and fetishism that contradicts the ephemeral value that Natives themselves attached to material things. Quite well in keeping with Western interests in anthropology and archeology, today we can appreciate the beauty of objects that would otherwise have been obfuscated by the living presence of their originators. Though the reality is quite different, what has been propagated in North America and Europe is the idea that Native American culture has vanished. Today it is an obviously different culture, but it continues a set of cultural realities that hold adaptation as their most elemental aspect and thereby negate any sort of photographic fixing. In other words, Native Americans are neither dead nor gone.

Along these very lines, I found myself thinking of what might have been happening in the places that some of the immigrants had left behind, and what the immigrants themselves might have thought of photography and its uses. Photographs were, and are, for migrants a fundamentally important object. Often deprived of all possessions, a migrant is likely to hold a photograph of his or her family and loved ones as a threadbare link to his or her world.

Aside from the record of photographs of the sort that Hine, Riis and countless other photographers accumulated, most of which foreground the basest conditions and habits of those they depicted, there exist personal archives of photographs that contradict them. Immigrants sought the help of studio and street photographers, and later of friends and relatives, to construct their own archives of life in their new homes. While indeed many of the photographs may show people at work, or in their everyday garb, a good portion of these photographs were meant to either reassure the folks back home that all was well, or to impress them with the newfound fortunes. In either case, it was more advisable to wear one's own Sunday suit, to look well-fed and clean-cut, everything in place and assertive of a new status. Some immigrants did own a Sunday suit of clothes but others did not, and so studios would also provide a change of clothes as an additional prop to their stylized backgrounds. Of course these archives are harder to analyze since they are privately held, and what might be found in the old photo studios is minimal at this point. Nevertheless, this alternative source of photographic images is of primary importance and defines a personal visual space that was not afforded by the aggressive and often invasive photography that met immigrants at the doors of the new nation, or chased them down in their ghettos.

In many ways that is what brought me to the photography of Giovanni Verga. Verga, Hine and Riis might seem to make up an odd grouping, photography being their only common denominator. However, with Sicilian emigrants constituting a large portion of those who left the Italian peninsula and found themselves entering the United States, the approximation begins to take on added significance. Historical circumstances make potential emigrants of Verga's subjects and, most likely, many became just that.

As I have previously suggested, while Verga's subjects are only potential emigrants who retain an identity and a place, Hine and Riis' portraits represent both sides of the coin of emigration: anonymity on one side, and erasure and transformation on the other. Theoretically, the effacement of both sides is what should over generations result in the recognition of the substance of each individual's worth held within the trace of the past culture and become valid currency in a diverse society. There is no doubt that Verga's images do as much to aestheticize his subjects as any photograph, but in large part that is a residual effect of what we might think of photography as a form that we relate to other forms of representation, such as painting.

Much as Curtis must have thought his images capable of preserving a "disappearing" reality, Hine and Riis must have thought it of great importance to record the events of immigration. The need to fix that which might vanish upon encountering a stronger, dominant culture, might tell us that the photographers recognized the effect of official policy toward those being assimilated. As Native Americans had been said to be a "vanishing race," so Hine and Riis might have thought to save the images of immigrant hordes from the effect melting pot. And Verga, whose Verist writings were also concerned with recording a world that he must have considered to be vanishing, most likely found in photography a more direct, and at times human, mode for recording presence.

## PHOTOGRAPHY'S STORY

As never before in history, photography made possible the technological appearance of the bodies that in themselves define the technology of empires and colonialism; the bodies that make possible the functioning of industry. Up until it was pictured, labor had only been fully visible to itself. The appearance of laboring bodies in photography marks the beginning point of ethical questions revolving around the uses of technology. It may therefore seem contradictory to state that this first stage also marks the decline of individual laborers' identities by their insertion into the realm of technological production. Photography opened the door to mechanical and/or technological memory, thereby expanding the only memory through which labor previously existed, which is to say the things it produced. Hine and Riis in part supported this emancipation by irrevocably casting immigrants and workers into the game as some of the first photographic memories of the nation's future.

Exactly how Hine and Riis succeed in their activation of images toward a national ideal might be explained by a perusal of the photographs themselves. The photographers depend on classical poses and compositions to make their foreign subjects palatable. There is no question as to the foreignness of those bodies shown in their "natural" habitats, but the rhetorical figuration of foreignness makes them both different and exploitable for the apparent lack of cultural specificity. Jacob Riis' depictions (*Mulberry Bend, Vagabond in the Heart of Baxter Street, Playground*) all show the dispossessed in a run-down, decrepit environment. There is of course no mention as to whether that environment was of the immigrants' own making or whether it is what was bequeathed them by their benevolent hosts.

Photographs can only ask or answer such questions tangentially; it is left up to the viewer to deduce whether or not the conditions in which these new arrivals find themselves are of their own making. It is how such things are interpreted that goes to shore up the American myth of the land of opportunity and individuals will be considered "American" only once they have been able to pull themselves "up by their bootstraps." Unfortunately, the socio-economic conditions of the dispossessed are translated as a lack of social and cultural value in the mind of those who are already part of the American landscape.

In any case, whether in a generalized landscape or in a more close-up and "intimate" depiction, Riis' subjects tend to be represented in orderly formations: in lines, seated, at tables, in sweatshops, in markets. *Jersey Street, Italian Mother and Child*, c. 1890, is one of those impressive photographs that turns to classical and religious imagery to establish a connection with its viewers. The mother and child are seated at the back of a storage area that may also function as their residence (Figure 5.1).

They are classical neither in body or expression, nor religious in the sense that they do not elicit adoration. Their pose is a trope that effectively evinces a familiarity that pulls us into the composition to elicit a sense of pity rather than compassionate identification. It is a photograph that requires the viewer to feel for the subject and then question the

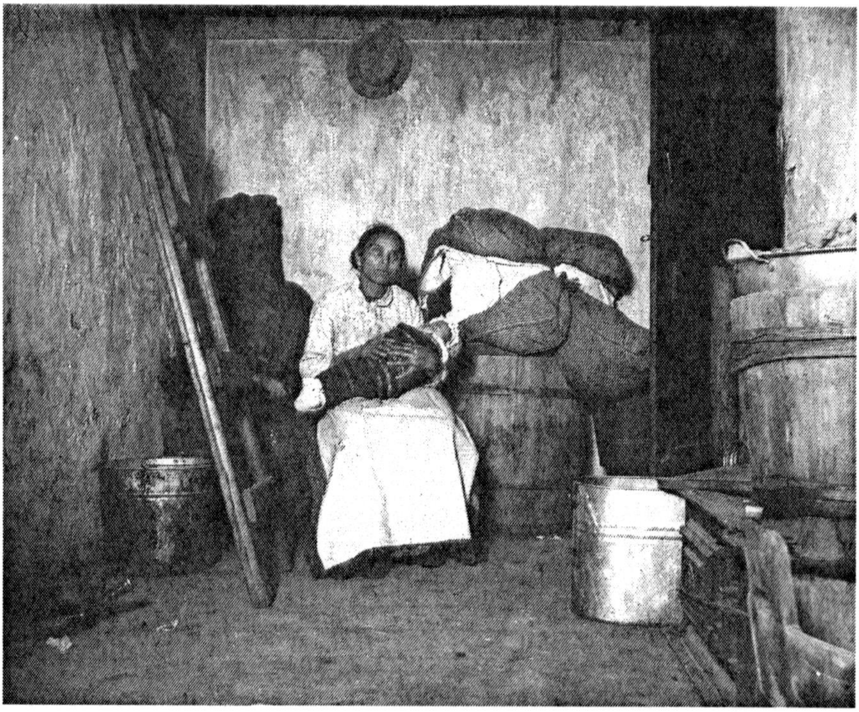

**Figure 5.1. *Jersey Street, Italian Mother and Child.* Jacob Riis, c. 1890. Permission granted by the Museum of the City of New York.**

conditions in which it appears, suggesting assimilation as a strategy for the betterment of their lot. What seems to keep the effective image of the mother and child steadfast in the place in which we see them might very well be the label that is attached to them. Being Italian functions almost as an obstacle to their assimilation, a challenge to the society that receives them. While these depictions want us to believe that their lot will improve once they become Americans, we know of course that it is not that simple. Change and assimilation will only be possible once the subjects themselves become willing to overcome their qualifying extra-national label.

Lewis Hines' photographs are not dissimilar to Riis' as far as settings and composition, but they do draw closer to the entities they capture and document. Hine seems to show more of an interest in the individual personalities of his subjects. Whether they are valued more or less socially is up for discussion, but there is no denying that we are drawn closer into the personal space of Hines' subjects, allowing us to scrutinize their eyes and faces with ease. Even if it is not directly documented in the legend of the photograph, or anywhere else for that matter, these people appear to have an identity that calls viewers to consider how it might be interpreted and how it might be incorporated into the American landscape. Have a look at *Young Russian Jewess*, Ellis Island, 1905, or *Arriving in the Promised Land*, Ellis Island, 1905, or *Italian Family at Ellis Island*, c. 1905, and Russian Steel Workers, 1907–1908, or Young Girl in Cotton Mill, N. Carolina, c. 1908. These photographs of workers and immigrants do not represent two distinct groups. There is an obvious and historically determined overlap that as time progressed blurred the "infiltration" of "foreign" laborers that will become a meaningful presence in American society.

Hine and Riis effectively tapped into culturally active and integrated imagery that rendered the reading of their images more immediate and meaningful. The two photographers made foreign figurative details apparent to "American" eyes foreign figurative details through familiar visual tropes and indices. In so doing, they also impressed on their viewing public a neutral and generalized image of the foreign bodies that was meant to facilitate their acceptance and eventual transformation into "American" bodies. Aside from the accidental appearance of a fraction of one of their shadows in a frame here and there, I know of no self-portraits by Hine and Riis posing with their immigrant subjects. And yet, this accidental inclusion might be more telling than a direct self-portrait because it expresses both the fear of being inversely assimilated into the amorphous immigrant mass and the notion that we are all immigrants to this place.

Hine and Riis created a compendium of laboring bodies for the nation by recording and cataloguing the immigrant masses as they transitioned into American society, a body of work that was of no direct use to those pictured. Because their photographs pay no attention to what is signified by the subjects beyond their predetermined use, the portrayal of these immigrant bodies becomes exploitative. There is no denying that the two photographers used their work to argue for the improvement of conditions in which the immigrants lived and worked. However, the immigrants functioned as little more than anonymous bodies over which to superimpose an idealized history of a culturally diverse and free nation, without necessarily giving them specific attention. An interesting dilemma this, in which photography serves doubly to historicize and de-historicize. The ideological imposition of a predetermined history, such as what the work of Hine and Riis serve, functions as a denial of Benjamin's acclamation of photography as a potential instrument of revolutionary value. Far from giving its subjects agency through presence, in such cases photography institutes their presence as part of a political/social discourse that is the photographer's own or emanates from the photographer's preconditioned response to his subjects. The subject is in fact made absent outside of the technology that records it and, as such, comes to represent the first threat to both its individuality and collectivity. Given the medium's ability to reproduce and create a series of similar images, the erasure is rendered complete. It does not take much of a leap of the imagination to relate this exercise to the generation of exploitable classes through racist and exclusionist immigration policies.

The photographic image involves its viewers in a recollection of form that is reminiscent of, but divorced from, remembering; in other words re-constituting, in a material and therefore socially and politically viable direction. The illusion of a recognizable and interpretative surface that is created by images erases the memory of depth that social activism requires and distracts from the fundamental questions that must be posed regarding the use and function of photographic representation. Photography might very well be a social tool of immediate impact but, with time, it always risks the acquisition of an aesthetic patina that could potentially reduce its efficacy. As an archive of the future, Hine and Riis' photographs of immigrants and workers give us the form of a condition that was the New York they saw; not a slice of their time, but their personal testimony to a situation. They offer us some of the first technological memories of ourselves as *not ourselves*, an archive of the future of their time in which the images themselves have become objects of American culture.

## NOTES

1. Holmes, Oliver Wendell Holmes, "The Stereoscope and the Stereograph" (1859), "Sun Painting and Sun Sculpture"(1861), "Doings the Sunbeam" (1863) in *The Atlantic Monthly*, Boston.

2. Walter Benjamin, "The Work of Art in the Age of Mechanical Reproduction," in *Illuminations: Essays and Reflections* (New York: Schocken Books, 1987), 20–21.

3. Ilaria Serra, *The Imagined Immigrant: Images of Italian Emigration to the United States between 1890 and 1924* (Madison: Fairleigh Dickinson University Press, 2010). Through the study of newspapers, film, popular and personal testimonies, Serra constructs a useful compendium of the elements that have gone to construct reciprocal iconographic signs within the Italian and American imaginary by which both populations relate to each other.

4. Naomi Rosenblum and Walter Rosenblum, *Lewis W. Hine* (Paris: Editions Nathan, 1992), 1.

5. Ibid., 3.

6. Bollati, *L'italiano*, 164.

# 6

# Imaginative Contradictions

## *Von Gloeden's Disruptive Bodies of Representation*

Nowadays, we have come to assume that, aside from specific examples such as Robert Mapplethorpe (and even there the exceptions are many), the subject of nude photography has always been mostly female. This has not always been the case; it has been demonstrated and well documented that the genre was originally dominated by images of male and female children.[1] With a greater concern and awareness of potential misuses of media and the connotations they have come to carry in association with child abuse and pedophilia, what might be objectionable to us today was quite an acceptable practice during the Victorian and Edwardian periods. Historically, it has been far more problematic and controversial for artists to photograph nude men and women rather than children.

Photographs of female nudes were considered rather transgressive and, as such, became easily absorbed by a booming industry of erotica, and into sometimes more specific subgenres such as what came to be known as "French postcards." On the other hand, in the usually convoluted logic of these things, these photos and postcards found justification in their subject matter since it was quite the common belief that adult female models who would pose for this sort of photography were nothing more than prostitutes. In the case of colonial subjects, viewed as racially inferior beings, the parameters of decency and morality were not thought to apply to them and so nude photographs of those subjects inflated the curio market during the late colonial periods.

The situation did change somewhat with the rise of the photographic school of *Photo Pictorialism* in the 1890s. The *Pictorialists'* evaluation of photography as an art *on par* with other arts allowed the new medium to borrow freely from painterly conventions and establish a closer link with the more noble art of painting. This crossing over of aesthetics also provided photographers with the opportunity to blend in an increased awareness of the physical beauty and sensual/sexual qualities of the male nude.

Nevertheless, male nude photography was strongly stigmatized by the perceived danger that to partake in photographing or viewing male nudes might influence one toward homosexuality. Even at the height of interest in the male nude, steps were taken to reduce the perceived threat of homosexuality by emphasizing the artistic concern and content of the work. Even before taking on the name, the *Pictorialists* came together to form a loose group that came to be called the "aesthetic school" of photography. Photographers who adhered to the "aesthetic school's" activities worked primarily in the United States, Italy, and Britain. They rejected Victorian dictates as they pursued their interests in the male nude and the out-of-doors, and sought inspiration and guidance from the arts of Classical Greece and Rome.

Representative of these concerns was Henry Peach Robinson, a member of the British Photographic Society. Frustrated by the failure of the BPS to recognize photography's artistic possibilities, Robinson founded *The Linked Ring Group* in 1892. Among the members of the *Ring* were Frank Sutcliffe and Alfred Stieglitz. These photographers not only sought to have their medium recognized as a legitimate art form, but also expressed their desire to distance themselves from the increasing popularization of the medium caused by the introduction of simpler, more portable and accessible cameras.

Members of *The Linked Ring Group* would eventually be among the founders of the *Pictorialist* movement, and proponents of a photography that would emulate painting and etching. Having become familiar with the group and its ideals, the American photographer Fred Holland Day soon became a member.[2] Widely recognized as the "grandfather of *Pictorialism*," Alfred Stieglitz would eventually move to the U.S. and extend the influence of this type of photography via his fine art journal *Camerawork* (1903–1917).[3]

Other photographers outside the *Ring*'s sphere of influence reflected similar interests and aesthetic concerns; Baron von Gloeden, a German expatriate living in Taormina, Sicily, was one of these artists. Taormina's history and location could be said to embody the ideals of the "aesthetic school," and it is not by accident that von Gloeden's choice of residence was also one preferred by Grand Tourists for its cultural connections to Classical Greece. So taken were the members of the *Ring* with the photographic results achieved by the baron that a group of them traveled to Sicily to visit with him. As a result, the *Linked Ring* journal *Photogram* published a special issue in 1894 on "photographing the nude," accompanied by von Gloeden's photos.[4] By this time, "the nude" had come to mean that the subjects were almost always exclusively male. As this type of photography found acceptance, the commercialization of the images and their increased circulation brought von Gloeden greater popularity and business, especially since his photographs not only insinuated but made visible idealized notions of a Mediterranean Arcadia.

## THE MEDITERRANEAN

The history of the attraction for Mediterranean men within the homosexual world is rich and long-standing, with plenty of literary and artistic works to document its effects and powers of inspiration. Robert Aldrich's *The Seduction of the Mediterranean: Writing, Art and Homosexual Fantasy* (1995) is an important contribution to the study of the phenomenon, its culture, origins, and lasting traces. In short, and so as not to repeat Aldrich's words, the Mediterranean represents an Arcadic environment indicative of what might have been either lost or never developed in Northern, more puritanical environments. Associated with Greek classical and Renaissance models, the Mediterranean was (is?) presumed to have maintained a cultural connection with those past ages. It offered Grand Tourists, artists, and writers a lingering glimpse and possible hope for the recuperation of situations that might be more open and accepting. The Mediterranean sphere appeared to them to be more accepting of what "civilized" nations deemed primitive, including homosexuality. One need only travel to the no-longer hidden corners of the near Mediterranean such as the Amalfi coast, Taormina, Mykonos, and various ports on the North African coast to confirm the legacy of assumptions regarding the region. Its place in the fulfillment of the North's desires through the firmly established tradition of the Grand Tour continues.

Taking Thomas Mann's *Death in Venice* as his point of departure, Robert Aldrich references that novel's main character, Aschenbach, as representative of the struggle of a middle-aged man with his homosexuality. His attraction to a younger man's idealized classical beauty is indicative of a generic condition applicable to any number of artists, writers and intellectuals who similarly struggle(d) with their sexuality.[5] Aldrich names the condition "Aschenbach phenomenon" and defines it as particularly interesting for its blending of an interest for classicism and southern climes with the justification and condonement of homosexuality. Classicism thereby provides a screen of respectability for those who may not be ready to claim their homosexual identity.

> Mann's novel came at the end of a period stretching back to at least the 1700s during which a number of European writers and artists had been drawn to the classic and contemporary Mediterranean with mixed motives, both cultural and homosexual. . . . They made a pilgrimage southward to find culture; they also wanted to find boys: they usually found both. Many of these writers and artists played a large role in forming general European ideas on such subjects as classical art, Renaissance history and contemporary Italy.[6]

As it stands, Mann's *Death in Venice* could be said to represent the struggle of many similarly positioned men of the period, including von Gloeden, with appropriately different conclusions to their situations. Since the situation was far from singular, it led to the creation and substantiation of a Mediterranean myth that forms its justifications out of classical texts and images.

The Italian Renaissance had filtered north mostly through the work of masters who were active in France, and by the influence of Caterina de' Medici's enthronement as Queen of France. The influential Renaissance philosopher Marsilio Ficino's (1433–1499) commentaries and translations of Plato into Latin are all important in having conditioned attitudes toward homosexual love during the Renaissance and beyond. Ficino's *De amore*, a rereading of Plato's *Symposium*, is plainly a treatise on homosexual love in which he is, nevertheless, very careful to separate sodomy out of the notion of Platonic love and attraction.[7] Ficino, and the Platonic revolution that he led in Florence under the patronage of the Medici, signaled a rebirth of culture that countered the decadent nature of classical Platonism.

The Renaissance constituted a more direct approach to Christianity that also offered an opening toward diversity and dialogue. The somewhat relaxed attitude of the Italian Renaissance toward same-sex male relations made it a source of inspiration and justification for homosexuality.[8] One of its effects was that it also established the necessary continuum to an idealized corporeal presence in the Mediterranean regions for future seekers of the remnants of that idyllic period.

Another enlightening trait of the "Aschenbach phenomenon" is that it also communicates the "ambivalent feeling authors held about the South, both its lands and its peoples."[9] It may well be that the Renaissance itself could have generated this ambivalence. The bodies that come to represent a neoclassical ideal are merely the shell of those ancient ones from which the Renaissance distilled an essence which, when blended with Christian mores, produced the doctrine of Neo-Platonism. As a result, the authors that dealt with the "south . . . its lands and its peoples," being well aware that they were dealing not with the creators or inhabitants of the classical period, must have felt that distance. But these surrogates, who happened to have been born in the places of antiquity, fulfilled, at least in part for such seekers, the desire for a closer proximity to that world.

One undeniable fact that must have been thoroughly frustrating was that, while they might be the descendants of ancient cultures, these young men were often ignorant of their heritage. The visitors' reaction to this is at times only lightly palpable, but usually such ignorance elicits nothing but an arrogant disgust. It is not surprising then to notice, in the nineteenth and twentieth centuries, the disturbing and insistent association between representations of sexuality and manifestations of illness: cholera, tuberculosis, typhoid, and eventually HIV and AIDS. Interestingly enough, contagious illnesses are assigned origins and popular names related to locales that are not the supposedly clean and pure environments from which the travelers arrive. Sexually transmitted diseases all carry qualifiers that situate their origins abroad, outside of the normative and disinfected environment of the First World, where in recent history AIDS and HIV are also said to have originated.

Such examples reflect an "ethnocentrism and cultural arrogance [that] are underlying motifs in much writing about the Mediterranean, coexisting with admiration, enjoyment and idolization."[10] The paradox however subsists in the notion that for individuals the likes of von Gloeden, as well as the travelers who populate the writings of the Grand Tour and beyond, the Mediterranean stands as a curative for northern ailments. Obviously, the real or imagined cure-all carries within it the potent counteractive and threatening dose of ailments for both sides of the equation.

## E. M. FORSTER

The British writer E. M. Forster expressed many a northern traveler's thoughts when he wrote that Italy was where "things prohibited in England became possible."[11] Yet, when proximity to the indigenous population is involved, a touch of danger is always felt and expressed which conditions the exhilaration of meeting the exotic. Travel literature often depicts Italians as primitive and brutal; their presence in the landscape seems to be rather incidental, if not downright bothersome. The excerpt from Forster's *Room with a View,* quoted herein in Chapter 2, offers a clear indication of the animalistic nature attached to Italians. It is a trait that is made to appear to assault the British sensibilities of Lucy and Emerson, as the close proximity of the danger of the situation sends a shiver of pleasure to rise through their bodies. Foster finds in Italy and Italians a potentially liberatory character that is as puzzling as it is exciting. *Room with a View,* but also *Where Angels Fear to Tread* and "The Story of Panic," all include moments in which the exalted culture is contrasted by the threatening presence of Italians who appear to function as catalysts for the collapsing and breaking of social limits and constraints. The Italians never seem to benefit from the relationships they establish with the visiting English folk. And, even though much of what the English fear is based on their being exploited by the shifty Italians, the latter do not garner much gain from any of the relationships. What is in any case clear is that Italy and the Mediterranean have served many for varied purposes, among which is the "continuing power of Italy to effect sexual revelation (whether hetero or homosexual)."[12]

It is very important that the Italian South in particular, which as part of Magna Graecia holds a close connection to classical Greek moral ideals, seems to allow greater freedoms. It is in that capacity that it brings travelers closer to an alternative to more rigid lives as they might be lived in the northern reaches of Europe. Unfortunately, these alternatives were often associated with a primitiveness and backwardness that not only seemed to negate modernization but to be fully incompatible with it, which in turn negated the possibility of exporting the lessons gained there.

E. M. Forster could, however, be said to have taken back with him at least some of that influence, as suggested by his posthumously published novel, *Maurice* (1971).[13] His only explicitly homosexual novel, *Maurice* qualifies that in the South one might find in "antiquity a model . . . that allows men to cross social barriers, not re-create an ancient culture."[14]

It is therefore fascinating to think that the recreation of that ancient culture finds some of its most effective results in the medium of photography, whose main characteristic is said to be the accurate recording of reality in the present. Before the advent of photography, Italy and the Mediterranean provided the subject matter for much homoerotic if not homosexual art, painting, and sculpture. Often, mythological narratives were used to skillfully disguise the homosexual subject matter but, as trends developed toward new technologies and movements, such as realism and impressionism, the more classical representations lost favor among painters and sculptors.[15] The homoerotic subject found a clean transition into the field of photography, and into the aesthetic field of view of Wilhelm von Gloeden as one the more popular photographers of the late nineteenth and early twentieth centuries.[16]

## THE BARON VON GLOEDEN

Wilhelm von Gloeden's art was influenced by the work of the German artists Hans von Marées and Adolf von Hildebrand, as well as Michetti, Burne-Jones, and Alma-Tadema, all of whose work von Gloeden had seen in exhibitions during his extensive travels.[17] Marées (1837–1887) was the clearest exponent of homoerotic Arcadian imagery of the period. Born in Dessau, Marées studied in Berlin and then frequented the artistic milieu of that city before moving definitively to Italy in 1864. Marées used classical mythology as inspiration for his homoerotic works. There is in fact a greater frequency of male nudes in Marées' work than in that of any other of his contemporaries. It is also interesting to note that the majority of Marées' works associate male nudity with oranges, a typically Mediterranean fruit. The orange trees in his works not only signify a Mediterranean and Arcadian setting, they are inspired by, and refer to, the still existing orange grove in Sorrento. Marées often visited the grove as a place for his encounters with the young men of the Neapolitan coast.[18]

Even with the preponderance of homoerotic subjects in his works, Marées' sexuality, or at least his own sense of it, remains mostly unclear. Despite this, the great "love" of his life appears to have been Adolf Hildebrand, a young aspiring German sculptor he met in Rome in 1867. Though their relationship was established on a father/son, teacher/pupil level, Marées' feelings for Hildebrand were expressed by him as being as meaningful and true as an expression of "the thing."[19] Marées was commissioned in 1873, with Hildebrand, to produce murals for the Naples Zoological Station. Marées' paintings in the station's library are deeply representative of an idealized relationship between Northern and Southern Europe, in this case Germany and Italy; "of classical and peasant life, on the one hand, and modern scholarly life on the other. . . . North and South, puritan and permissive, nature and art (or science) are contrasted."[20] Of course, these designations and contrasts are constructed by the German in relation to an idealized South whose population has fallen from grace and contradicts its past by its present. It is at this juncture that von Gloeden finds a coincidence not only with Marées but with most artists, writers and intellectuals who traveled to the southern reaches of Europe.

Wilhelm von Gloeden's biography is a mixture of fact and myth, documentation and conjecture that nevertheless goes toward forming the image of a man who, unwilling to conform to life in his native Germany, strikes out in search of a place where he could be himself. Born in 1856 in Volkshagen, he is encouraged in his artistic interests by his stepfather, Baron von Hammerstein. Von Gloeden enrolled in the Weimar Arts Academy, where he became involved in the Beaux Arts and Music. At this point in his life, the unrest caused by his sexuality is referred to by his biographers as "an illness"; listed variously as consumption, a lung ailment and tuberculosis, the condition eventually led von Gloeden to Berlin to seek out medical help. Whether as a result of the doctor's suggestions that "he leave Prussia for a warmer, drier climate," or due to the fact that in Berlin he meets the expatriate painter Otto Geleng, von Gloeden leaves for Sicily in 1876.[21] Geleng had lived in Taormina since 1863, and upon hearing of von Gloeden's "illness" he suggested that the baron move there to discover "the key to everything."[22]

There is in the two men a correspondence of interests that suggests that their initial understanding was based on more than just a helpful suggestion for the baron's health. The Grand Tour being at the time a requirement toward a complete education to which many Northerners subscribed, Geleng's descriptions of the "idealized Greek world" of Taormina were not wasted. His friends and acquaintances, who also sought to discover the heritage of Western culture that was still to be found in all its innocence in Italy, were very much taken by his tales. But Geleng and von Gloeden's meeting and sharing of aesthetic interests falls into a pattern of homosexual mentorship that is recognizable by the markers of a well-established pattern in its relationship with the Mediterranean. Additionally, writers such as Leslie and Weiermair support the notion that Taormina represented for von Gloeden an escape from a repressive and oppressive society where homosexuality was disdained. As an example these writers cite the downfall of von Gloeden's stepfather, a successful newspaperman and advisor to the Kaiser Wilhelm. Various sources report von Hammerstein's decline as having been due to a number of different causes. Whether as a result of financial finagling, the publication of sensitive materials related to the Kaiser, or a homosexual scandal, the mere mention of this last possibility gives an indication of the status of homosexuality within that society. Again, a cumulative consideration of the events that led to von Gloeden's departure suggests that his less-than-specific illness may have been his homosexuality. Could "consumption" also be taken to be a term describing the "ailment" of homosexuality that sent many in search of better climes? The prescription of the warmer and drier regions of the Mediterranean would fit perfectly as a cure. The availability of a mythic cure, a pharmakon of mythical stature located where life was more simple, more primitive, more in touch with the past, stimulates the exploratory spirit. The additional presence of a classically influenced philosophy arising from those same places justified homosexuality's relation to a more ancient, classical era, and its continued existence and practice. Just as those geographical regions stereotypically appear to negate production in a capitalist, industrial sense, so homosexuality's stereotypically leisurely manner and negation of biological reproductivity might also appear to run counter to the interests of modernity and finds more affinity with pre-modern societies. Whether this is anthropologically true, as some intellectuals such as Pier Paolo Pasolini and writers like Paul Bowels have intimated in their works, or whether it is a romanticized projection on the part of a privileged population remains an open question. Whatever defines this relationship, it is by this sense of apparent congruency that homosexuality often comes to participate in systems that structurally resemble aspects of colonialism and imperialism.

Taormina presented the perfect setting for someone striving to escape the dictates of a conventional society and begin their life anew. The town is situated on the side of Monte Tauro, on the east coast of Sicily, high above the sea. The railroad line reached the Giardini Station on the shore below, but the town of Taormina itself was only accessible via a rough path up the side of Monte Tauro until Geleng, who had married locally and had been elected mayor, constructed the first carriage road up to the town.[23]

The late-medieval town is constructed on a base of Greek temples, theatres and roadways. Roman aqueducts, archways and cisterns are overlaid on the Greek matrix. Its Greek amphitheatre is situated over the Ionian sea, with the volcano Etna looming in the background. A vegetation of grape vines, oranges, lemons, fig trees, and cascades of bougainvilleas growing among crumbling walls and narrow streets was nothing if not attractively romantic and filled with the atmosphere of Magna Graecia. All this in one place, and isolated at the furthest reaches of Europe.

Today, the ancient town of Taormina has retained some of the lure of the past. As one internet tourist guide confides, Taormina is a "city of art and a seaside resort, a place that fascinates and enraptures you, that seduces you and ties you to it, is still an elitist tourist resort today . . ."[24] Unfortunately, while the guide mentions Johann Wolfgang Goethe's visit to Taormina, and goes on to name some famous homosexual artists who have visited the town, the longtime resident and patron of Taormina that was von Gloeden is referenced nowhere.

It didn't take long for von Gloeden to establish himself in Taormina and to gain the sympathy of the locals. The story goes that, given the baron's permissive lifestyle and the traffic of young men in and out of his home, and the town's more conservative and conventional mores, he and Geleng soon fell out of sorts. There seem to be some discrepancies regarding von Gloeden's own practices. Charles Leslie asserts that "Wilhelm von Gloeden was a self-acknowledged and fervently practicing homosexual. The midnight revels in the Villa Gloeden and in the high meadows of Monte Ziretto were, in fact, orgies . . . ."[25] On the other hand, Charles-Henri Favrod reports that "the baron never organized orgies, even if he did receive all of the homosexual gentry of the time. His home was managed by the daughter of his mother's first nuptial bed. She was an austere old maid from the Mucleburg who would not have tolerated any excesses. According to his models, there never were any."[26] Von Gloeden's disaccord with Geleng may have come about as a result of the older artist's jealousies toward his newly arrived, younger and more successful friend. As with most information regarding von Gloeden's life, we have often multiple and contradictory memories. Let it suffice here to say that the baron's own living quarters were separate from his half-sister's, and that she "always retired and always rose much earlier than Wilhelm—undisturbed, leaving her brother and his male guests to their cigars and brandy. She was usually not aware—or chose not to be aware—of still other guests, local youths—who arrived even later."[27] As for his models, posing for photographs that could be justified as classical studies to make a little money was one thing, but to admit to having participated in homosexual orgies would be quite another, especially in a small Sicilian town.

Another area in which information is vague is in relation to von Gloeden's experiences with photography. The baron's initiation into the medium was probably the result of a number of different events that must have led him to choose it as an alternative to painting, with which he had not been very successful. After having settled in Taormina von Gloeden traveled frequently to Rome, Capri and Naples. It is in Naples that in 1878 he met his cousin Wilhelm (Guglielmo) Plüschow, who was already an active photographer. Plüschow's specialty was in male nudes, sometimes posed in classical contexts. A passing comparison between his photographs and the baron's readily show a deep difference. Plüschow's are much more raw, less abstracted images than his cousin's eventual soft, sensual photographs that seem to arise from the imagination rather than present themselves as stimuli to the eye. Nevertheless, it could be said that von Gloeden found in Plüschow an initial spark.

Other important meetings for von Gloeden took place in 1880 when he first encountered the Abruzzese artist Francesco Paolo Michetti (1851–1929), whose realist work had achieved international fame. Michetti had taken up photography around 1871, as an aid for his painterly studies before exploring the medium's own qualities. He seems to have had some influence on von Gloeden's art in that it was he who explicitly expressed the idea of celebrating Mediterranean classicism through photography. The baron's meeting of the photographer Giovanni Crupi (1859–1925) in Taormina, who is said to have provided him with basic lessons in photography, its technology and chemistry, might very well have been a fundamental professional relationship.

Von Gloeden's work quickly attracted the attention of foreign and Italian writers and artists such as Oscar Wilde, Matilde Serao, Gabriele D'Annunzio, and Eleonora Duse. This fame brought requests for his work from journals, photographic exhibitions and competitions. In 1893 he showed at the *Linked Ring* Gallery and with the *Royal Photographic Society* in England, where he was awarded a Gold Medal, the result of which was the publication of a selection of his photographs in the journal *The Studio*. That same year he traveled through Germany, Sicily, and Turkey, and the German journal *Kunst für Alle* published some of his photos with the telling caption "naked natives of the island of Sicily."[28] The photographs von Gloeden makes in Turkey begin to show some of the compositional elements and attire that will become common in his reconstructions of classical environments back in Taormina. There is a discrepancy that should be pointed out here regarding his travels and photographs from this period, one that emerges occasionally and which the Alinari Archives staff helped me resolve somewhat. It has been widely reported that von Gloeden traveled to Tunisia sometime between 1893 and 1900; many of his photos have been reported as being from there. However, some of the staff at the Alinari Archives were very adamant about the fact that the baron had not traveled to Tunisia, even though photographs at the Archive show "Tunisian" landmarks. This conundrum demonstrates that there is still a swirl of confusion about von Gloeden's activities. This issue in particular goes to show that either his Turkish photographs have been enlisted by Western homosexuals as a way to fulfill an extension of the Grand Tour, and expand the horizons of permissiveness as Southern Europe became "modernized," or the baron's ethnic cross-dressing was so effective as to dupe most observers. Of course, the possibility of a misinformed technician at the Alinari Archives also stands forth since in further communications I was told that the place in question was Tunisia.

The devastating earthquake of December 1908 in Calabria and Sicily gave von Gloeden another subject through which to show his concern and dedication to the place he had chosen as a home. He traveled about the region to photograph the effects of the quake and a selection of those was published by the Italian Photographic Society under the title "Messina and Reggio after the earthquake" (1909). Von Gloeden was unquestionably the king of the "hermaphroditic peninsula," as the art historian Carlo Bertelli defined the regions where foreigners settled to live the Hellenic ideal of same-sex love.[29] Nevertheless, the images of the earthquake helped von Gloeden establish himself beyond the Arcadian reconstructions as a photographer with a wide range of interests and skills. His historical documentation, journalistic reportage and aesthetically dictated reconstructions rounded out his palette and helped von Gloeden achieve a stable professional and artistic presence.

There is no doubt that the support of respectable institutions for his work beyond the ephebic reconstructions helped to legitimate von Gloeden's photos beyond their sexual erotic aspects. There is however another more subtle and culturally determined frame of reference that lends support to his work. Most of von Gloeden's models were local boys who were extracted from their social and cultural context to be placed and posed in a constructed one. The cast of a foreign gaze situated these young men within an idealized representation alien to their bodies. While von Gloeden's sense of the local inhabitants was not the same as what the caption "naked natives of the island of Sicily" suggests, it is that very attitude that facilitated and popularized his activity. As Roland Barthes noted of von Gloeden's work, his practice reflects an almost "ritualistic manner [toward the subjects that allows it] to become socially acceptable."[30]

## THE BARON'S PHOTOGRAPHS

Robert Aldrich sorts von Gloeden's photographs into three main categories: ancient ruins and landscapes, peasants, and boys. The photographs suggest to him a sense of comradeship among the boys (and the photographer?). While some photos may be suggestive, as a result of their open display of frontal nudity and sensual interaction between the subjects, there is an absence of explicit sexual activity and the contextual atmosphere is strongly Arcadian.[31]

Von Gloeden himself identified four main elements within his own work: the classical ideal, peasant boys, Italian landscapes, and explorations into the technological potential of the camera. The baron never makes direct mention of his sexual interest in the boys, but I would venture to say that it is that sexual tension to establish the narrative link between the four elements he proposes as guides to approaching his photographs.

Aside from the available reference materials, my experience in directly viewing von Gloeden's photographs is limited to those available in the Alinari Archives in Florence. Out of a total holdings of approximately three thousand prints and negatives, I analyzed over one thousand images printed from the archive's negatives. While not all the prints are archival, most are and two hundred of these were organized into a traveling exhibition in the year 2000. Alinari also published a selection for the exhibition catalogue, accompanied by an introduction by Charles-Henri Favrod. To reiterate, the range of von Gloeden's subjects is quite extensive and contradicts common categorization of him as only a photographer of male nudes.

Aldrich's categories cover the range of the baron's images in general terms, but the Alinari Archives reveal a greater variety within each grouping that might be broken down into more specific areas. What follows is my own division as suggested by my consultation of the Alinari Archives:

1. Photographs depicting ancient ruins and landscapes, such as the photographer might also use for the reconstruction of classical scenarios for his models. Sicily keeps perhaps the best preserved architectural landscape of Magna Graecia. The Greek temples and building complexes found on the island are in better shape than in any other area, and with those there is also a wealth of Roman remains. Taormina itself is rich in this architecture, which no doubt gave von Gloeden an instant insight into the possibilities of readily accessing the symbols of neoclassicism for his paintings and photographs. As one travels south along the Italian peninsula and approaches Naples, the light and pastoral landscape of ancient Greece begins to manifest itself. The atmosphere becomes more intense and settled in Sicily, where it provides a ready-made palette.

2. More generalized landscapes from around Sicily and places of his travels, such as Naples. These would include his early photographs of the massive 1908 earthquake in Sicily and Calabria.
3. Photographs of peasants and the general population in and around Taormina, as well as from other places he visited (Figure 6.1).

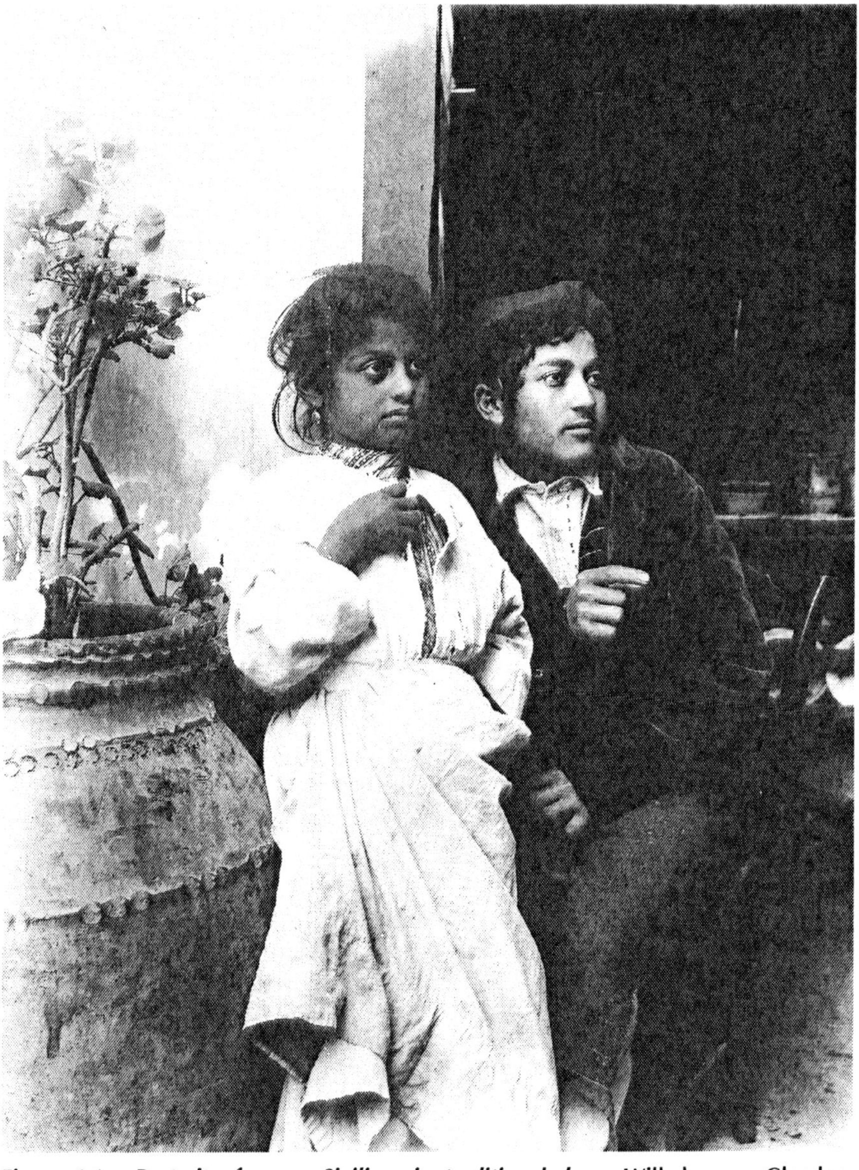

Figure 6.1. ***Portrait of young Sicilians in traditional dress.*** Wilhelm von Gloeden, 1895–1905. Fratelli Alinari Museum Collections-von Gloeden Archive, Florence. Credit: Alinari Archives, Florence.

4. Nude photographs of boys (and occasionally women) in classically reconstructed poses or otherwise. Within this last section we might also define three subsections: a. portraits of individuals, b. group portraits, c. scenes with a vague theme or plot (Figure 6.2).
5. Photographs from his visit to Tunisia and/or Turkey, c. 1909. These include photos of market places and mostly city streets. They show men in their daily attire of cloth capes and turbans, all of which will make up the range of von Gloeden's range of accessories for his photographs. The composition of one photograph in particular is interesting in this series. It is a shot of two young men standing on a roof-top and holding each other close. They are rather small, right in at the center of the composition and what is mostly visible is the city (Istanbul?) as their background. But they are nevertheless the most important element in the photograph because they could be lifted out of the photograph and placed in a Sicilian landscape, Arabic attire and all. These photos are meaningful for their suggestion of von Gloeden's hybridization of Mediterranean cultures.

The silence of postcolonial critics regarding the exoticized and exploited racialized European subjects is rather puzzling since, by overlooking the possibility of an imperialism that is intra-national as it is inter-national, it enables the emergence of a sort of proto-global imperialism. The topic of subaltern realities within the so-called First World has been neglected, and subalternity has been considered only within immigrant or extra-national groups. The result is that it ends up protecting the over-riding dichotomy between European and non-European cultures and precludes the possibilities of more expansive alternative alliances.

Von Gloeden's photographs are a case in point in how they have been used by cultural critics to demonstrate a European tendency to "orientalize" North Africans, all the while neglecting the fact that his Sicilian subjects were in fact orientalized "Europeans."[32] Such an analysis would be very instructive in that the rapport between populations within European countries might unveil within each an *in nuce* expression of their eventual external colonial activities and attitudes.

Roland Barthes, one of our most important thinkers with regards to the creation of mythologies and their function within cultural systems, when faced with von Gloeden's photographs seems to fail to heed his own lessons. Barthes' text in the Twelvetrees edition of von Gloeden's photographs comments that von Gloeden fills his photos "with African bodies. . . . Delacroix used to say that ancient togas were presentable only on Arabs. This notwithstanding, the results here are delectable in the contradiction of all this literary apparatus of an ancient Greek version and the dark bodies of these little peasant gigolos (if anyone of them is still living I hope they can forgive me, I do not mean to insult them) with their dense,

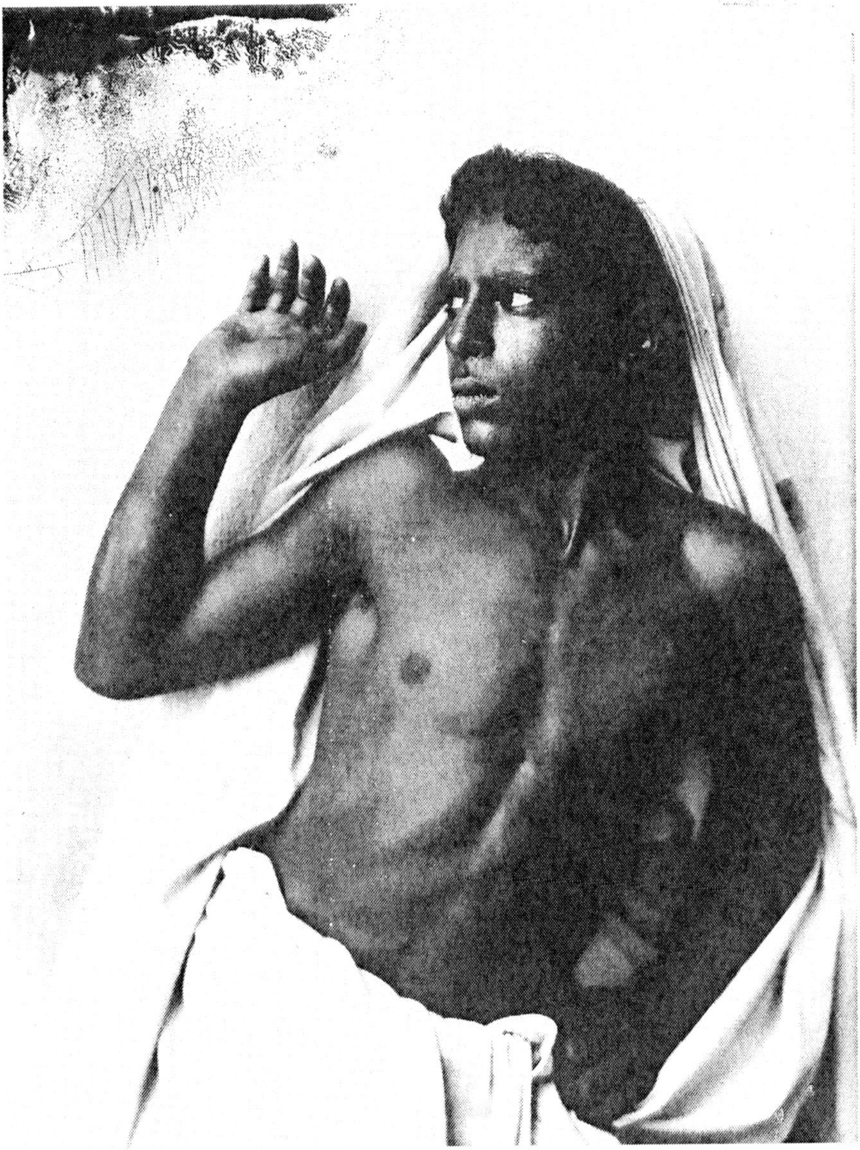

**Figure 6.2.** ***Portrait of a young Sicilian man.*** **Wilhelm von Gloeden, 1895–1905. Fratelli Alinari Museum Collections-von Gloeden Archive, Florence. Credit: Alinari Archives, Florence.**

dark gaze . . ."[33] Barthes goes on to observe that, given photography's direct and unmediated approach, the baron's photographs represent "a collection of details without any hierarchy, without an order. These little Greek gods (contradictory in their darkness) have the dirty hands of peasants, with roughly manicured nails, worn and dirty feet, swollen prepuce in clear view, not stylized (in other words pointed and shrunken)."[34]

Obviously seduced by the photographs, Barthes overlooks his own objectification of the boys through a filter that is an extension of the mythologies of colonialism. As a result, his gaze repeats the systematic (and therefore hierarchical) reinforcement of a taxonomical system imposed by a "superior" viewer onto an "inferior" subject. This may be the function of the baron's photographs, to which Barthes assigns the qualities of "sublime and anatomical at the same time."[35] The sublime that veils the anatomical element fundamental in the definition of power relationships is one of photography's original uses as a tool through which to classify inferior groups by their anatomical differences.

Another troubling aspect of Barthes' description is that he puts the responsibility for seduction on the young men by defining them as "little gigolos." This effectively exculpates the baron and other outsiders of the responsibility for the established order of things. The photograph that follows ideally illustrates the mixing and negation of heterogeneity that Northern European obsession with the Mediterranean tends to produce.

6. Finally, there is a rather small but extremely important category made up by von Gloeden's self-portraits. This is directly indicative of his (Northern) desires in adopting the other's superficial (assigned) qualities, while dismissing their present culture, and assigning value to a past that fulfills the dominant's logocentric desires (Figure 6.3).

Perhaps, the best place to begin in reading von Gloeden's photographs is with a few that directly illustrate the influence of Arcadian aesthetics. It is easy to find poses that suggest statuary that von Gloeden might have seen at the Naples Museum of Anthropology, a place he visited with some frequency. And there are certainly compositions in which we might discern the influence of Caravaggio, Dubufe, Eakins, Fortuny, and Alma-Tadema.[36] However, I think it more important to first cite two important homoerotic paintings that may have had a certain influence on von Gloeden's own compositions, and that find direct correspondents in his photographs. They are Anne-Louis Girodet's *Le sommeil d'Endymion* (1791) and Hippolyte Flaudrin's *Jeune homme nu assis au bord de la mer (étude)* (1835). The recreation of the paintings as photographs shows the baron's interest in following a classical aesthetic. Von Gloeden expands the influence of the classical beyond its philosophical/aesthetic attraction. By peopling his photographs with individuals considered to be the descendants of a lost classical culture, the baron breathes life into mythologicalized figures.

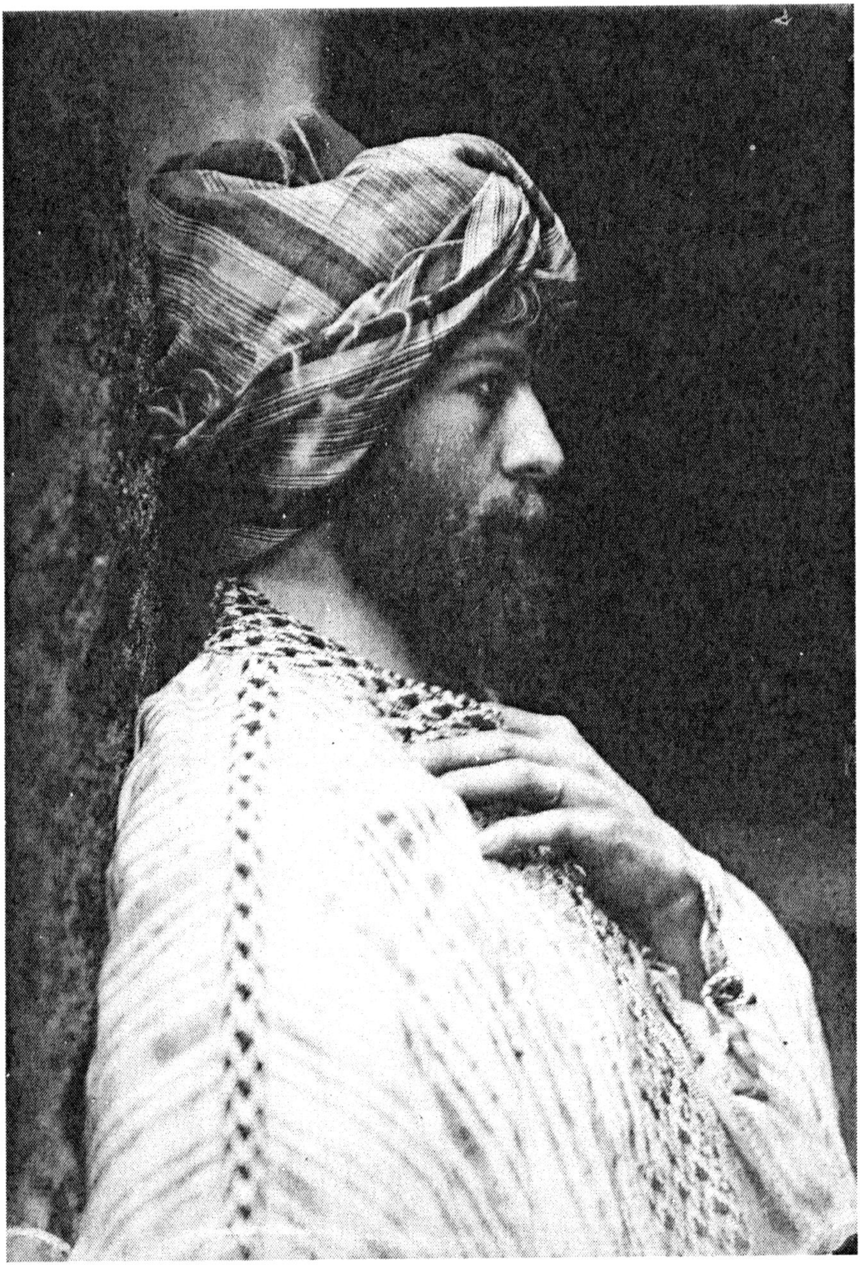

Figure 6.3. ***Self-portrait in oriental dress.*** Wilhelm von Gloeden, c. 1900. Fratelli Alinari Museum Collections, Florence. Credit: Alinari Archives, Florence.

The young men who pose for von Gloeden are mostly identified by the generic titles of the photographs rather than by their real names: *Sicilian Boy, Three Boys, Arab Boy, Two Nudes, Group of Boys, Youth on Tigerskin, Youth with Roses, Youth Sitting on Two Rocks*, all of whom are rendered equal and nameless by circumstance and physicality. These young men are, after all, not themselves but reflections of von Gloeden's desires. Photography thus becomes the cultural mediatory medium between classes, sexes, races, ethnicities, and any other category that is defined as different from that of the photographer himself.

Again, even while most of the baron's favorite subjects were young peasants, fishermen, and shepherd boys, his range of subjects was quite varied. And it goes without saying that the class differences between the baron and his subjects must have facilitated von Gloeden's task. Of course the baron might have in time come to feel close to the people of Taormina, and they to him. There is no question however that von Gloeden's is a self-referential and representational response to subaltern classes for his own use, in his own terms, and toward his own ends.

Victorian resistance to male nudes led the baron to make his work acceptable but overlaying it with an aura of classicism. Von Gloeden's compositions appear to be almost ritualistic in their organization, an aspect that tended to make them more socially acceptable. The Italian art historian Boatto identifies the undressing of models by Rodin as one of the first acts of *dénouement* of the subject in painting, by which the figure remains "dressed" in the sense that it is covered by the veils of mythology.[37] This is precisely von Gloeden's tactic. By draping the veil of mythology and classicism over the bodies of his subjects he participates in this undressing by introducing it into photography, thereby saving his works from being categorized as obscene and pornographic. By thoroughly centering the male body within local, historically marked scapes and representing indigenous physiognomies to gain status by their association to mythology, the baron captivates an otherwise cautious audience. This is what makes his images a valued and respected expression.

A number of the questions that should be asked regarding the possible exploitative aspects at play in the photographic processes discussed in this study have to do with the posing, positioning and compositional aspects of the images. Such questions are even more interesting when applied to a photographer such as von Gloeden, whose work and fame seem to have generally escaped these accusations. Granted, the case is not as clear, given his personal relationship with the town and its inhabitants and the economic compensation that he provided for his models and assistants. Nevertheless, even as his photos depict a constructed "reality," they are advantaged by the well-hidden and more immediate socio-economic situation of his models. We must in the end ask if the baron's portraits, the eventual use of which was recognized to be for the enjoyment of privileged classes, does not also participate in the designation, formation, control and maintenance of social categories.

Photography has been characterized as a mirror with a memory, but this must be qualified in that, while it may be an apparently direct memory, it is never neutral. The memory of photography is socio-anthropological. The way a subject is situated within the photographic space defines the viewer's relationship to it which, in turn, is a reflection of ideological spaces. As democratic as photography may initially appear to be, all the choices made in producing a photograph, to its exhibition, collection and interpretation, all represent subjective and interested systems of signification.

The popularity of *cartes* in the second half of the 1800s, photographs used as calling cards, and as a way to leave one's presence behind, parallel the custom of collecting *cartes* into albums. The desire was to create a familiar space and environment of visual iconology that reassured its holder of belonging to a certain social class, and of being in some way related to people of similar background. These albums, much like photography itself, became the exclusive domain of a middle or upper class. Excluded from their pages were the poor, the sick, and those deemed to be inferior due to racial or ethnic difference.

Yet, the exclusion extended only to the pages of socially meaningful collections, not by any means from the gaze of the camera. During this same period there is an extensive catalogue of racial and ethnic types, popular costumes and traditions, that is accumulated through the enterprises of colonialism, imperialism, and labor exchange. Photography and anthropology became very closely allied in the task of defining hierarchical norms that continue to dominate global relations.

The conventions that reflect the ideology of colonialism and the evolution of the disciplines that helped create some of their supporting structures, by engaging with the subjects to be subsumed, are many. A common convention in ethnographic photography is the positioning of the head at a three-quarter profile in order to facilitate the recording of specific physiognomic details. The fine details made available through subject positioning, and the clear, sharp prints from large-format cameras, provided the evidence needed to communicate a subject's "otherness": skin pigmentation, facial and physical features, dress, and other visible cultural signs.

The context in which the photograph may have been taken is also of paramount importance. While the portrait pose of a respected businessman and that of a Native American tribal elder may differ only slightly, the photos differ greatly in how they were ideologically prepared. The first would most likely be taken at the request of the subject, or someone who has an interest in being associated with the subject's achievements in order to advertise that person. The latter would almost without question be the result of a seating prepared by the photographer, or at the request of an agency, for purposes that the subject himself did not control.

Examples of photography that fall into the last category are not too distant in our historical past, where we find plenty of examples of visual typecasting and categorization at the service of some ill-defined ideology. T. H. Huxley, an early supporter of Darwinism, was hired by the British Colonial Office to devise a set of instructions for the training of photographers who would participate in the "formation of a systematic series of photographs of the various races of men comprehended within the British Empire." The system he conceived of called for unclothed subjects to be photographed full and half-length, frontally and in profile, standing beside a clearly marked measuring stick.[38]

Von Gloeden's photographs do not of course explicitly fall into the intentionality of Huxley's system, but they do not escape it completely. Von Gloeden's work can be said to be colonizing, at least in part, by his use of a socially subaltern population that was almost completely invisible and manipulating it into an historical context that is foreign to it.

It is true that intentionality is often difficult to determine, as there are always unknown and uncontrollable elements at work that tend to turn the actions of imposition against themselves. For example:

> In 1850, Louis Agassiz, a Harvard University natural scientist commissioned daguerreotypes of black slaves in the American South to demonstrate what he considered the inherent inferiority of the black race, but these daguerreotypes served instead to document the social system under which they were produced.[39]

The same could also be said of von Gloeden's photographs by reading the boys' stance and gaze. Their participation in the making of the images might be said to represent a sort of concept of *arrangiarsi* or making do, but it also could be read as a temporary retaliation against the classical system that has led to their contemporary world, and their exclusion from it. When the gaze of the subject does not engage the viewer, it could be interpreted in two ways. First, as the photographer's way of denying the subject's individualism or, secondly, as the subjects' taunting of the viewer from the confidence of their subaltern bodies. Further, in the second case, we might ask to what extent the subjects themselves might be aware of the fiction in which they are asked to participate.

It would be interesting to compare von Gloeden and Pier Paolo Pasolini for their similar relationship to Southern Italian and Third World young men. Compelling to think how the representation of their subjects might compare, and about how they might insert their own image into the social landscape they are recording as outsiders. While I will not go into a consideration of Pasolini here, I will review the latter part of my proposal vis-à-vis von Gloeden and his self-portraits.

There are only a few known self-portraits of the baron. One is of him as a Christ-like figure, in another he is dressed in a fairly conventional gentlemanly manner, and in others von Gloeden has adorned himself with "oriental" attire. The latter require the viewer to truly consider what the role of self-portraits might be. If we assume that the subjects of photography reflect the vision of the photographer, then we could also assume by these photographs that there is at least a certain amount of desirous thinking involved in the baron's self-identification with his subjects. And, since von Gloeden chooses on occasion to dress himself like his models, I am also curious as to the possible existence of any nude self-portraits. The baron's use of layers of Arabic and classical drapery, which he loved to use so sparingly on his subjects, could in his personal use of it be meant to hide/veil his figure and thereby betray a latent fear of exposing his sexuality.

Many of von Gloeden's photographs have never been published, including some truly interesting ones in the Alinari Archive, within a subset of photographs from the supposed 1909 visit to Turkey. As I previously mentioned, often these photographs are identified as having been taken in Tunisia; photographs of landscapes, village life, market scenes and buildings. And, there is no shortage of photographs of local Turkish youths obviously posing, and resembling very much those of the baron's Sicilian boys. The Alinari archivists thought it possible that von Gloeden purchased many of the "Arabic" costume accessories for his Sicilian models during this visits to Tunisia and/or Turkey.

Having already mentioned the roof-top photograph that resembles in pose the future classical photographs of Sicilian boys, there are also photographs of male youths in female Arab garb. Striking very feminine poses and casting an enticing gaze, the boys are adorned with veils, jewelry and arabesque decorations. Such photos are the most explicit example of von Gloeden's attempt to cross-dress ethnicity, meaning that as he cross-dressed his subjects into femaleness, he cross-dressed himself into ethnicity and explicitly expressed his desire to ethnically feminize the male body. It is here that von Gloeden is at his most Dionysian, most playful and most disruptive of the masculine culture of his day. Nevertheless, by cross-dressing the bodies he desires (or that he creates to stimulate the desires of others) the baron is making the appropriation unambiguous and direct, and collusive with a sort of undeniable colonialism. The insertion of himself into the formula by dressing in Arabic style and naming these shots "self-portraits," puts into question not only the whole category of the self-portrait by displacing the subject/object outside of his culture but directly plays with the notion of the self as other. *Je suis autre* is nowhere as true as it is here.

Unlike Modotti's representation of herself as a woman of Tehuantepec, von Gloeden's self-portraits are less an expression of solidarity and more an attempt to construct an aesthetic. The baron's is a double representation by which he inscribes the young men into an imaginary and mythological Mediterranean history into which he then inscribes himself. His self-portraits are representative of a questioning of the homoerotic gaze, an analysis and definition of a homoerotic aesthetic that offer him the only alternative to the oppressive environment in which he had been born.

## NOTES

1. Emmanuel Cooper, *Fully Exposed: The Male Nude in Photography* (New York: Routledge, 1995).
2. Ibid., 149.
3. Alfred Stieglitz, *Camerawork. A Pictorial Guide* (New York: Dover Publications, 1978).
4. Cooper, *Fully*, 151.
5. Robert Aldrich, *The Seduction of the Mediterranean: Writing, Art and Homosexual Fantasy* (London: Routledge, 1993), 8.
6. Ibid., 12.
7. Marsilio Ficino, *Sopra lo amore o ver' Convito di Platone: Comento di Marsilio Ficini Fiorentino sopra il Convito di Platone* (Milano: Celuc, 1973), 38.
8. Ibid.
9. Aldrich, *Seduction*, 10.
10. Ibid., 11.
11. Ibid., 94.
12. Ibid., 100.
13. Ibid., 97.
14. Ibid., 99.
15. Ibid., 143.
16. Ibid.
17. Charles-Henri Favrod, "L'innocenza di Eros e di Dionisio," in *Von Gloeden: Fotografie* (Firenze: Alinari, 2000), 8.
18. Aldrich, *Seduction*, 141.
19. For more information on Marées see Kurt Liebmann, *Hans von Marées* (Dresden, 1972) and Wayne R. Dynes, *Encyclopedia of Homosexuality* (New York, 1990).
20. Aldrich, *Seduction*, 140.
21. Charles Leslie, *Wilhelm von Gloeden, Photographer: A Brief Introduction to his Life and Work* (New York: Soho Photographic Publishers, 1977), 14.
22. Favrod, "L'innocenza," 5.
23. Leslie, *Wilhelm*, 26.

24. "Taormina," www.taormina_guide_dolce_vita.htm.
25. Leslie, *Wilhelm*, 42.
26. Favrod, "L'innocenza," 8.
27. Leslie, *Wilhelm*, 38.
28. Francesco Faeta, "Wilhelm von Gloeden: Per una lettura antropologica delle immagini," in *Fotologia 9* (Museo di Storia della Fotografia Fratelli Alinari, 1998), 94.
29. Carlo Bertelli, "La penisola ermafrodita," in *Storia d'Italia. Annali 2. L'immagine fotografica 1845–1945* (Torino: Einaudi, 1979), 84–86.
30. Roland Barthes, "Introduction," in *Baron Wilhelm von Gloeden* (Santa Fe: Twelvetrees Press, 1997).
31. Aldrich, *Seduction*, 147.
32. Here I would cite as indicative of this trend Joseph A. Boone's "Vacation Cruises; or, The Homoerotics of Orientalism," in *PMLA* (Vol. 110, number 1, 1995), 89–107.
33. Barthes, "Introduction," 9.
34. Ibid.
35. Ibid.
36. Aldrich, *Seduction*, 149.
37. Alberto Boatto, *Eros Mediterraneo* (Bari: Edizioni Laterza, 1999), 17.
38. John Pultz, *The Body and the Lens* (New York: Henry N. Abrams, 1995), 24–25.
39. Ibid., 25–26.

# 7

# Tina Modotti

## *Life Through the Ground-Glass*

Born in Udine, Italy, in 1896, Tina Modotti made her way to the United States in 1913 to join part of her already emigrated family. Their situation was no different than that of many other Italians who left their homeland in search of opportunity. As an evolved artist and social activist, Tina traveled to Mexico with the eminent American photographer Edward Weston in 1923. She remained there until 1930, well after Weston had returned to the U.S., when she was cast out as a foreign undesirable and communist agitator. After years spent working on behalf of the Soviet state in support of revolutionary causes in Europe, including the Spanish Civil War, Tina returned to Mexico in 1939 and died there in 1942.[1]

These are the basic facts that encapsulate perhaps one of the most active, influential, and productive lives of the early part of the twentieth century. Today, in the early part of the twenty-first century, the massive displacement of peoples across the globe remains a concern that calls for continued attention and compassion. Tina Modotti's activism and commitment to a collective consciousness is in this context that much more important and necessary as a point of reference and discussion.

As for many inhabitants of the then impoverished northeastern Italian region known as Friuli, Modotti's nomadic experience began at an early age when her family moved to Austria in 1898 in search of a more stable life. They returned to Udine in 1905 and, just a year later, Tina's father Giuseppe and her sister Mercedes left for the U.S. The family followed at intervals; Tina joined her father and sister in San Francisco in 1913. As to where and how Tina might have become familiar with photography, it is quite possible that the fascination with photography as an instrument of representation and potential livelihood began in her youth. Not only was her uncle Pietro the successful proprietor of a photography studio in Udine, where Modotti's father had also worked, but he, Giuseppe, had then established his own photography studio in San Francisco.

Upon her arrival in San Francisco, Tina plunged into the life of the city. As a resident of the "Italian quarter" known as North Beach, Tina was quickly enticed by the lively political and artistic scene. Despite her position as an overworked seamstress in the cramped I. Magnin production rooms, Tina made time to explore every opportunity available to her. One of the major turning points in her search for self-expression came with the opening of San Francisco's 1915 Panama-Pacific Exposition. There she came to know some of the art and artists that would most impress her, but, most importantly, it was there that she met Robo, the poet and painter Roubaix de l'Abrie Richey.

Tina's relationship with Robo was founded on their shared ideals and aesthetics, and on their strong and mutual physical attraction. His bohemian persona and lifestyle were attractive to Modotti, whose sensibilities and character were too strong to be caged by a traditional woman's role within the immigrant community. Her activities in the local theater scene drew much attention; her name and exploits made almost regular appearances in *L'Italia*, San Francisco's Italian newspaper of the time. Encouraged by her success, and possibly by the fact that Robo's family lived there, Tina moved to Los Angeles with him in 1918. The land of orange groves and petroleum, of Hollywood glamour and post-World War I social freedoms, was also the land of image-making. The "city of angels" would add a layer of mystery to Modotti's life, and provide her with more artistic and intellectual challenges and opportunities.

The bohemian art circles of Los Angeles were influential for both Robo and Tina. They made the acquaintance of many of the renowned characters with whom her name in particular is associated to this day. During this period, Tina successfully made her way as a film actress, playing characters that reflected Hollywood's fascination with women of mystery that embodied a dark, sensual fire that fulfilled the expectations of the period's art of Decadentism. Among the films in which she appeared, *The Tiger's Coat* (1920) cast her unfailingly as a brooding, lurking and sensually dangerous Italian or Latina. While her appearance in films was symptomatic of the sort of casting that might be expected for the period, it is also likely that these representations helped propagate Modotti's mysterious aura.

One of the artists she frequented in Los Angeles was Robo's friend Edward Weston. Their meeting would mark and important transition for Modotti. Tina and Edward's friendship developed into a romantic affair in 1921, the year in which Robo traveled to Mexico. His eventual death there caused Tina to also travel south to take care of her friend's funeral arrangements, and her initial foray into Mexico lasted only a few weeks. However, the exciting post-revolutionary atmosphere she found there was enough to instill a sense of potential artistic and personal freedom that would bring her back.

Unfortunately, only a month following Robo's death, tragedy struck again when Tina's father died in March 1922. Modotti's return to San Francisco, to the security of her family and to an environment she had known, almost ended her relationship with Weston. However, even after a letter dated October 1922 in which she bade good-bye to Weston forever, their relationship became closer. While it had been Robo to initially suggest that Weston join him in the "artists' paradise" that was Mexico, it was Tina who eventually led him there. In July 1923, in a turn of events that for some lent even more weight to Tina's "dark seductress" reputation, Weston left his wife and family and traveled to Mexico with her and his son Chandler.

Tina's relationship with the American photographer has been the subject of much speculation. Weston's role as her artistic mentor, his influence on her photography, her role in introducing him to Mexico, and the impact that such a stay might have had on Weston's aesthetics and composition, are all topics that continue to fascinate both scholars and admirers. However, it is their affair, and Weston's extensive use of Modotti as a model, often in erotic nude studies, that seems to grab the imagination and to have determined how Modotti is referenced in history.

Tina's Mexican home soon became a gathering place for artists, writers, and political activists. During this period, the names of Frida Kahlo and Diego Rivera became forever associated with Tina's. Weston and Modotti quickly blended into the artistic life of post-revolutionary Mexico. Tina was particularly impressed by the participation of the population at large in defining its own future. The capital, Mexico City, and its central *Zócalo*, its main plaza, became focal points for both social action and artistic representations of the new era. Weston and Modotti's time together in Mexico was quite successful and productive. Weston's photographs received unprecedented attention, and Tina began to photograph full-time. The two of them also appear to have successfully initiated a number of affairs that sometimes strained the relationship, but which did not hinder a deeply felt friendship. Weston left Mexico in December 1924 to return to California for a time; when he found his way back to Mexico eight months later with his son Brett, little had changed.

Having become more and more involved in socialist causes, Modotti had begun to use her camera as a tool of activism. Upon his return, she and Weston traveled throughout Mexico exploring life outside the capital. It was during this time that Tina, Edward and Brett photographed Mexican art and objects for Anita Brenner's book *Idols Behind Altars*. While the two photographers had found ways in which to work together, their relationship had taken a turn toward separation. And so it was that in 1926, as Weston again left Mexico, Tina began a new period of her life.

Modotti's relationship with the revolutionary artists of Mexico had started with her acquaintance of painter Xavier Guerrero in Los Angeles in 1922. While her family's socialist background had exposed Tina to the ideals of revolution, her time in Mexico clearly brought into focus the importance of political involvement and activism. It was during her residence there that Modotti had become associated with specific causes and organizations. The *Hands off Nicaragua Committee* against U.S. interventionism, the *Anti-Imperialist League of the Americas*, and the *Communist Party*, were all organizations in which she participated, and which brought her into close contact with an international cast of political refugees and revolutionaries.

Among the left wing activists and artists that Modotti came to meet and befriend was the Italian communist Vittorio Vidali, a dedicated anti-fascist. Vidali had spent several years in the U.S., where he had been deeply involved in the socialist cause in general, and in the defense of Sacco and Vanzetti specifically. Only months before the anarchists' execution in 1927, Vidali had been deported and, as fate would have it, he and Modotti met at a rally in Mexico, in support of Sacco and Vanzetti. Their mutual devotion to Communism and to anti-fascism motivated a strong friendship.

Tina's important service to the causes she espoused is emphasized by the inclusion of her figure in the revolutionary murals of Diego Rivera at the Chapingo Agricultural School and at the Ministry of Education, in Mexico City, and by the homage paid to her by many of Mexico's revolutionaries. These inclusions should not be read only as an appreciation of Tina's famed beauty, which would be rather dismissive of her contributions, but as testimony to her political commitment and participation. Her photography appeared in the official publication of the Mexican Communist Party *El Machete*, in the travel magazine *Mexican Folkways*, and in the radical leftist American journal *New Masses*, which illustrates Tina's successful amalgamation of political commitment, social commentary and art.

It was at this point that Modotti also came to know Julio Antonio Mella. Having previously also met him at a Sacco and Vanzetti rally, their formal introduction took place in June 1928 at the offices of *El Machete*. Mella was a young Cuban revolutionary who lived in Mexico as an exile, and was active against the government of Cuban dictator Gerardo Machado (1925–1933). Mella and Modotti quickly capitalized on their mutual attraction and began living together only months after their first meeting.

Her association with Rivera and other Mexican muralists fed a cultural-political aesthetics and ideology that became her all-consuming passion. Modotti's activism and strong criticism of the Mexican government made her a target of governmental investigations, which culminated with the assassination of Mella in 1929.

On the evening of January 10, 1929, as he and Tina were strolling, two shots rang out and Mella fell to the ground critically wounded. He died at the Hospital San Jerónimo later that night. The murder was covered extensively in the press, and Modotti became a primary suspect accused of either having organized or participated in the assassination. This was a great opportunity for the Mexican right to revile all that it deemed offensive and dangerous: "those without patriotism or national solidarity," "the Jewery of Russian Bolshevism," "nomadic foreigners," and so on. Six days after the assassination, Diego Rivera accompanied Modotti to court for an official interrogation. It soon became clear that the Mexican government's intention was to cover up the assassination as a crime of passion, pitting Mella's interest in Tina against those of her ex-lover, Xavier Guerrero. Various pieces of evidence were trotted out, first in support of the love triangle, then to portray the event as infighting among Communist factions in which Modotti was said to be a co-conspirator. Among the trumped-up charges, it was said that she had in her possession the Colt .45 that had killed Mella, and that she had acted as a Fascist spy. While Tina's name was eventually cleared, enough damage had been done and suspicion aroused about her to put her in a precarious legal situation as a foreigner.

In the meantime, Modotti's photography received more and more attention. The publications in *Mexican Folkways* had attracted interest outside of Mexico, and her work was solicited by many other journals. In November 1929, at the invitation of the Dirección de Acción Civica, Modotti exhibited her work at the National Library, in Mexico City. As a result of this, Modotti gained new status as a photographer and recognition for her original photographic eye. In December of that year, before the closing of the exhibition, artist and revolutionary David Alfaro Siquieros gave a talk on her photography entitled "The First Revolutionary Photographic Exhibition in Mexico," thereby acknowledging the power of Tina's images in a socio-political context.

These events took place in a climate in which Mexico's relationship with the Soviet Union was definitely taking a turn for the worse. Formal relations between the two countries broke off, and the mood against Mexican Communists worsened. In early 1929, the Communist Party was declared illegal. The Mexican government was eager to rid itself of Modotti and other "nomadic foreigners" who had become influential figures among the rank and file of the Communist party. The opportunity came on Sunday, February 5, 1930, following Pascual Ortíz Rubio's inauguration as Mexico's new president. A young man made an attempt on Ortíz Rubio's life and, while the would-be assassin was apprehended, Modotti was accused of taking part in the conspiracy. She was arrested and given the option of remaining in Mexico if she were to publicly denounce her beliefs. Tina's refusal to do so led to her expulsion from the country.

Not being in possession of a passport, Tina sought asylum and an entry visa for the U.S. Once more, she was given the opportunity by the American government to denounce her political activities in exchange for a visa and, again, she refused. Her request for an Italian passport was granted with the proviso that it would be valid only for re-entry to Italy, which for a Communist during Fascism's reign could have been fatal. She eventually found passage out of Mexico aboard the Dutch ship *Edam*. Her status on board being that of a detained deportee, she was under constant watch for the duration of the voyage. As it turned out, the route to Holland was rather circuitous. The ship made a call in the port of New Orleans, where Modotti was held under strict surveillance on port grounds for the eight days that it took for the ship to discharge and change its cargo. At other ports, she was not even allowed to set foot on shore.

The *Edam* reached Rotterdam after more than a month. Having been notified of Modotti's plight, Dutch workers' organizations were ready to receive her. Mussolini's government requested that she be extradited to Italy, a situation that was avoided through the Dutch courts, with the help of the Dutch Red Aid. A request to the Dutch for asylum was also denied and, while permitted to set foot ashore, she was ordered to leave Holland that same day. Through arrangements made by the Communist party, Modotti was admitted into Germany and arrived in Berlin in April 1930.

During this period Tina's relationship to photography seems to have been uneasy. Whether her attitude was conditioned by her state of mind, or by the need to involve herself deeply in the socialist cause, or the pressure to adapt to the new, smaller 35 mm cameras, different from her beloved Graflex, Modotti's letters to Weston discuss her consternation. She is offered "reportage" work by the German periodical *Workers' Illustrated Journal*, but is uncertain of her aptitude at such photography.[2]

It appears that during this short stay in Germany, Modotti was able to take short trips into France and Switzerland, the reasons for which are not quite clear. Italy, however, remained a distant, dangerous, and impossible destination. Meanwhile, the political climate in Germany was quickly shifting. Hitler continued to gain support, and the deteriorating economy made it hard for Tina to find employment. So it was that after six months, with the help of her friend Vittorio Vidali, who had transferred his activities there, Modotti left Germany for the Soviet Union. There she seems to have found renewed energy, and her last letter to Weston is written in an excited tone that mentions her whirlwind activities. Modotti and Vidali renewed their friendship and became lovers in Moscow. She dedicated herself to political activity and became involved with the International Red Aid in Moscow and elsewhere in Europe.

In 1933 Modotti undertook a three-month mission into Spain which was cut short when she was arrested and expelled. After her return to Moscow, until 1935, she and Vidali carried out a series of clandestine missions into various European countries, sometimes as a couple, at other times alone. Modotti spent part of this period in Paris, where she earned her living by translating and continues to work for the International Red Aid. The list of causes she supported and organized in France are quite impressive.

At the end of 1935 Tina and Vidali entered Spain for their most extensive stay in order to participate in the struggle against the undoing of Republican Spain. Prior to their arrival, events had led to an alliance between the Communists, the Socialists, the *General Workers' Union*, and other smaller entities, to form the *Popular Front* as representative of a united working class. With the escalating civil war Modotti joined the Fifth Regiment, a crack Communist military unit, and worked with the International Brigades. She was active at all levels of the struggle and continued her work as a reporter for the journal *Ayuda*.

With the end of the war, the defeat of the Republicans and official recognition of the Nationalists by a number of governments, Tina made her way out of the country among the thousands of refugees who filed into France. Living in Paris under an assumed identity she received a visa for entry into Mexico which, having supported the Republican cause, was accepting refugees from Spain. Her visa provided for a transit stay in the U.S., where she had hoped to visit with her family. However, upon arrival Modotti was refused admission, and the long-awaited reunion with her sister Yolanda was precluded. Almost a decade after her expulsion, Modotti once again entered Mexico on April 19, 1939.

Once again, Vidali had arrived on location before Tina and, in Mexico, they were once more reunited. Undaunted, she resumed her political activities, notably her anti-fascist work with the Giuseppe Garibaldi Alliance, and her relationship with friends both old and new who had also found refuge in Mexico. With their help, she was able to have her expulsion of 1930 annulled by then president Làzaro Cardenas, which enabled her to reclaim her name and identity. Only a few years after her return to Mexico, Modotti died prematurely in 1942. Official reports list the cause of death as a massive heart attack; others suggest that her death was nothing short of a political assassination. Whatever the cause, in death as in life, Modotti's legacy is one of activism, intrigue, mystery and fascination all tightly bound by a strong sense of duty to justice and artistic expression.

She was laid to rest in the Pantheon de Dolores graveyard in Mexico City and honored by the words of Pablo Neruda, who rightly noted about her that "fire does not die."[3]

## A REVEALING LIFE

Modotti stands as an early example of the breaching of conventional political affiliations and the redefinition of identity that necessarily take place once the confines of nationalism, citizenship, gender roles, and activism are challenged. Modotti's photography and writing served as instruments in support of this activity and they developed acutely over her lifetime. Yet, because of other strong personalities with whom she associated, such as Frida Kahlo, Diego Rivera, Edward Weston, and Vittorio Vidali, her work is greatly undervalued. In addition, as it has been veiled by an aura of nostalgia, romanticism and mystery, its more socially committed aspects have almost been erased and Modotti herself has come to lose some of her definition as a person.

Modotti's work as artist, writer and activist forms an important part of the cultural legacy of the early part of this century, a period during which much of the nomadism and transculturalism that define our contemporary society began to take shape. Long pigeon-holed as Weston's pupil and protégé, Modotti has been relegated to the secondary ranks of art history until recently. It was most likely her friendship with Weston that influenced Modotti in her choice of photography as a tool of expression, however we cannot discount the influence that her uncle's photo studio in Italy, or her own father's commercial photographic career in San Francisco, might have had. While Weston created a niche for himself between the pictorialist, documentarist, and avant-garde photographic movements of his time, Modotti's sensibilities and interests drew her closer to street photography, and the documentation of popular lifestyles and customs. As it has become apparent, the use to which Modotti was to extend photography was uniquely hers, influenced in part by her background and in part by her ideology. Having grown up for part of her life in the Friuli, an underdeveloped agricultural region, she would have had a rather direct contact with the hard life of its inhabitants. This undoubtedly led to her identification with Mexican urban poor and rural populations as part of a global class of marginalized peoples and cultures.

Definitely touched by a sense of aesthetics that is almost classical in its composition, Modotti's photographic work is no less a statement of protest against the social conditions of the time in Mexico and around the globe. If to "show poverty and injustice is to protest against it," as the Italian Neo-realist Cesare Zavattini suggested in post-World War II

Italy, then Modotti's photographs form part of a cultural legacy that still holds an important place not only in art history but in political history and activism.[4] While "realist" or documentary photography that depicted the "suffering masses" is said to have begun with photographers such as Lewis Hine in and around 1935, Tina Modotti had been hard at work, producing exactly that sort of socially relevant photography, already for almost a decade. What distinguishes her work from that of documentarists is that her subjects are directly representative of historical and political events, be it the failures of the Mexican Revolution or the struggle against Fascism.

It must be pointed out that Modotti's interest in this class is reminiscent of the Italian Marxist Antonio Gramsci, whose writings on folklore are in general traceable to the mid-1920s. In contradiction to the accepted myths regarding the peasant classes and their beliefs, their *folklore*, Modotti and Gramsci proposed a view of "folklore as a concept of the world and life . . . distinct from official concepts of the world" and that "only in folklore does one find the truncated and contaminated documents" of history which make folklore kinetic.[5] It is exactly this kinetic energy of culture that radicalizes folklore, and all its associated beliefs in myth, magic, the supernatural, and the natural world, and identifies within it a revolutionary potential.

The use of photography to engage folkloric subjects and products might seem contradictory. However, Modotti's art acts in the appropriation of that technology to offset its uses in support of cultural determinism, as defined by ethnographers and anthropologists, in the service of imperialistic or colonial interests. The work of Wilhelm von Gloeden, in a not so obvious manner, and that of J. W. Lindt, more overtly, formed a hierarchy in both racial and cultural terms as they became studies of "indigenous peoples." Modotti instead turns that same technology to express a continuously manifesting and undeniable human and cultural presences as equal, and alternatively available, to officially recognized ones.

However, her time behind the camera was short. During her life of forty-six years, Modotti dedicated approximately seven years to photography and fifteen to political activism. Her interests in these two fields are not so well defined chronologically; there was, in fact, a very obvious overlap of interests and activities. Modotti's photography cannot by any means be considered a purely aesthetic exercise, as both her photographic subject matter and her writings reveal, but a rather close interweaving of ethical and aesthetical attitudes.

As such, maybe too much has been made of the fact that Modotti gave up photography during her residence in the Soviet Union and for the rest of what remained of her life. Photography had been, for the nomadic Modotti, a means of culturally constructing herself; viewing, capturing, and ideologically assessing her subjects; a way for her to emphasize her own presence/absence in Mexico, and the absence/presence of a precise cultural context of her own. Many different reasons have been given for her abandonment of photography, enough to continue feeding the mythology that surrounds her. The list of reasons ranges from the dramatic, her having thrown her camera into the Rhine as a declaration of political activism vs. art, to her inability to produce photographs for political papers, to her supposed inability to adapt to new, small format cameras (the use of a Leica 35 mm format rather than her view camera). Topping the list, among those blamed for having caused her to dismiss photography, is the Italian communist Vittorio Vidali. He is assigned the bad-guy status for having insisted that Tina dedicate her life to political activism. However, any one of these versions unjustly undermines and underestimates Modotti's own ability and character, as well as her commitment to the causes she chose to support.

The question that must be posed with regard to Modotti however goes to the issues that feed her art and ideology, those that in turn reflect art and ideology to form a holistic sense of being in the world. Uppermost among these must be her twofold status as a twice over emigrant, and the nomadicism it implies. Modotti's work is the site of specific discourse that reveals aspects of her particular views on personal identity as a product of engaged hybridity. Which is to say, it enacts a foregrounding of hybrid influences in all their variations and engages them toward a definition of a social self. Repeatedly hailed and acknowledged as a singularly important figure and influence in contemporary Mexican photography, Modotti was not Mexican. Sought by Mussolini's Fascists under accusation of crimes against the Italian state, she had left Italy as a teenager never to set foot on Italian soil again. As an important American artist and activist, she was designated *persona non grata* and refused entry into the US on her return from Europe following the Spanish Civil war. This list of non-definitions and exclusions according to nationalist designations should make clear that identity is an amorphous concept, hardly sustainable by notions of citizenship. Rather, as Chantal Mouffe has suggested, "by resisting the ever-present temptation to construct identity in terms of exclusion, and recognizing that identities comprise a multiplicity of elements, and that they are dependent and interdependent, we can 'convert an antagonism of identity into the agonism of difference' and thus stop the potential for violence that exists in every construction of 'us and them.'"[6]

Modotti appears to have been predisposed to activities that led to a valuation of alternative social strategies. In other words, Tina's activities emphasized an "agonism of difference" that found her less attached to more conventional political modes and the commonly felt need to antagonize purely along positional or ideological categories. She showed remarkable insight into the limits and contradictions of Marxism itself, especially in the relationships between the proletarian, the peasant, and the sub-proletarian classes. Through her photography, Modotti raises into prominent view the social by-products of capitalism and its influence on the working class and socially marginal groups, while also giving prominence to the bodies and activities of sub-proletarians and peasants. This is particularly important in Mexico, since the two categories tend to include indigenous peoples or "Indian" populations who suffer extensive exclusions at all levels of society. It is through this representation of a hardly considered reality within the Mexican landscape that Modotti forges that hybridity of concern that undermines "us vs. them" paradigms. Tina's work and activities redefine social spaces by shifting the focus of oppressive forces via the presentation of a potential series of alliances within the field of hegemonic struggles. Her photographs are representative of a manner in which the explanatory power of what might define community, society, or nation might be redistributed; they reestablish the coordinates not only for photography as a viable social practice, but for the position of the subjects portrayed within it.

Influenced by her disinterest in conventional nationalisms, their congruent prescriptive identities, and by her own obvious experience of migration, Modotti's photography is strongly marked by her interest in hybridity. While she neither artificially creates examples of hybridity nor defines the term, Modotti seeks out subjects that represent it. I am aware that this strays close to claiming for photography an objectivity that is hard to negotiate, but Modotti seems to succeed in her task to represent cultural dimensions not defined from *within* hegemonic practices but as something exercised from *without*: without power, without citizenship, without privilege, without voice. It is the subject matter, which she values culturally, socially, and ideologically, that lends hybridity *to* her exercise, a process through which "By accepting that only hybridity creates us as separate entities, it affirms and upholds the nomadic character of every identity."[7]

Hybridity as a concept cannot of course be applied as an umbrella qualifier to any and all situations; it requires that it be expressed anew in relation to every single situation in which it is thought to be pertinent. At first this may seem an odd concept to couple with photography. Supposedly, the act of taking a photograph is straight forward and singular, and Modotti herself, although we know otherwise both in general terms and for Modotti's own manipulation of certain images, thought it to be an objective exercise. But, if there is no manipulation, then the hybridity must manifest in some other manner, and the artist, the product or the subject are all potential sources. Modotti's early work, and let us remember that she apparently produced less than three hundred images over a period of about eight to ten years, has been criticized as being apolitical, of having purely aesthetic preoccupation, and of being merely a reflection of Weston's work. But it may be in those very still-life exercises of her early period that we might find the clue to lead us closer to Modotti's ideology as reflected in her work. Besides the obvious sense of something that is "not moving," *Still life* could also be read literally to mean that the subject matter is still living, culturally or otherwise. Ideologies are one thing, humanity, on the other hand, is a whole other matter, and human subjects are still lives in the sense of living culture. It is at that juncture that hybridity takes form, in the meeting of the photographer and her subjects, both through the camera and in personal relationships.

The early still lifes were a training ground for her humane photography during which, differently than for some other photographers, Modotti was able to befriend her subjects. The photographs show that there is no timidity and no reluctance on the part of her subjects to be photographed. It is this hybridity that informs Rivera's opinion that her work was a truth of great pedagogical power for its immediacy, and its particularly strong support of revolutionary ideals, even as she became disillusioned with the bureaucratic aspects of the communist hierarchy.

It is this confident consciousness that makes of Modotti a figure of great importance. She smoothly brings together, as tightly functioning and inseparable, aesthetics and ethics. Does it diminish the significance of the photographs if she writes something completely and utterly mundane on the back of them? Not unless we forget that the photographer too is a living human being. Read as such, Modotti's photography reclaims its stature as a political and ideological product that enacts a social critique, something very distant from the commodification it has undergone within the art market. Over a period of only a few years, the value of her work skyrocketed to bring in 1989 one of the highest auction prices in photographic history.

Much of the critical work on Modotti has been from an art history perspective, which, besides the importance of the cultural/historical context that it provides, also functions to stoke the fires of the art market machine. Tina Modotti's value today is still primarily the value attached to her photos by the market, greatly boosted by the very limited number of vintage prints available. That value must be clarified and enhanced beyond that, to recontextualize her art and to expose the nullifying and neutralizing effects of the market on the socio-cultural and political implications of it.

Art historians have almost exclusively concentrated on the relationship between Edward Weston and Tina Modotti to revisit the concepts of originality and influence, for these are the elements by which hierarchies within disciplines is defined. Thus, Modotti's history has been outlined in the shadow of this great photographer and could be said to have suffered for it. The market does not recognize the confluence of political, cultural, and other forces that go to inform the photographs it commodifies. It thrives on terms of authenticity and originality established for its own benefit, terms that are in full contradiction of Modotti's life and activism.

## MODOTTI'S VISUALLY TACTILE IDEOLOGY

The series of photographs entitled "The Women of Tehuantepec" was taken by Modotti in 1929. After being acquitted of charges that had attempted to tie her to the conspiracy in the assassination of her then companion, the Cuban Antonio Mella, and as the campaign against her continued to mount and would eventually reach a climax with her expulsion from Mexico, Tina traveled to the region that was well known for its matriarchal culture. Tehuantepec had become an exemplary symbol of post-revolutionary Mexico, for it seemed to have distilled in its local culture all that was valued as being quintessentially Mexican. Artists and others sought to touch this culture and visited the area to experience it first hand. Diego Rivera himself spent time there sketching the everyday life of a population that was to become emblematic in his many muralist representation of Mexico. However, while most were attracted to a romanticized notion of Mexico that was said to be found in Tehuantepec, Modotti's photographs, and her own understanding of that culture, seems to bear some distinguishing traits (Figures 7.1 and 7.2).

It is, for example, singularly interesting that most all the photos from that particular series are, aside from some crowd scenes, conspicuously devoid of the presence of men. At a time in her life when her position as an independent woman and activist was being put into question and her life at risk, Modotti found in the women of Tehuantepec a way in which to represent a moral and physical strength that was quite different from how others had pictured them. While most other artists and photographers concentrated on producing beautiful portraits of the women, Tina focused her efforts on their everyday life and activities.[8] She was especially attentive in selecting situations that would foreground women's work with and for the family. Therefore we find in this series images of nurturing women, of women socializing and sharing day to day tasks and pleasures, of young women and older women, of mothers, sisters, friends and compañeras. Modotti's strong identification with these women and their matriarchal society culminates in her attempt to identify with them more directly and explicitly in a self-portrait that will be discussed later.

Andrea Noble's book *Tina Modotti: Image, Texture, Photography* (2000) offers a reading of the photographer's images that goes a long way toward recognizing a differently defined function for them, outside the conven-

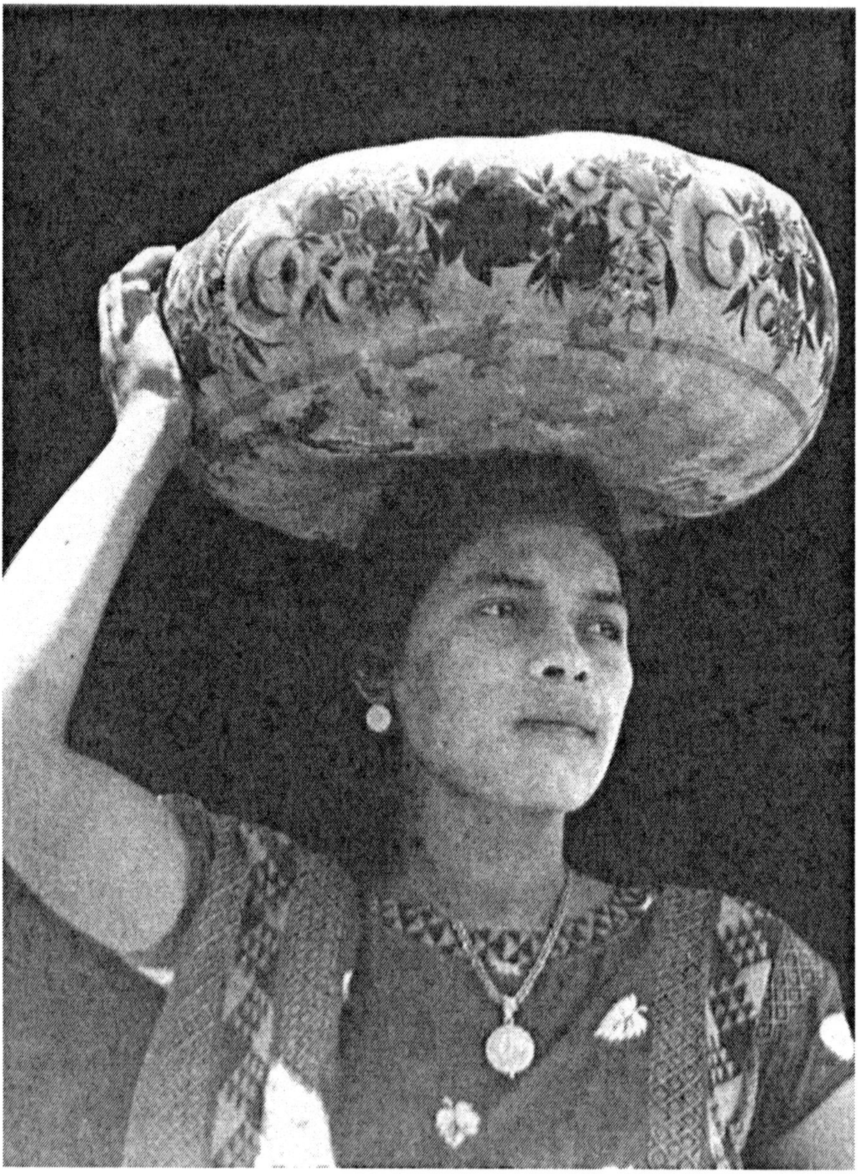

Figure 7.1. *Woman of Tehuantepec.* Tina Modotti, c. 1929. Permission granted by Throckmorton Gallery.

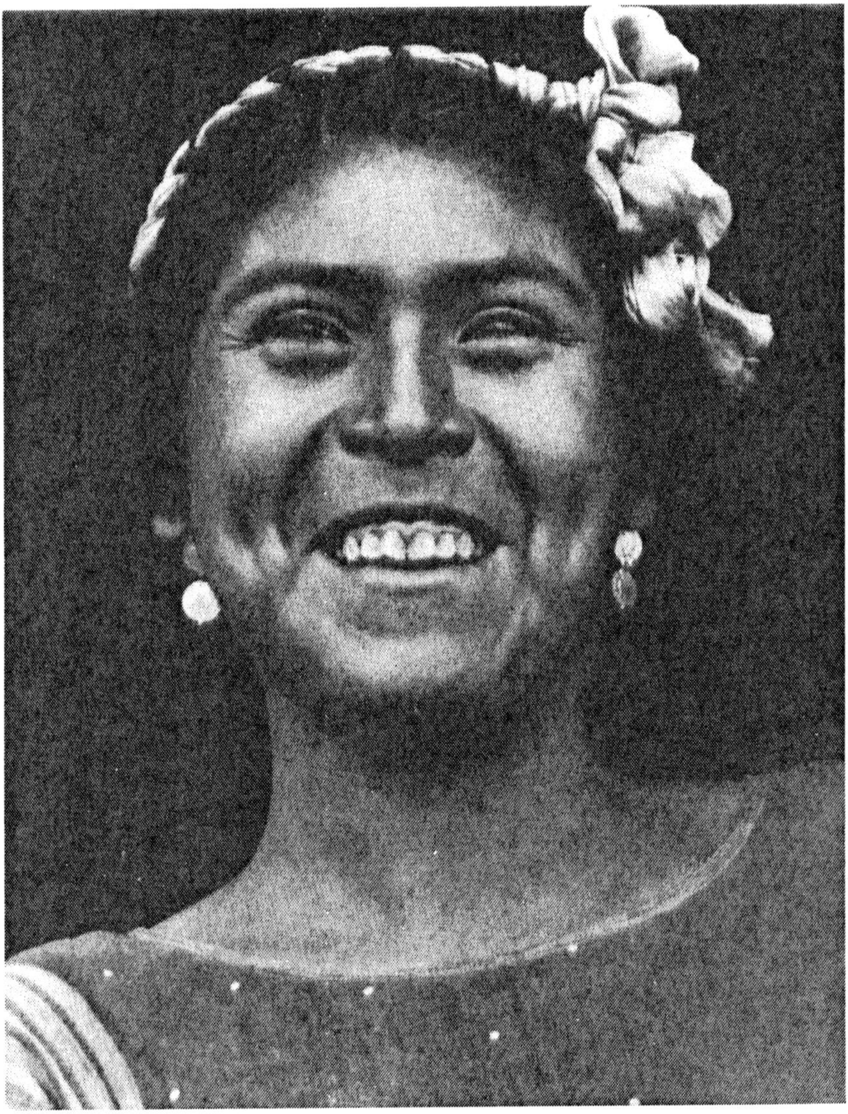

Figure 7.2. ***Tehuantepec Woman Smiling*****. Tina Modotti, c. 1929. Permission granted by Throckmorton Gallery.**

tions of art history and artistic practice. Within those normative contexts, the artist's signature demarcates the work's authenticity and originality, and a declaration of the intention of wanting to participate in its mandates.

Modotti's case is particularly interesting, given her relatively short period of production and the limited availability of archival prints. That, associated with her strong ideological bent, and the diminishment of her work on the part of a number of critics, some of which I will address later, resulted in an almost complete erasure of her "signature" from the history of photography.[9] Her relationship with photography was also problematized by her personal relationship with Edward Weston, whose body of work is so emphatically marked by female subjects and feminized objects. Weston's photographs form a site for the male photographer's signature to stand as a declaration of a recognizable aesthetics of controlled production, predicated on the imposition of the male gaze for its own enjoyment.

Another recent reading of Modotti's photography, which also foregrounds her use of the medium toward an explicitly female view of the world, is Carol Armstrong's "This Photography Which is Not One: In the Gray Zone with Tina Modotti" (2002).[10] Armstrong makes the case for a Modotti whose photographic production contrasts that of Weston. Through a reading of journals and letters, both Modotti and Weston's, as well as through portraits of the photographers taken by each other, Armstrong delineates two photographic modalities that point to diverging life philosophies. Most importantly, by looking at photographs that might on the surface appear to be similar, Armstrong's inclination is to show "how divergent each one was from the other in their photographies."[11] Her approach

> proposes, finally, to find Modotti's celebrated otherness in her photographs, rather than in her person, and to locate her sedition in the subliminality of her formal strategies rather than in the politics that she consciously avowed.[12]

We find in Modotti's photographs the clue to a reciprocal influence that has always been buried, never acknowledged, and often simply derided. Armstrong convincingly traces out a parallel path through subject matter, and in their personal relationship as photographer and model, that speaks volumes as to Modotti's influence on Weston. While this influence might not be relatable to the technical side of photography, where Weston was undoubtedly more experienced, Armstrong makes the case for a reciprocal influence on Weston by Modotti. This might have come in a less tangible manner, in a way of seeing and giving value to certain aspects of what they might have chosen to place in front of the camera, ones that Weston might not have previously considered. Contrasting Weston and Modotti's photography alongside the work of Stieglitz and O'Keeffe, Armstrong poses a convincing progression of influences that sets male "straight" photography against the female intimacy of Modotti's *Roses* and *Calla Lily* and O'Keeffe's genital flowers. By following a timeline of their photographs it becomes demonstrable that "it was from Modotti . . . that Weston got the idea for the close-up, frontal, view-to-the-core photograph, rather than the other way around."[13] All the while, it is the very softness of Modotti's photographs, their sense of integrative visualization, that makes them *appear* as "anything but tributary, it is almost impossible to conceive of them as originary."[14]

According to Armstrong, Modotti's famous 1924 *Roses* photograph is exemplary of the difference between the two photographers, and determining in its characterization of what might be considered Modotti's vision. The subject and composition of *Roses* is all important in that it appears to set the parameters for all of Modotti's photographs or, at least, offer us a key through which to read them. The mass of crowded roses gives no clear-cut form to any one of them, making it difficult "to tell where one rose ends and the other begins" (Figure 7.3). Such a vision of interconnectedness and "petalled pluralism," that Weston might find too tight-fitting, is almost an ideological declaration on Modotti's part.[15] It is here then that we can begin to determine a difference in how Modotti chose to wield her camera in a socio-political context. Modotti's photographic subjects (and we might here think again of the "Women of Tehuantepec") are not meant to be captured and held, which could be considered a contradiction of the medium itself.

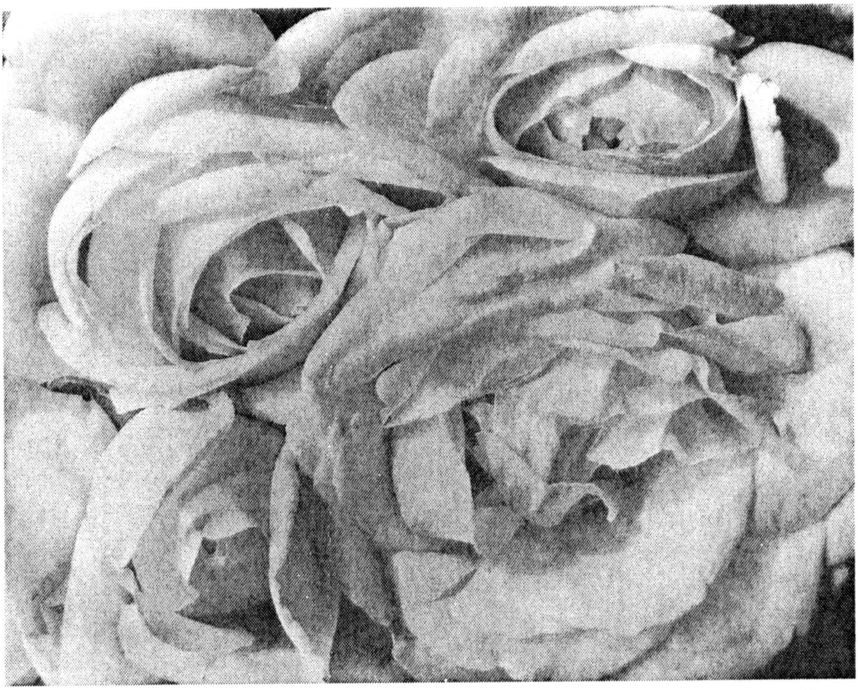

**Figure 7.3.** ***Roses.*** **Tina Modotti, 1925. Permission granted by Throckmorton Gallery.**

Along these lines, Lucy Lippard has suggested that "feminist landscape" photography is "more attuned to the local/personal/political than the god-like *big picture*."[16] And, while Modotti's optic is not that of landscape, a similar observation could be made regarding her photography which Armstrong suggests is "not transcendent in its opticality: it is too devoted to the frailty and mortality of what it records and to the very temporality that the photograph is supposed to freeze and overcome."[17]

I cannot help but visualize *Roses* and *Mother and Child* side by side (Figure 7.4). The intimacy of one speaks to the intimacy of the other; the

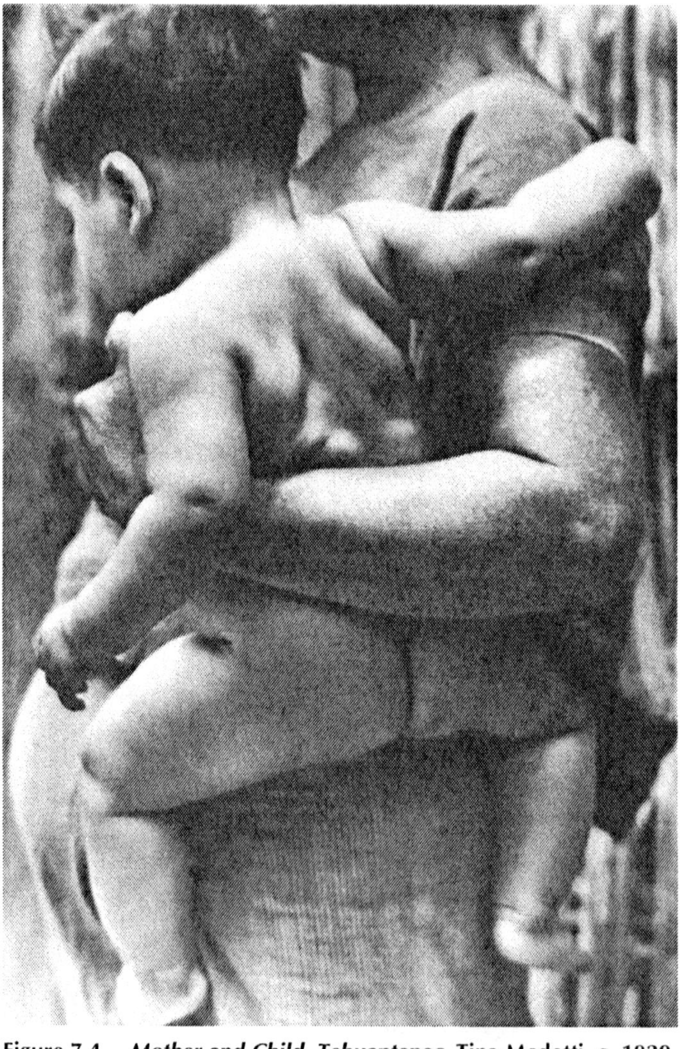

**Figure 7.4.** ***Mother and Child, Tehuantepec.*** **Tina Modotti, c. 1929. Permission granted by Throckmorton Gallery.**

wrinkled undifferentiated petals spill for me into the proximity of the mother and child that is further emphasized by the mother's expectant belly. Modotti gives full and substantial value to the materiality of her subjects and their bodies, which speaks to

> her unsublimated attraction to a tactile field and the flaws within it; her preference for frangible materiality over the metallic or the adamantine, for the mutable and mortal over the immutable and immortal, and for in-between gray tones over the full black-and-white range.[18]

The full black-and-white tonality range that Weston investigated, and that later would evolve into the "Zone System" developed to masterful perfection by Ansel Adams among others, is what designated a contrast to all other photographic activities as lesser. Definitely, given that context, Modotti's range of grays situated her in a lower rung of technical ability. More likely than not, this is what has influenced art historians in their approach to her work, especially Weston scholars and those who champion so-called "straight photography." I would suggest however that Modotti's tonality scale is also an ideological signifier that works to level the social, political and human playing field upon which she situated herself as an active agent.

## THE SELF-PORTRAIT AS POLITICAL IDENTITY

Tina Modotti's "fame" has been established away from her own work and her own capabilities and deeds. There has been a tendency to give value to her image only as it was re-created and re-presented by male artists who may or may not have been her acquaintances, lovers and partners. As Robo's muse, Tina was a quintessential symbol of female evanescence, she was Edward Weston's subject for the period of their relationship, she was Diego Rivera's symbol of revolutionary creative forces, she was the fertile figure that gave forth a virile world of struggle and natural resistance. But she was rarely depicted as anything more than a posed product of the male imaginary, all of which tended to diminish the value and effort of her own political activism and creative work. This reading of Modotti has been so long the norm that it has settled deep into the minds of traditional art historians. It still finds cause among those who, such as Weston historian Amy Conger, have declared that Modotti's photographs during the years of Tina and Weston's residence in Mexico are merely the work of a student strongly influenced by a master. During the course of a 1996 conference on Modotti at the University of California San Diego, Conger went so far as to suggest that some of Modotti's photographs may in fact have been either Weston's or his son's. Even at that young age, Conger's belief is that Brett was a much more sophisticated photographer than Modotti could ever have been. And just to show how deeply the Modotti-light image has filtered, the 2002 film *Frida* showed Tina in a fleeting sequence as nothing more than a party animal.

The obvious problem with such declarations is that they illustrate their own prejudice and limitations by being able to declare only the greatness of the photographs by their association with Weston father or son. Modotti's works are magically transformed into poor copies or amateurish exercises. There is no question as to Weston's influence on Modotti. It can be traced through comparative studies of their works, as Amy Conger has done, and it is well documented in Weston's diaries, in their reciprocal letters, and through the facts of their relationship. But their trajectories were quite different. Modotti's use of photography, though it by no means avoided aesthetic and compositional studies, was mostly tied to its ability to communicate Modotti's own social and cultural ideology. Her photography was closely tied to her own evolution as a social being and eventually to her activism, even in its most imperceptible moments. That is most likely the reason that stands behind her abandonment of the medium after her departure from Mexico. While she may very well have continued to photograph at some capacity (though almost nothing of these images is known), it could not have been in the vein of her obvious participatory style in post-revolution Mexico. Mexico was in many ways her initiatory experience into the interactive nexus of art and politics.

After all the speculation on the influence of her biography on her art, the question remains as to how Modotti's art may have been or become self-representational. Usually, the best indications we have regarding an artist's vision of his or her own image within the body of their work are autobiographical writings or self-portraiture. In Tina Modotti's case the samples that fall into this category are extremely limited. Her writings are exclusively political in nature, aside from her correspondence with a variety of individuals and one piece on the practice of photography. This last too, however, is a piece that considers the uses of photography as a political tool. We may want to consider her cinematographic or dramatic roles as self-representations of sorts. To these we might even add the roles she played as a model for Robo, Weston, Rivera and others. While there is no denying that, even in her poses as a model, Modotti always brought to bear her strong personality and figure, what all that might have to do with these aspects of her self and her body would be little more than speculation.

So far, in the large but still largely traditional body of scholarship on Tina Modotti the experts have uncovered only one, possibly two, self-portraits. We know that the 1942 posthumous exhibition of Modotti's works at the Galeria de Arte Mexicana, in Mexico City, contained a self-portrait that is listed in that exhibition's manifest simply as "Autoretrato."[19] However, in recent history, Patricia Albers tracked down and brought to light the traveling trunks that had been in the possession of Robo Richey's cousins in Oregon for decades. These containers held, among dozens of letters, other such documents and photographs, one particular image that appears to be a self-portrait. Uncertain as to which photograph was listed as a "self-portrait" in the Mexico exhibit, Albers suggests that the new found one and the catalogued image might be one and the same. If this is so, then we can count on the existence of only one known self-portrait. If the two are in fact dissimilar then there may be two self-portraits in circulation of which we so far know only one.

The self-portrait uncovered by Albers is published in *Vocio*, the catalogue of the Modotti exhibition that was installed at the University of California San Diego's Art Gallery from November 1996 to January 1997. Entitled *Costume from Tehuantepec*, the photograph depicts the smiling Tina in the traditional dress of the women of Tehuantepec. Her left hand is behind her back, supposedly handling the bulb of the long cable release that will enable her to realize the photograph (Figure 7.5).

How can we read this self-referential photograph beyond the obvious admiration that Modotti wants to communicate for the women of Tehuantepec. It is self-conscious, like all self-portraits, yet it is also a fully expressive ideological declaration. The subject seems to revel in the fact of its making, yet tries to mask the nature of the portrait by hiding the shutter release bulb in the left hand behind her back. We see the cable following the folds of the skirt until is falls past the skirt's material and out of the frame. Modotti's right arm and hand are perched in an odd fashion as the arm moves upward and the hand comes to rest on her right shoulder. The photographer's gaze is concentrated in a somewhat anxious manner upon the lens of her camera. Her face shows delight at what we might take to be a passing thought of pleasure in her exercise in making of her body a site of personal and collective history.

Instantly available to us is a Modotti whose *latinità* is a personal statement rather than a depiction rendered by another's eye, as it had been first in her film roles and later by Edward Weston. Here Modotti has covered her body in the dress of women representative of a matriarchal culture, and this dress tends to almost obliterate the male-constructed image we might have of her by blending her body into the background. The dress is itself suggestive of the layering in *Roses* and, as such, might be taken to imply how Modotti could have envisioned the function of her photography and her activism as somewhat imbricated in the reality of the revolutionary struggle of Mexico and women in particular. Read in this manner, Modotti's self-portrait falls into line with many of her other photographs in that it "proposes, finally, to find Modotti's celebrated otherness in her photographs, rather than in her person, and to locate her sedition in the

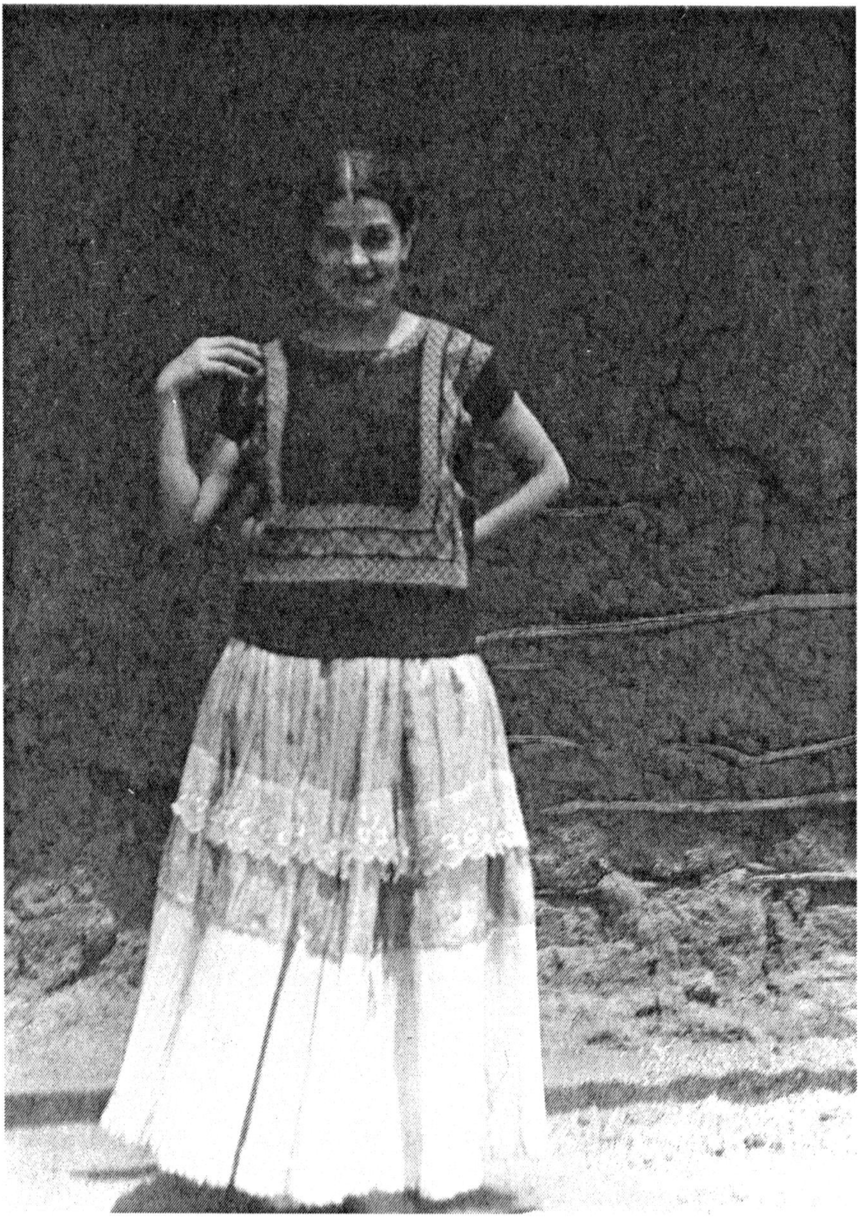

Figure 7.5. *Tina Modotti, self-portrait in costume from Tehuantepec,* c. 1927. Permission to reprint granted by the San Francisco Museum of Modern Art.

subliminality of her formal strategies rather than in the politics that she consciously avowed."[20] Indeed, *Autoretrato* situates Modotti's celebrated otherness in one of her photographs, a photograph of herself as other.

## NOTES

1. While there are many sources for Tina Modotti's biography, for this book I have depended upon an unpublished manuscript on Modotti by Christiane Barckhausen. Barckhausen, from what was formerly East Germany, had access to Soviet archives before the fall of the wall that had theretofore not been scrutinized by anyone. The result of this research was published as *Verdad y leyenda de Tina Modotti* (La Habana: Casa de las Américas, 1989) as a winner of the Cuban *Casa de las Americas Prize*. The version made available to me by Barckhausen in 1997 is a shorter biographical essay, an Italian translation from an original German text. Other books that have been fundamental for the chapter are: Mildred Constantine *Tina Modotti: A Fragile Life* (New York: Chronicle Books, 1993); Letizia Argenteri *Tina Modotti: Between Art and Revolution* (New Haven: Yale UP, 2003); Margaret Hooks *Tina Modotti: Photographer and Revolutionary* (New York: Harper Collins, 1995).

2. Amy Stark, "The Letters from Tina Modotti to Edward Weston," in *The Archive* (Tucson: University of Arizona, 1986), 74. Also see Edward Weston, *The Daybooks of Edward Weston* (New York: Aperture, 1973).

3. Pablo Neruda, "Tina Modotti ha muerto," in Vittorio Vidali, *Retrato de Mujer* (Puebla: Universidad Autónoma, 1984), 111.

4. Cesare Zavattini.

5. Antonio Gramsci, *Folclore e senso comune* (Roma: Editori Riuniti, 1992), 6.

6. Chantall Mouffe, "For a politics of nomadic identity," in *Travellers' Tales. Narrative of Home and Displacement* (New York: Routledge, 1994), 111.

7. Ibid.

8. Mariana Figarella, *Edward Weston e Tina Modotti in Messico.* (Pordenone: Cinemazero, 2003), 193.

9. Andrea Noble, *Tina Modotti: Image, Texture, Photography* (Albuquerque: University of New Mexico Press, 2000), 61.

10. Carol Armstrong, "This Photography Which is Not One: In the Gray Zone with Tina Modotti," in *OCTOBER 101*, Summer 2002, 19–52.

11. Ibid., 23.

12. Ibid.

13. Ibid., 27.

14. Ibid.

15. Ibid., 28.

16. Lippard, *The Lure*, 58.

17. Armstrong, "This Photography," 29.

18. Ibid., 33.

19. Patricia Albers, "Tina Modotti and the Indians of Mexico," in *Dear Vocio: Photographs by Tina Modotti* (San Diego: University of California Gallery, 1997), 51.

20. Armstrong, "This Photography," 23.

# Autobiographical Post Face as a Way of Conclusion

## *Belabored Bodies, Believable Fictions, Belated Images*

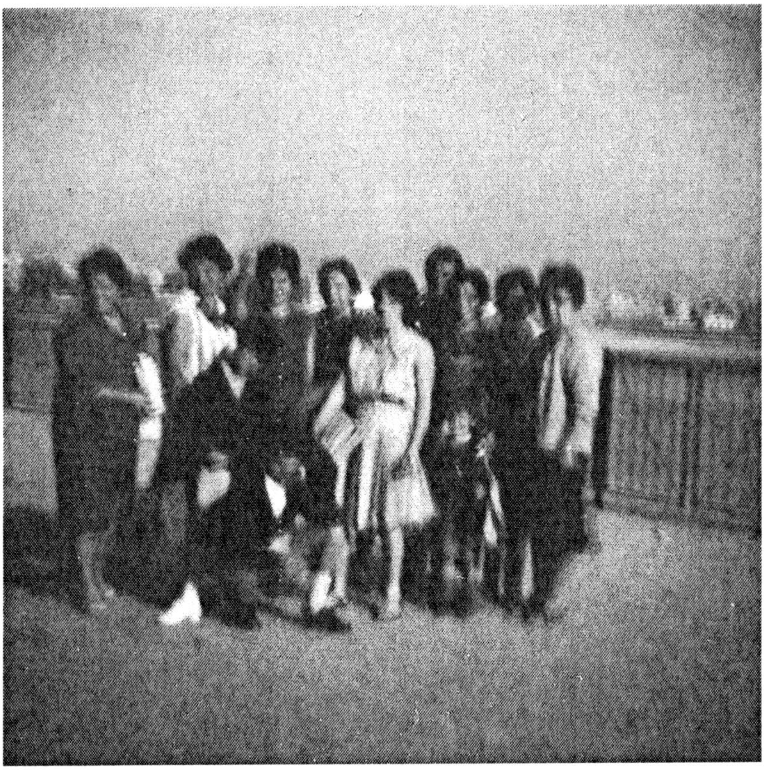

Figure C.1. *Napoli, departure.* Credit: P. Verdicchio.

We mostly live our lives as a series of postscripts, addenda, after thoughts and after images. Figure C.1 is a photograph of my family and friends on the day of our departure from Naples' Ciampino Airport for Canada. It is a photograph that I have misplaced, found, lost, and found again. I have read it over and over, and continue to read without exhausting its stories. It is a photograph of once intimately connected bodies that distance transformed into strangers. It is an image of a past that remains insistently present, one that defines the border between presence and absence, belonging and non-belonging, attachment and impermanence and, on a different referential level, citizenship. Looking at photographs like this one, I am reminded of Gianni Celati's observation that "we are not what passes through us, and yet that is all we are."[1]

This out-of-focus photograph was taken long before the onset of the digital age, with an inexpensive Diana that I had been given as a going-away present. It is the sort of plastic camera with plastic lens that has today become a sort of nostalgic collector's and curio item reminiscent of an early stage in the popularization of photography. The camera takes 120 mm film and produces 2 ½ x 2 ½ negatives that enthrall me now as they did then by their size and the visibility and materiality they give the contrasting black and white of the images. This was most likely the beginning of my fascination with the magic of photographic image production. It being my camera, I feel a sense of proprietorship in relation to the images that it produced. I am the photographer within an image recorded by someone else; since this is a group photograph, and very unclear, it also becomes a self-portrait without an explicit presence. Placed in the context of a family history, it becomes a substitution for one's self.

Family and friends are there to see us off; it would be the last time that some of us would see each other. And, while this photograph represents a moment of leaving and separation, it is inherently a representation of re-unification, with a father who had left before us and awaited our arrival in a place about which we knew almost nothing. Everything we had learned about our destination was nothing more than an accumulation of myths and imagination, a few photographs and a handful of coins my father had sent home. My mother was about to leave behind her own mother, sisters, brothers and relatives, which meant the almost complete disintegration of all she had known, for integration into another, more compact reality made up of her husband and children. It was for her a progressive shift from a clear knowing to an out of focus remembrance. It is of little importance that the people in this photograph are hardly recognizable. To those familiar with the event, the group, the bodies of those within it, their stance and gestural expressions are enough to bring them to life.

Six out of the twelve people in the photograph are now dead and gone, a fact that weighs heavily on the right side of the photograph from the viewers' point of view. Of the remaining six, three are my brothers and myself, one is our widowed mother, and two are aunts (one of them also widowed). It would not be far fetched to think of this photograph as being fully expressive of the impermanence of residence (only one person is still alive in Naples), and the multivalence of the term. Familial belonging, citizenship and the very issue of identity are suspended in uncertainty; with five of those depicted having become Canadian citizens.

This photograph seems to speak to many of the things that I have done in my life, up to and including this book. It is representative of a reply to these pages even before their being written. Contrary to its position in the body of this book, this snapshot is an actual face before the book, a physiognomy of visibility and invisibility of the various stages of growth, education, integration, adaptation and assimilation that looks to the book as part of its expression. These out of focus bodies, closely linked by community and blood, are belabored by the impositions of class constrains, by the socio-economic circumstances that result in emigration. The out-of-focus faces are an expression of the uncertainties before each individual, whether staying behind or emigrating, and inform their status and continued struggle with poverty, marginality, self-doubt, and lack of opportunities. These are belated images that may or may not manifest as fully "developed" into a focus expressive of their full potential. And even while belatedness might seem to imply an eventual resolution, as if it were moving toward clarity, in the case of a photograph, belatedness is "fixed" within the image and is also expressive of class distinctions.

While a photograph is the expression of a momentary manifestation, that may or may not form a continuum, it also holds a sense of promise. The photograph expresses the promise of emigration as a believable fiction that leads to the event of departure, which in turn fulfills the making of the photograph as a document of the moment. Yet, fictions too tend to have a life span that with time transforms them more and more into fragments of memory and diminish their sense of "reality." Even with drastic improvements in the socio-economic status brought by emigration to most of its subjects, the believability of the fictions becomes dependent on the diminishment of the subjects' previous condition as a lived "reality."

Although not usually referred to as such, I consider emigration and immigration to be forms of labor that exert immeasurable influence on the lives of those who live them. Often regarded only in terms of what they add to or subtract from a particular national context, the effect of this labor upon those who suffer it is generally neglected. The ground upon which the rhetoric of migration constructs the believability of its fictions is that of nationalist forces. The nations and populations unable or unwilling to take responsibility for that portion of themselves that emigrates, and those that receive immigrants with promises of freedom, work, prosperity, and opportunity, both participate in maintaining a constant view of laboring bodies, that are in themselves expressive of other social and cultural situations, as belated images that await the promise of focus and clarity.

This photograph, with its subjects celebrating a moment of promise for the future, fits solidly into the schema of nationalist discourses. As Italians preparing to leave for a world of better opportunities, the subjects have donned new (homemade) clothing that helps them "cut a proper figure" (*fare una bella figura*) and thereby fulfill a respectable and exportable image of Italy. As immigrants, they fulfill the requirements of what Canada has established to be good potential citizens. This image of neither departure nor arrival, accidentally out-of-focus as it is, could not better express this as a transition from one national "reality," the dissolution of the subjects' histories to that point, and the uncertainties beyond the blurred moment of their pose.

## NOTES

1. Gianni Celati, "Studenti nelle acque," in *Cinema naturale* (Milano: Feltrinelli, 2001).

# Bibliography

Agosta, Giovanni Garra. *Verga fotografo*. Prefazione di Paolo Mario Sipala, con uno scritto di Vincenzo Consolo. Le Pietre d'Angolo. Documenti. Catania: Giuseppe Maimone Editore, 1991.

Agostinis, Valentina, ed. *Tina Modotti: Gli anni luminosi*. Pordenone: Cinemazero. Edizioni Biblioteca dell'immagine, 1992.

Albers, Patricia. *Shadows, Fire, Snow: The Life of Tina Modotti*. New York: Potter, 1999.

Aldrich, Robert. *The Seduction of the Mediterranean: Writing, Art and Homosexual Fantasy*. London: Routledge, 1993.

Alighieri, Dante. *La divina commedia di Dante Alighieri*. Introduced by Raffaello Fornaciari. Milano: Hoepli, 1991.

Alloula, Malek. *The Colonial Harem*. Translated by Myrna Godzich and Wlad Godzich. Introduction by Barbara Harlow. Theory and History of Literature, Volume 21. Minneapolis: University of Minnesota Press, 1986.

Anzoino, Tommaso. *Pasolini*. Il castoro. Firenze: La Nuova Italia, 1971.

Argenteri, Letizia. *Tina Modotti: Between Art and Revolution*. New Haven: Yale University Press, 1993.

Armstrong, Carol. "This Photography Which is Not One: In the Gray Zone with Tina Modotti." In *OCTOBER 101*, Summer 2002, 19–52. Cambridge: MIT Press, 2002.

Baldwin, Gordon. *Looking at Photographs: A Guide to Technical Terms*. Los Angeles: J. Paul Getty Museum, 1991.

Barckhausen-Canale, Christiane. *Verdad y leyenda de Tina Modotti*. La Habana: Casa de las Américas, 1989.

———. *Tina Modotti: Leben, Werk, Schriften*. Kiel: Agimos Verlag, 1996.

———. *Tina Modotti: Una biografia*. Unpublished manuscript provided by the author, 1997.

Barthes, Roland. *Roland Barthes by Roland Barthes*. New York:
———. *Mythologies*. London: Granada, 1980.
———. *Camera lucida: Reflections on Photography*. Translated by Richard Howard. New York: Hill and Wang, 1982.
———. Introduction to *Taormina: Baron Wilhelm von Gloeden*. Santa Fe: Twelvetrees Press, 1997.
Behdad, Ali. *Belated Travelers: Orientalism in the Age of Colonialism Dissolution*. Durham: Duke University Press, 1994.
Benadusi, Lorenzo. *Il nemico dell'uomo nuovo: L'omosessualità nell'esperimento totalitario fascista*. Prefazione di Emilio Gentile. Campi del sapere. Milano: Feltrinelli, 2005.
Benjamin, Walter. "The Work of Art in the Age of Mechanical Reproduction." In *Illuminations: Essays and Reflections*. Edited and with an Introduction by Hannah Arendt. Translated by Harry Zohn, 217–51. New York: Schocken Books, 1987.
———. *The work of Art in the Age of its technological reproducibility and Other Writings on Media*. Cambridge: Belknap Press, 2008.
Berger, John. *About Looking*. New York: Pantheon, 1980.
———. *And our faces, my heart, brief as photos*. New York: Vintage, 1991.
Bertelli, Carlo. "La penisola ermafrodita." In *Storia d'Italia. Annali 2 L'immagine fotografica 1845–1945*, edited by Carlo Bertelli e Giulio Bollati. Vol. 1. 84–86. Torino: Einaudi, 1979.
Boatto, Alberto. *Narciso infranto: L'autoritratto moderno da Goya a Warhol*. Bari: Edizioni Laterza, 1998.
Bollati, Giulio. *L'italiano: il carattere nazionale come storia e come invenzione*. Biblioteca studio, 31. Torino: Einaudi, 1996.
Boone, Joseph A. "Vacations Cruises; or, The Homoerotics of Orientalism." In *PMLA*. Special Topic: Colonialism and the Postcolonial Condition. January 1995. Volume 110, number 1, 89–107. New York: MLA, 1995.
Bufalino, Gesualdo. *Il tempo in posa*. Introduction by Diego Mormorio. Palermo: Sellerio, 2000.
Burfoot, Annette. 2002. "Surprising Origins: Florentine Eighteenth-Century Wax Anatomical Models as Inspiration for Italian Horror." In *Kinoeye* 9, 1–9, 2002.
Calvino, Italo. *The Path to the Nest of Spiders*. Preface by the author. Translated by Martin McLaughlin. Fifth printing. New York: Ecco Press, 1985.
———. *Mr. Palomar*. Translated by William Weaver. New York: Harcourt Brace Jovanovich, 1985.
———. "L'avventura di un fotografo." In *Gli amori difficili*. Milano: Oscar Mondadori, 1993.
———. "Visibilità." In *Lezioni americane: Sei proposte per il prossimo millennio*. Milano: Oscar Mondadori, 2003.
Campanella, Tommaso. *La città del sole*. http://www.liberliber.it/biblioteca/c/campanella/la_citta_del_sole/html/la_citta.htm
Canon. "Canon U.S.A. Consumer Site." http://www.usa.canon.com/consumer/controller?act=ModelInfoAct&tabact=ModelFeaturesTabAct&fcategoryid=138&modelid=9831&pageno=1
Cattaneo, Carlo. "Sulle scoperte lucigrafiche di Daguerre e Niepce; estratto del Rapporto del sig. Arago [Giugno 1839]." In *Storia d'Italia. Annali 2. L'immaginefotografica*

*1845–1945*, edited by Carlo Bertelli e Giulio Bollati. Vol. 1. 207–11. Torino: Einaudi, 1979.

Cattanes, Luigi and Alessandro Riva. *The Anatomical Waxes by Clemente Susini of the University of Cagliari.* (Bilingual Italian/English edition). 25 color plates. University of Cagliari: Edizioni della Torre, 1993.

Celati, Gianni. *Cinema naturale.* Universale Economica Feltrinelli. Numero 1731. Milano: Feltrinelli, 2003.

———. *Narratori delle pianure.* Universale Economica Feltrinelli. Numero 1027. Milano: Feltrinelli, 2000.

Cerami, Matteo and Mario Sesti, editors. *La voce di Pasolini: I testi.* Real Cinema BiM. Milano: Feltrinelli, 2006.

Cerroni, Umberto. *Lessico gramsciano.* Universale 99. Roma: Editori Riuniti, 1978.

Chastain, Sue. "Screen Shots of JPEG Save Options for Various Software." *About.com: Graphics Software.* http://graphicssoft.about.com/od/formatsjpeg/ss/jpegoptions.htm.

Chevrier, Jean-François. "The Image of the Other." In *Staging the Self: Self-Portrait Photography 1840s–1980s.* Edited by James Lingwood. Plymouth: Plymouth Arts Centre, 1986.

Chiarelli, Brunetto and Paolo Chiozzi, editors. *Etnie: La scuola antropologica fiorentina e la fotografia tra '800 e '900.* Firenze: Alinari, 1996.

Cirese, Alberto Mario. *Intellettuali, folklore, istinto di classe: Note su Verga, Deledda, Scotellaro, Gramsci.* Torino: Einaudi, 1976.

Clarke, Graham, editor. *The Portrait in Photography.* London: Reaktion Books, 1992.

Constantine, Mildred. *Tina Modotti: A Fragile Life.* San Francisco: Chronicle Books, 1993.

Cooper, Emmanuel. *Fully Exposed: The Male Nude in Photography.* New York: Routledge, 1995.

D'Autilia, Gabriele. *L'indizio e la prova: La storia nella fotografia.* Le scene del tempo. Milano: Bruno Mondadori, 2005.

Düring, Monika v., Georges Didi-Huberman and Marta Poggesi, editors. *Encyclopaedia Anatomica: A Complete Collection of Anatomical Waxes.* Museo di Storia Naturale dell'Università di Firenze, sezione di zoologia La Specola. Köln: Taschen, 1999.

Dynes, Wayne R. *Encyclopedia of Homosexuality.* New York: Garland, 1990.

Evans, Jessica and Stuart Hall, editors. *Visual Culture: The Reader.* London: Sage Publications Ltd., 1999.

Ewing, William A. and Nathalie Herschdorfer, editors. *Face: the new photographic portrait.* London: Thames & Hudson, 2006.

Faeta, Francesco. "Wilhelm von Gloeden: Per una lettura antropologica delle immagini." In *Fotologia.* Museo di Storia della Fotografia Fratelli Alinari. Volume 9, maggio 1988, a.c. di Italo Zannier, 88-104. Firenze: Alinari,1998.

Favrod, Charles-Henri. "L'innocenza di Eros e di Dionisio." In *Von Gloeden: Fotografie.* Capolavori delle collezioni Alinari. Firenze: Alinari, 2000.

Ficino, Marsilio. *Sopra lo amore o ver' Convito di Platone: Comento di Marsilio Ficini Fiorentino sopra il Convito di Platone.* Edited by G. Ottaviano. Milano: Celuc, 1973.

Figarella, Mariana. *Edward Weston e Tina Modotti in Messico.* Pordenone: Cinemazero, 2003.

Flusser, Vilém. *Toward a Philosophy of Photography*. Göttingen: European Photography, 1983.

Fofi, Goffredo. "Premessa." In *Lo sguardo da sud*. Edited by Alessandra Mauro. Napoli: l'ancora, 1999.

———. "Introduction." In *Humana: La presenza dell'uomo in fotografie*. Moreno Gentili editor. Udine: Art& - Parole e figure, 1996.

Fossati, Paolo. *Autoritratti, specchi e palestre: Figure della pittura italiana del Novecento*. Milano: Bruno Mondadori, 1998.

Forster, E. M. *Maurice*. New York: Norton, 1971.

———. *A Room with a View*. Introduction and Notes by Malcolm Bradbury. Penguin Twentieth Century Classics. New York: Penguin Books, 2000.

Gallini, Clara and Francesco Faeta, editors. *I viaggi nel sud di Ernesto De Martino. Fotografie di Arturo Zavattini, Franco Pinna e Ando Gilardi*. Nuova Cultura, n. 71. Torino: Bollati Boringhieri, 1999.

Gentili, Moreno editor. *Humana: La presenza dell'uomo in fotografia*. Udine: Art& - Parole e figure, 1996.

Gilardi, Ando. *Storia sociale della fotografia*. Serie sintesi. Milano: Bruno Mondadori, 2000.

Girard, René. *Violence and the Sacred*. Translated by Patrick Gregory. Baltimore: Johns Hopkins University Press, 1977.

Gramsci, Antonio. *The Southern Question*. Translated and introduced by Pasquale Verdicchio. Toronto: Guernica Editions, 2006.

———. *The Modern Prince and Other Writings*. New York: New World Paperbacks, 1967.

———. *Folcolore e senso commune*. I piccoli. Roma: Editori Riuniti, 1999.

Grazioli, Elio. *Corpo e figura umana nella fotografia*. Milano: Bruno Mondadori, 1998.

Holmes, Oliver Wendell. "The Stereoscope and the Stereograph." In *Atlantic Monthly*, Boston, III, 1859, 738–48.

———. "Sun Painting and Sun Sculpture." In *Atlantic Monthly*, Boston, VIII, 1861, 13–29.

———. "Doings the Sunbeam." In *Atlantic Monthly*, Boston, XII, 1863, 1–5.

Hooks, Margaret. *Tina Modotti: Photographer and Revolutionary*. San Francisco: Pandora Books, 1981.

Jonas, Susan editor. *Ellis Island: Echoes from a Nation's Past/A Celebration of the Gateway to America*. Third Printing. New York: Aperture Books, 1997.

Jordanova, Ludmilla. *Sexual Visions: Images of Gender in Science and Medicine Between the Eighteenth and Twentieth Centuries*. New York: Harvester Wheatsheaf, 1989.

Krauss, Rosalind. *Teoria e storia della fotografia*. Elio Grazioli editor. Sintesi. Milano: Bruno Mondadori, 1990.

Leopardi, Giacomo. *Discorso sopra lo stato presente dei costumi degl'italiani*. Classici della BUR, L1187. Testo critico di Marco Dondero. Commento di Roberto Melchiori. Milano: BUR, 1998.

———. *Lo Zibaldone*. Archivio Centro Nazionale di Studi Leopardiani. www.leopardi.it/zibaldone.php.

Leslie, Charles. *Wilhelm von Gloeden, photographer: A Brief Introduction to his Life and Work*. New York: Soho Photographic Publishers, 1977.

Lévi-Strauss, Claude. *The Raw and the Cooked.* Translated by John and Doreen Weightman. New York: Harper and Row, 1969.
Liebmann, Kurt. *Hans von Marées.* Dresden: Verlag der Kunst, 1972.
Lingwood, James, editor. *Staging the self: Self-portrait Photography 1840s–1980s.* A National Portrait Gallery & Plymouth Arts Centre Exhibition, 1986.
Lippard, Lucy. *The Lure of the Local: Senses of Place in a Multicentered Society.* New York: The New Press, 1997.
Malossi, Giannino, editor. *The Icon of Italy in Global Pop Culture.* New York: The Monacelli Press, 1999.
Marcenaro, Giuseppe. *Fotografia come letteratura.* Milano: Bruno Mondadori, 2004.
Marchese, Angelo. *L'officina del racconto.* Milano: Mondadori, 1983.
Marchi, Gian Paolo. *Le bellezze diverse: storia delle edizioni illustrate di Giovanni Verga.* Palermo: Sellerio, 1991.
Marra, Claudio. *Fotografia e pittura nel Novecento: Una storia "senza combattimento."* Milano: Bruno Mondadori, 1999.
———. *Le idée della fotografia: La riflessione teorica dagli anni sessanta a oggi.* Milano: Bruno Mondadori, 2001.
Marzocchini, Vincenzo. *Letteratura e Fotografia: Scrittori, poeti, fotografi.* Bologna: Clueb, 2005.
Mauro, Alessandra. "La voglia di narrare." In *Lo sguardo da sud: conversazioni su sud e fotografia.* Edited by Alessandra Mauro. Napoli: l'ancora, 1999.
Melloni, Marcello. "*Relazione intorno al Dagherrotipo,* letta alla Regia Accademia delle Scienze nella tornata del dí 12 novembre 1839." In *Storia d'Italia. Annali 2 L'immagine fotografica 1845–1945,* edited by Carlo Bertelli e Giulio Bollati. Vol 2. 212–32. Torino: Einaudi, 1979.
Mignemi, Adolfo. *Lo sguardo e l'immagine: La fotografia come documento storico.* Saggi: Storia, filosofia e scienze sociali. Torino: Bollati Boringhieri, 2003.
Miraglia, Marina and Italo Mussa editors. *Le fotografie di Von Gloeden.* Con una nota di Goffredo Parise. Tea Fotografia. Milano: TEA, 1996.
Morello, Paolo. *Briganti: Fotografia e malavita nella Sicilia dell'Ottocento.* Diorama 5. Palermo: Sellerio, 1999.
Mormorio, Diego. *Una invenzione fatale: breve genealogia della fotografia.* Prisma 78. Palermo: Sellerio, 1985.
Mouffe, Chantall. "For a politics of nomadic identity." In George Robinson, *Travellers' Tales. Narrative of Home and Displacement.* New York: Routledge, 1994.
Muzzarelli, Federica. *Formato tessera: Storia, arte e idée in photomatic.* Milano: Bruno Mondadori, 2003.
Natter, Tobias G. and Peter Weiermair. *Et in arcadia ego: Wilhelm von Gloeden, Guglielmo Plüschow and Vincenzo Galdi.* Turn of the Century Photography. Zurich: Oehrli Editions, 2000.
Noble, Andrea. *Tina Modotti: Image, Texture, Photography.* Albuquerque: University of New Mexico Press, 2000.
Nolan, Leslie. *Jacob A. Riis.* Collection Photo Poche 72. Paris: Editions Nathan, 1997.
Palazzoli, Daniela editor. *Ignoto a me stesso: Ritratti di scrittori da Edgar Allan Poe a Jorge Luis Borges. La fotografia vista da Leonardo Sciascia.* Milano: Bompiani, 1987.
Paltrinieri, Elisa. *Tina Modotti: Fotografa irregolare.* L'Altra Metà dell'Arte, n. 15. Milano: Selene Edizioni, 2004.

Pericoli, Tullio. *L'anima del volto*. Milano: Bompiani, 2005.

Pirandello, Luigi. *Quaderni di Serafino Gubbio operatore*. Liber liber. http://www.liberliber.it/biblioteca/p/pirandello/quaderni_di_serafino_gubbio_operatore/pdf/quader_p.pdf

Poggio, Pier Paolo. "Unificazione nazionale e differenza razziale." In *Nel nome della razza: Il razzismo nella storia d'Italia, 1870-1945*. Alberto Burgio editor. I percorsi. Bologna: Il Mulino, 1999.

Pultz, John. *The Body and the Lens*. New York: Henry N. Abrams, 1995.

Re, Lucia. "Calvino e l'enigma della fotografia." In *Calvino e l'italianistica attuale*. Franca Bizzoni and Mariapia Lamberti, editors. Mexico City: Cátedra Extraordinaria Italo Calvino – Facultad de Filosofia y Letras, Universidad Nacional Autonoma de México, 2007.

Ricci, Franco. *Painting with Words, Writing with Pictures: Word and Image in the Work of Italo Calvino*. Toronto: Toronto University Press, 2001.

Riis, Jacob A. *How the Other Half Lives: Studies Among the Tenements of New York*. Preface by Charles A. Madison. New York: Dover Publications, 1971.

Robertson, George. *Travellers' Tales. Narrative of Home and Displacement*. New York: Routledge, 1994.

Rodler, Lucia. *Il corpo specchio dell'anima: Teoria e storia della fisiognomica*. Testi e pretesti. Milano: Bruno Mondadori, 2000.

Rosenblum, Naomi and Walter Rosenblum. *Lewis W. Hine*. Collection Photo Poche 50. Paris: Editions Nathan, 1992.

Rossellini, Roberto. *Rome Open City*. DVD. New York: Criterion Collection, 2009.

Ruberto, Laura and Christi Wilson, editors. *Italian Neo-Realism and Global Cinema*. Detroit: Wayne State UP, 2007.

Sciascia, Leonardo. "Il lungo viaggio." In *Il mare colore del vino*. Fabula 91. Seconda edizione. Milano: Adelphi, 1998.

———. "Verismo e fotografia." In *Opere 1971-1983*. Edited by Claude Ambroise. Milano: Classici Bompiani, 1999.

Settimelli, Wladimiro editor. *Giovanni Verga: Specchio e Realtà. 84 foto inedite dello scrittore siciliano*. Poetica dell'immagine fotografica. Collana diretta da Francesco E. Ferrito. Roma: Editrice Magma, 1976.

———, and Filippo Zevi, editors. *Gli Alinari: Fotografi a Firenze 1852–1920*. Firenze: Edizioni Alinari, 1977.

Sipala, Paolo Mario. "Prefazione." In *Verga Fotografo*. Edited by Giovanni Garra Agosta. Catania: Giuseppe Maimone Editore, 1991.

Sironi, Marco. *Geografie del narrare: Insistenze sui luoghi di Luigi Ghirri e Gianni Celati*. Il castello di atlante, number 18. Reggio Emilia: Edizioni Diabasis, 2004.

Steichen, Edward. *The Family of Man*. New York: Museum of Modern Art, 1955.

Stieglitz, Alfred. *Camerawork: A Pictorial Guide*. Edited by Marianne Fulton Margolis. New York: Dover Publications, 1978.

Stark, Amy. "The Letters of Tina Modotti to Edward Weston." In *The Archive*. Research Series. Number 22. January 1986. Tucson: University of Arizona,1986.

Strand, Paul and Cesare Zavattini. *Un paese: Portrait of an Italian Village*. New York: Aperture, 1997.

Sullivan, George. *In the Wake of Battle: The Civil War Images of Mathew Brady*. New York: Prestel Verlag, 2004.

Taormina. *Taormina Travel Guide*. www.travelplan.it/taormina_guide.htm.
Taramelli, Ennery. *Mondi infiniti di Luigi Ghirri*. Il castello di Atlante, number 22. Reggio Emilia: Diabasis, 2005.
Teti, Vito. *La razza maledetta*. Torino: Manifesto, 1990.
Verga, Giovanni. "L'amante di Gramigna." In *Le novelle*. Vol. 1. 212–20. Milano: Garzanti, 1980.
Verdicchio, Pasquale. "Tina Modotti: Life Through the Ground-Glass." In *Dear Vocio: Photographs by Tina Modotti*. Catalogue of the exhibition, Nov/Jan. 1996–1997, 8–19. San Diego: UC San Diego, 1997.
———. "Tina Modotti: Toward a Politics of Culture and Displacement." In *Devils in Paradise: Writings on Post-emigrant Cultures*. Toronto: Guernica Editions, 1997.
———. *Bound by Distance: Rethinking Nationalism through the Italian Diaspora*. New Jersey: Fairleigh Dickinson University Press, 1997.
———. "La lupa" in *Le novelle*. Vol. 1. 206-211. Milano: Garzanti, 1980.
———. *La lupa*. Collezione di Teatro, no. 259. Torino: Einaudi, 1982.
Vidali, Vittorio. *Retrato de mujer: Una vida con Tina Modotti*. Puebla: Universidad Autónoma de Puebla, 1984.
von Gloeden, Wilhelm. *Taormina*. Introduction by Ulrich Pohlmann. *Masters of the camera*. New York: Te Neues, 1998.
Weston, Edward. *The Daybooks of Edward Weston*. Edited by Nancy Newhall. New York: Aperture, 1973.
Zannier, Italo. *L'io e il suo doppio: Un secolo di ritratto fotografico in Italia, 1895/1995*. Firenze: Edizioni Alinari, 1996.
———. *Il sogno della fotografia*. Milano: Skira, 2006.
Zevi, Filippo, editor. *Alinari, Photographers of Florence, 1852–1920*. Introduction by John Berger. Florence: Edizioni Alinari, 1978.

## PHOTOGRAPHY WEBSITES

Hine, Lewis. "Lewis Hine." *Masters of Photography*. www.masters-of-photography.com/H/hine/hine.html
Modotti, Tina. *Tina Modotti*. www.modotti.com
Riis, Jacob. "Jacob Riis." *Masters of Photography*. www.masters-of-photography.com/R/riis/riis.html
Susini, Clemente. *Clemente Susini: VAA-F-004483-0000*. Alinari Archives. www.alinariarchives.it
Verga, Giovanni. "Le fotografie del Verga turista come un ponte tra nord e sud." *Alibi on line*. http://www.alibionline.it/mostre/fotografia/1475-le-fotografie-del-verga-turista-come-un-ponte-tra-nord-e-sud.html
von Gloeden, Wilhelm. *Wilhelm von Gloeden*: *GWA-F-0010570-0000*. "Ritratto di ragazzo." Alinari Archives. www.alinariarchives.it
Weston, Edward. *Edward Weston*. www.edward-weston.com

# Index

# About the Author

**Pasquale Verdicchio** teaches literature, film, and cultural studies in the Department of Literature, University of California at San Diego. He received a Ph.D. from UCLA. He is a founding member of the Association of Italian Canadian Writers and sits on the editorial board of journals such as *Testuale* (Italy) and the *Journal of Italian Translation*. As a translator, he has published the work of Pier Paolo Pasolini, Antonio Gramsci, Alda Merini, Andrea Zanzotto and Giorgio Caproni. His *Bound by Distance: Rethinking Nationalism through the Italian Diaspora* was published by Fairleigh Dickinson in 1997.